The M.E. Sharpe Library of Franklin D. Roosevelt Studies

Volume One

The M.E. Sharpe Library of
Franklin D. Roosevelt Studies

Franklin D. Roosevelt
and the Shaping of American Political Culture

Volume One

Nancy Beck Young,
William D. Pederson,
and Byron W. Daynes
Editors

M.E. Sharpe
Armonk, New York
London, England

Library of Congress Cataloging-in-Publication Data

Franklin D. Roosevelt and the shaping of American political culture / edited by Nancy
Beck Young, William D. Pederson, and Byron W. Daynes.
     p.cm.
   Includes bibliographical references and index.
   ISBN 0-7656-0620-8 (cloth : alk. paper)
     1. Roosevelt, Franklin D. (Franklin Delano), 1882–1945—Influence. 2. Political
culture—United States—History—20th century. 3. Politics and culture—United
States—History—20th century. 4. Popular culture—United States—History—20th century.
5. United States—Politics and government—1933-1945. I. Young, Nancy Beck. II.
Pederson, William D., 1946– III. Daynes, Byron W.

E806 .F692 2000
973.917′092—dc21   99-088090

Printed in the United States of America

The paper used in this publication meets the minimum requirements of
American National Standard for Information Sciences
Permanence of Paper for Printed Library Materials,
ANSI Z 39.48-1984.

BM (c)   10   9   8   7   6   5   4   3   2   1

TABLE OF CONTENTS

Introduction and Summary 1
Nancy Beck Young

Part One: FDR
  1. The Popular Iconography of FDR 9
     Lynn Y. Weiner and Ronald T. Tallman
  2. The Sun Comes Out Tomorrow 19
     Ron Briley

Part Two: Art, Architecture, and Music of the 1930s
  3. Federal Arts Policy and Political Legitimation 42
     Graham Barnfield
  4. A Reassessment of New Deal Art 63
     Francine Carraro
  5. Heroes in Texas Post Office Murals 73
     Philip Parisi
  6. WPA Frescoes: Louisiana's Depression Era Economy 81
     Mary R. Zimmerman
  7. WPA Buildings in Northwest Louisiana 88
     Mary R. Zimmerman
  8. The WPA's Forgotten Muse 98
     Arthur R. Jarvis, Jr.

Part Three: Popular Culture
  9. Don't Let Hitler (or the Depression) Kill Baseball 119
     Ron Briley

Cultural Chronology 134

Biographical Digest 136

List of Contributors 145

Index 147

Introduction and Summary

Nancy Beck Young

Franklin D. Roosevelt and the Shaping of American Political Culture results from the conference *FDR After 50 Years*, held at Louisiana State University in Shreveport in September 1995. The volume contains a variety of important chapters detailing the new work and new questions being asked and answered about the various intersections between politics and culture. Targeted for a wide audience, the collection includes chapters about the representation of Franklin D. Roosevelt in film and in household objects, about art and politics, about professional musicians suffering from lost employment opportunities using New Deal relief programs to create new cultural forms, about construction of public buildings and their social and political meanings, and about the implications of military policy for mass culture with regard to baseball's future during World War II. Historians of the New Deal, political historians and political scientists, cultural and social historians, art historians, and literary critics all will find material of interest to their specialties. These distinct chapters, individually insightful, taken together prove the dynamism of a new field of scholarship—political culture. How did Americans respond to the economic catastrophe that beset them in 1929? In what way or ways did the social and cultural responses inform the politics of the period and vice versa? How did changed political beliefs alter cultural activities? These are just a few of the questions posed and answered in the chapters of this volume.

Lynn Y. Weiner and Ronald D. Tallman provide an intriguing analysis of Franklin D. Roosevelt's representation before the public. This process happened in two ways. First, the president established various representations of himself, all of which allayed public fears about the economy and international security. Second, Americans, enamored with strong emotions toward FDR, used their understanding of his life to craft their own methods of memory and interpretation. The authors suggest that projecting a positive public image was of primary importance to Roosevelt. Their chapter examines the four personas FDR adopted—Sphinx, Father, Doctor, and Captain of the Ship of State—and the manner in which FDR partisans interpreted each in souvenir iconography. These personas represent or reflect both the key points the president wished the American public to understand about his leadership and the reactions of individuals so motivated to enshrine the various concepts in handwork. Through each of these images, the president appeared in complete control of himself and the nation. Furthermore, the authors have examined numerous examples of common objects ranging from toys to pillowcases in which the various images of FDR were translated and transferred to the American public. The chapter that results provides scholars with important clues in understanding the linkages among images as conveyed and received, politics, and the culture out of which each flowed.

Ron Briley's chapter, "The Sun Comes Out Tomorrow: Hollywood's Depiction of Franklin D. Roosevelt and the New Deal, From *Gabriel Over The White House* to *Annie*," analyzes the film industry's image of FDR and his times. Like Weiner and Tallman, this essay indicates the multifaceted—sometimes contradictory—nature of popular culture representations of FDR. Unlike Weiner and Tallman, Briley casts a wide net. His concern is not with artifacts and memorabilia generated by FDR partisans, but with the exchange between movie depiction and critical reaction to FDR, his programs, and the fictional representation of them to moviegoing audiences. The latter circumstance ensured a wider distribution than was true of the FDR iconography. More importantly, Briley analyzes the veracity of conservatives who defile the liberal government activism FDR helped to forge and indict the movie industry as a coconspirator in the cultural and social decline of "traditional American values." To the contrary, Briley convincingly demonstrates that Hollywood's attitude toward FDR was not always supportive. He cites examples such as Louis B. Mayer and Irving Thalberg, who helped defeat Upton Sinclair's 1934 quest for the California governorship as a Democrat. Mayer and Thalberg feared Sinclair's liberalism, like that of FDR, would weaken their competitive position in the film industry. However, Briley argues that most filmmakers "prefer[red] to work through political allegory, assuming that the audience would be able to make some rather obvious connections." Briley asks and answers numerous questions about the contextual political comment and commentary in films made during and after Roosevelt's years in office. In this way, the chapter demonstrates the wealth of knowledge that resulted from analyzing the intersections between politics and culture.

Part II moves away from evaluating FDR in popular and political culture media. The chapters in this part look instead at how the New Deal interacted with art, architecture, and music. The Great Depression proved the old maxim that cultural outlets are often the first to suffer funding cuts when the economy tightens. However, New Deal policy makers responded with alacrity to this problem. A total of over $35 million was appropriated for support of the arts in the 1930s. With the exception of Graham Barnfield's chapter, all the chapters in Part II look at the interaction between the New Deal and the arts on the local level. In this, the scholarship that follows is representative of larger trends in New Deal studies: examination of policy on the micro level to test the accuracy of the macro theoretical framework.

Graham Barnfield's chapter, "Federal Arts Policy and Political

Legitimation," analyzes how policy makers legitimized their decisions and programs to a changing population. The problem of political legitimation was heightened by the economic crisis of the Depression. Barnfield also assesses the tensions between different branches of the government. Finally, he uses the topic of his case study—cultural policy—to examine how "government officials . . . sought to link their arts policies to a distinctive national identity." He demonstrates that FDR's greatest ideological concern was with preserving a belief in democracy. As such, it was only the presence of communists that caused FDR to worry. Barnfield's chapter explores the various interpretations of government cultural programs, specifically the Works Progress Administration Federal Project Number One. Despite rave reviews, federal patronage of the arts generated much criticism, both at the time and by later writers. However, Barnfield warns against the latter. He argues that an interpretation of Federal One based on the social and cultural climate of a more recent decade "risk[s] reading history backwards." Instead, Barnfield asserts that cultural policies in the 1930s were rooted in the social and intellectual milieu of the 1920s, which included a rise in nativism, repression of foreign-born immigrants, and prohibition. The political upheavals of the 1930s flipped the 1920s out-groups into a more important social and political position. The result was a different perspective on cultural production. Part of the richness of Barnfield's chapter comes from his successful use of state theorists to position his interpretations about New Deal art policy.

In "A Reassessment of New Deal Art," Francine Carraro takes the tenure of the Public Works of Art Project and its successor, the Section of Painting and Sculpture of the Treasury Department, and examines their activities in Texas. PWAP provided a government wage to artists who created for federal buildings, offices and post offices as well as a myriad of state structures such as schools and prisons. Artists won jobs only after submitting their designs in competition for the available commissions. PWAP combined its central mission, relief for starving artists, with the development of state-sanctioned culture. All work created became the property of the federal government. The seemingly incongruous purposes of PWAP also predicated much of the criticism of the art that has resulted since, as Carraro argues, "PWAP founders belie[ved] that art for the public must be understandable and accessible." Indeed, much of the art generated represented local, regional, and historical themes popular with average Americans. Texas historians will enjoy Carraro's description of the politics surrounding subjects depicted within post office murals. Most noteworthy was the removal of the mural by Jerry Bywaters and Alexandre Hogue from the Houston Parcel Post Building in the mid-1950s. The art depicted dockworkers loading and unloading freight as part of a larger visual history of the Houston Ship Channel. However, Cold War political concerns about labor unions and strikes prevailed and the murals were taken down. The episode demonstrates the potential for difficulty concomitant with state intervention in art and illustrates Carraro's larger argument that "art, chosen on sociological grounds in the name of cultural egalitarianism, will not long remain art."

Philip Parisi's chapter also examines the relationship among the federal government, depression relief, and public art patronage. Whereas Carraro explored the evolution of the entire program in Texas, Parisi concentrates on "didactic mural art" in the state's post offices. He argues that a common theme—heroes and their heroism—permeated the images that were represented. Local heroes and/or pioneers, cowboys, Native Americans, Texas Rangers, and outlaws all became the subject of post office murals. Post office patrons were supposed to reflect on those icons as they combatted the Depression. Parisi argues that the intellectual genealogy of the mural program is traced to Diego Rivera and other Mexican artists who captured the history of their country and its revolution in mural form, as well as American painters Thomas Hart Benton and Grant Woods, who dominated the American Scene movement's painting of local subjects in an accessible manner. Parisi suggests that the Treasury Department Section on Fine Arts encouraged "only positive images . . . for post office murals." He asserts that the murals succeeded in their foremost aim of providing and reinforcing democratic values of a citizenry in crisis.

Mary R. Zimmerman's chapter on Works Progress Administration (WPA) frescoes looks at the intersections between art and government from yet another perspective. Her laboratory for study is not Texas but Louisiana. Read in conjunction with the Carraro and Parisi entries, much can be learned about the development of public art projects in the South. She argues that the lasting value of the frescoes—their depiction of workers—also generated hostility from conservative critics who doubted the merits of federal sponsorship for the arts. Most of Zimmerman's evidence is drawn from the fresco panels in the Louisiana State Exhibit Museum in Shreveport. She also suggests that the fair murals "added a classical feature to the museum's façade," which was "a superb example of modern architecture." The murals depict the work of lumberjacks, paper production, the oil industry, and agriculture. The most important sections of this paper analyze the career of Conrad Alfred Albrisio, the artist who painted the murals. In this way, Zimmerman provides the context for understanding the economic and social history of Louisiana as represented in the murals.

Zimmerman's second chapter illuminates another aspect of New Deal political culture—the construction of new public buildings in Louisiana with Works Progress Administration funding. After summarizing the history of the WPA, Zimmerman demonstrates the ways in which the building projects resulted in architectural advances. She also explores the influence of modern architecture on the WPA construction boom. The result, according to Zimmerman, created "a national architecture that was not rooted in the past." The author suggests that the new structures, with their emphasis on usable space as opposed to ornamental space, communicated that the government took its responsibilities for Depression relief seriously. The body of her chapter will be especially useful to

Louisiana historians concerned with details of Shreveport and northern Louisiana architectural history. Zimmerman provides descriptions of the representative styles of buildings erected. Beyond the primary goal of job creation, the WPA building program achieved cultural success by encouraging modern architecture and providing public gathering space. Zimmerman forces her audiences to remember the latter as well as the former.

Arthur R. Jarvis Jr. takes another component of New Deal relief for the arts as his topic—funding for the Philadelphia Civic Symphony. Using Philadelphia as his laboratory, Jarvis constructs a chapter that, read in conjunction with the others in this volume, demonstrates the nationwide catastrophe that the Depression wrought for the arts. He explains that modern technology, specifically the advent of the motion picture soundtrack and the concomitant decline of live film music, intensified unemployment problems for musicians during the Depression. He charts the various federal programs that provided employment-specific relief for musicians. Under the Civil Works Administration, Philadelphia gained a City Symphony in 1934. The result was a competition between the federally funded relief project and the privately funded Philadelphia Symphony Orchestra. The City Symphony achieved nationwide acclaim but was disbanded along with the CWA. The Works Progress Administration's Federal Project Number One filled the void with the Federal Music Project. Under the FMP, Philadelphia again gained a federally supported symphony—the Civic Symphony. This WPA Civic Symphony became the most important classical music outlet in Philadelphia by the late 1930s. Jarvis highlights accomplishments, which included promotion of American leadership and American music. These innovations reinforced important cultural values during a period of economic crisis. Likewise, the Civic provided an outlet for young talent not contracted out to the established, professional orchestras. Jarvis notes that the Civic's popularity was most easily measured by the large audiences who attended concerts. Attendance became a problem only when the orchestra was forced to play in unpopular locations. Jarvis argues that relief programs such as the WPA's Civic Symphony ultimately served a broader purpose than job provision for unemployed musicians—the program added new dimensions to the cultural offerings within America, and, as a result, he suggests that government-sponsored art can have positive consequences.

The third part of this anthology moves beyond the New Deal to look at the war years as well. Ron Briley's chapter, "Don't Let Hitler (or the Depression) Kill Baseball: Franklin D. Roosevelt and the National Pastime, 1932—1945," analyzes the ways in which FDR "used the national pastime to ward off despair and retain American pride and morale during a period of crisis." Even as FDR preferred other sports, such as sailing, he recognized the centrality of baseball to most Americans. As a result, he often employed baseball metaphors to explain Depression Era policies. Briley's chapter has even more nuance. He juxtaposes FDR's use of baseball imagery against analysis of that sport's problems and development in the 1930s and 1940s. He explores how the Supreme Court decision arguing that baseball was not a business affected the players' demands for raises and the owners' implementation of salary reductions during the Depression. At just the time when a distraction like baseball would have been beneficial to the national psyche, Briley asserts the game faced a serious internal challenge. Baseball owners welcomed the opportunity to cooperate with the New Deal. The result is a rich tapestry from which the reader can discern how politics influenced popular culture and vice versa.

I

FDR

1

The Popular Iconography of FDR

Lynn Y. Weiner and Ronald D. Tallman

No American president was more concerned about how he was portrayed than Franklin Delano Roosevelt. He shrouded himself in dozens of disguises, including Sphinx, Father, Doctor and Captain of the Ship of State. One main theme was consistent. FDR invariably represented himself, and was portrayed by others, as hale, hearty, optimistic, and healthy, his most brilliant disguise. That image of vigor makes ironic the debate over the depiction of Roosevelt in his memorial statues in Washington, DC, and raises complex issues about the portrayal of the best-known but most enigmatic president of the twentieth century. Should his physical disability be featured or hidden?[1]

This controversy is one of the many expressions of the iconographic complexity of the 32nd president of the United States. Hundreds of thousands of material artifacts—not only memorial statues, but also paintings, political buttons, toys, and utilitarian objects—have presented the president in varied ways for the past sixty years. The U.S. government has enshrined FDR's likeness on the fifty-dollar savings bond, postage stamps, and, of course, the ubiquitous Roosevelt dime. Symbols relating to FDR have also abounded in speeches, cartoons, and other printed matter. This essay introduces some of the myriad images of FDR both in the historical literature and in surviving examples of FDR memorabilia, and suggests how their construction has contributed to the enduring reputation of Roosevelt in the collective memory of the nation.

Material objects related to presidents and their campaigns have existed since the beginning of the republic, but especially since about the 1880s, when participation in electoral politics became relatively high. The existence of utilitarian objects representing the virtues (or flaws) of a politician, according to the Museum of American Political Life, "suggest[s] the public's wide-spread involvement in the presidential selection process."[2] Presidential campaign objects also represent the increasing commodification of the electoral process, as well as the growing consumer culture in the United States. By the late nineteenth century, political parties began to run their campaigns much like businesses, using advertising and the image of the candidate as tools of campaign strategy.[3] Moreover, for a few presidents whose reputations were shaped by such national emergencies as war or martyrdom, public veneration led not only to perpetuating their names through children, highways, schools, bridges, and museums, but also to the crafting of iconographic items displayed in the homes of ordinary citizens. These included political textiles (such as banners and pennants), campaign ceramics (such as commemorative china and glassware), lapel pieces, political paper, clothing, novelties, and games. One scholar suggested that such political Americana provides an invaluable personal and material link between the public and those who have been elected to office.[4]

No president generated as many iconographic objects as did Franklin Delano Roosevelt. Because of the length of his term in office, his unprecedented four astonishing campaigns, objects like political buttons and posters, coins and medals, busts, wall plaques, and paintings exist by the thousands, but so do such mundane items as matchboxes, trays, drums, bottles, dishes, cups, neckties, license plates, pillowcases, figural clocks, toys, and dolls. These artifacts often identify a singular achievement. One bust, for example, is entitled "Our 'New Deal' President"; sets of china memorialize specific treaties or election victories; a figural clock presents FDR behind a bar observing a festive party celebrating the end of prohibition. These varied objects were produced both during FDR's lifetime and in the years immediately after his death.

Material artifacts relating to FDR are preserved in several places. These include organizations that collect national political memorabilia, such as the Smithsonian Institution; the Roosevelt Presidential Library and Franklin and Eleanor Roosevelt Institute in Hyde Park, New York, and individual or smaller collections, including that of the Center for New Deal Studies at Roosevelt University in Chicago. At Roosevelt University, the FDR artifact holdings are dominated by the collection of Joseph M. Jacobs, a Chicago labor lawyer. Jacobs amassed a huge 4,000—item collection of memorabilia relating to FDR, including such personal items as cigarette holders, shot glasses, and playing cards. This collection is considered the largest private FDR memorabilia collection in the world.[5] Many of the objects in the collection were produced commercially for souvenir or political purposes, but some are handmade, rare, or unique. A similar but smaller collection of memorabilia, the Lowery Collection, was donated to the University in 1996 by the Roosevelt Institute.

Shortly after FDR's death in 1945, Jacobs began to collect the kind of items that were, he said, "icons" of FDR produced or displayed by ordinary Americans. He wanted to see the varied ways in which FDR was portrayed or venerated in the American home.[6] Jacobs was as interested in seeing the third or fourth copy or reworking of a painting or bust as he was in securing the original artifact. This collection is therefore a fascinating resource for understanding how Americans commemorated FDR both before and after his death, and offers a way to supplement the more conventional use of print material for the interpretation of American political culture.

For a rare few venerated presidents, powerful symbols have emerged to express popular and simplistic conceptions of their place in American history. These images help to both create a mythology of American leadership and maintain a collective memory of the presidency. Although these memories change over time, for these special presidents, their ranking at the top of the list of American presidents seems secure. According to one historian:

> Each of the three centuries since the founding of the American republic has produced a president whom the public reveres as an irreproachable paragon of leadership. The eighteenth century gave the nation George Washington, the . . . Father of his Country. . . . The nineteenth century witnessed the emergence of Abraham Lincoln . . . Great Emancipator. . . . The twentieth century has seen the elevation of Franklin Delano Roosevelt, Doctor New Deal and Doctor Win-the-War, his county's leader in the best and worst of times.[7]

Historians have consistently ranked Roosevelt as one of the greatest presidents of the United States along with George Washington and Abraham Lincoln. But this elevated ranking began in his own time, as seen in commercial items associating Roosevelt with a pantheon of exemplary presidents. A typical example is a cardboard fan held in the Center for New Deal Studies, which advertises Edinger's Bakery in Philadelphia. Dated 1933, this object portrays a painting of FDR seated in front of a radio microphone on one side, surrounded by the approving visages of six previous "great" presidents, including Andrew Jackson, Abraham Lincoln, Theodore Roosevelt, Woodrow Wilson, Thomas Jefferson, and George Washington. On the back of the fan, the text suggests that this "president of all the people" has already (by 1933) been placed "on a par with great Presidents of the past. He stands today as a symbol of America, of the fighting, courageous, gallant America built by our leaders of the past." There are also trays, dishware, and other items portraying FDR not only with past presidents, but with world leaders such as Winston Churchill.[8] That FDR assumes this stature seems appropriate, for he was deeply aware of his reputation in American history.

Roosevelt often quoted Oliver Wendell Holmes: "We live by symbols." He was a crafty manipulator of the symbolic image of past presidents, particularly of Abraham Lincoln. Just as Ronald Reagan later ignored political party lines to appropriate FDR for his own, so FDR did the same in shrewdly appropriating the mantle of the Republican Lincoln. In his speeches, Roosevelt often quoted Lincoln; he made a well-publicized visit to the log cabin where Lincoln allegedly was born, and in 1935 on Lincoln's birthday, he "made a public display of meeting with the only surviving man who had guarded Lincoln's body when it lay in state" a century earlier.[9] That in the 1980s and 1990s FDR's memory was freely evoked by politicians of both parties—from the Democrat Senator Edward Kennedy on the one hand to the Republican House Speaker Newt Gingrich on the other—suggests that his function as a historical symbol, like that of

Abraham Lincoln, remained powerful long after his lifetime.[10]

There is not yet a comprehensive study of portraits of FDR, but a multiplicity of images exist in memorabilia collections. Very few photographs or artifacts depict the president's physical disability. Many portraits, representations, and objects instead show an optimistic man clearly in control. Even the caricatures emphasize a strong jaw, often clenched around a cigarette, good humor, a man clearly in command. Caricatures were created not only in posters and buttons, but also in items like bottletops, dolls, smoking pipes, and even the cloth arm patches worn by FDR's personal airplane pilots. The latter is particularly rich in symbolism. A "Mr. Peanut" icon with FDR's aristocratic face wears a top hat and monocle, and leans on a cane, though the bottom half of the body is configured into a bomb. FDR's beloved dog Fala hovers in the clouds above. Some of the representations, however, take on more specific iconographic or metaphoric meanings to suggest strength, power, and mastery. At least four such images appear in the memorabilia of FDR: Roosevelt as Sphinx, Father, Doctor, and Captain. Although we suggest interpretations to fit these images, we are aware that—appropriately—sometimes an image of FDR can be perceived in more than one way.

FDR as Sphinx

"The Sphinx" is a good example of a focused representation of FDR that has a historical context and survived well after FDR's death in the shape of souvenir iconography linking the president to a powerful and ancient symbol. There exists in the Center for New Deal Studies a miniature reproduction of a papier-maché caricature of FDR now held at the FDR Library in Hyde Park. The original is over seven feet tall and built in the shape of a pyramid. It portrays FDR's smiling face, teeth gripping a cigarette in a sphinxlike caricature. This sphinx was created by James D. Preston of Washington, DC, and was first displayed in December 1939 at the annual winter dinner of the Gridiron Club, the organization of White House press correspondents.

According to FDR Library notes, Roosevelt at this time was sometimes referred to as "The Sphinx" because he refused to say if he would seek nomination in 1940 for an unprecedented third term as president. The reproduction was sold at one time at the FDR Library museum shop. The imagery is also used in political cartoons, such as the example by Ross Lewis of the *Milwaukee Journal* that pictured FDR as a sphinx giving such "cryptic answers to third term queries" as "abracadabra."[11] Although not a particularly widely used image of Roosevelt, this is an interesting symbol suggesting the enigmatic and shifting nature of the president. The popularity of the sphinx artifact long after memories of the third campaign dimmed also evidences that the image of FDR as an enigma remained potent for decades.

FDR as Father

A second image of FDR is that of Father. In 1932, when FDR told listeners in Detroit that "six million children do not have enough to eat," critics called his programs "paternalistic." His simple reply: "All right; I am a father."[12] The Jacobs Collection holds a remarkable portrait of FDR, which can be interpreted as Father of the New Deal. In this WPA-like painting, almost cartoonish in style and signed by a "J.M. Robinson," a strong and vigorous FDR (standing on his two legs!) holds a blueprint or plan in his hand. He is surrounded by adoring Americans of many kinds: farmers, the elderly, working men and women, children, the sick, the blind, immigrants, soldiers, the African American domestic servant and Pullman porter. Looming in the background are planes and ships of the American military. Because the soldiers are dressed in the style of World War I, it appears that this undated painting was crafted sometime during the 1930s. Clearly, the president is in control and in a paternalistic position of protection and leadership of this family of citizens.

FDR as Doctor

The portrait just referred to might also be interpreted as Doctor of the New Deal—the kindly old-fashioned family physician healing the sick. A common representation of FDR during his lifetime (but apparently not so much thereafter) was as a doctor: either Doctor New Deal or Doctor Win-the-War. This symbolism of FDR as a healer was consciously crafted by the president himself. Medical metaphors came into frequent use in presidential press conferences as well as in political cartoons. One example can be seen in a cartoon by C. K. Berryman, published in the *Washington Star* in December 1943, and captioned "There's an Odd Family Resemblance Among the Doctors." Dr. New Deal stands by the ailing John Q. Public; on the bedside table are potions and bottles of various welfare remedies. Dr. Win-the-War strides into the sickroom to further tend the patient, while Dr. Fourth Term hovers behind in the doorway.[13]

In printed material, the term "Doctor Roosevelt," "Old Doctor Roosevelt," "Doctor Win-the-War," and "Dr. Brain Trust" are much used, although this imagery does not proliferate in the artifacts. Nevertheless, this iconography is part of the larger picture of FDR. A doctor has mastery over illness, and, possibly as a victim of polio, FDR's attempt to doctor himself and others translated into efforts to heal the nation economically and militarily. His remarkable success in combatting a debilitating physical illness contributed to his effective use of images of mastery and control.

Roosevelt's speeches reflect this crafting of the image of president as doctor. For example, in the well-known Quarantine Speech of October 5, 1937, FDR states that "War is a contagion" and that the United States must oppose violations of treaties by quarantining lawbreaking nations just as one would a sick patient "in order to protect the health of the community against the spread of the disease."[14] In another example, he discussed the fate of the New Deal during wartime in a December 1943 press conference:

> How did the New Deal come into existence? It was because there was an awfully sick patient called the United States of America. . . And they sent for the doctor. . . . And there were certain specific remedies that the poor old doctor gave the patient, and I jotted down a few of these remedies . . . But since then, two years ago, the patient had a very bad accident. . . Old Dr. New Deal didn't know "nothing" about legs and arms . . . So he got his partner, who was an orthopedic surgeon. Dr. Win-the-War to take care of this fellow who had been in this bad accident.[15]

Writers quickly appropriated this imagery. Presidential speech writer Samuel Rosenman recalled in his memoirs how "Dr. New Deal and Dr. Win-the-War soon became very well known and oft-mentioned practitioners." John Gunther noted how "Dr. New Deal" gave way to "Dr. Win-the-War" by 1943, and Geoffrey Ward titles a chapter in his book on FDR, "Old Doctor Roosevelt."[16]

FDR As Captain of the Ship of State

Perhaps the clearest example of an iconographic use of FDR in the material culture is as ship's captain. Roosevelt's inaugural medals are inscribed "sail on o Ship of State: Sail on o Union strong and great."[17] Additionally, many paintings and other objects depict the president as a ship's captain or helmsman.

This captain imagery emerged as much from FDR's own self-conception as from the imposition of a symbol by the public. FDR was always interested "in ships, in sailing, and in tales of the sea."[18] As a child, his love of the sea led him to build sailing ship models; as an adult, he collected books and prints on naval history. Sailing dominated his summers at Campobello Island as a child and young man. From 1913 through 1920, he served as Assistant Secretary of the Navy. "I love to be on the water," he once said. "All my life I have loved ships and have been a student of the Navy."[19]

FDR often used the language of the helmsman. During the Depression, while referring to an economic downturn, "He made it quite clear . . . as he had said so often in private conversation—that instead of pulling in or trimming sails, the way to beat the recession was to go ahead full speed."[20] In another example, he said in an April 1938 Fireside Chat about the New Deal:

I believe we have been right in the course we have charted. To abandon our purpose of building a greater, a more stable and a more tolerant America, would be to miss the tide and perhaps to miss the port. I propose to sail ahead, I feel sure that your hopes and your help are with me. For to reach a port, we must sail—sail, not tie at anchor—sail, not drift.[21]

After Pearl Harbor, FDR wrote out in his own hand the passage from Longfellow's 1849 poem, "The Building of the Ship," which was used on his inaugural medals, and sent it along to Winston Churchill:

> Sail on, O Ship of State!
>
> Sail on, O Union, strong and great!
>
> Humanity with all its fears,
>
> With all the hopes of future years,
>
> Is hanging breathless on thy fate![22]

Other representations of Roosevelt as helmsman of variously the New Deal and the United States at war exist in metal figured clocks. The clocks depict FDR as a strong captain standing upright and gripping the wheel of a ship. The clock face is often embedded in the wheel. Some of the clocks present the faces of FDR along with other U.S. presidents, such as George Washington and Abraham Lincoln. Others are also configured into lamps. Some are inscribed "Captain of the Ship of State," "Steersman of the U. S. A.," or "Captain of the New Deal." Joseph Jacobs stated these clocks were raffled off in saloons during the 1930s and 1940s.[23] They are an outstanding example of how mundane objects were used to express iconographic expressions of venerated public figures.

A final example of this metaphor of ship's captain can be seen in a portrait held in the Jacobs Collection, copied from a well-known war poster. In this picture, a masterful FDR surveys his domain, cape blowing in the wind. The captain identifies this portrait as the "Commander-in-Chief Reviewing the Troops, Oct. 1944" and is signed "A.L., May 1946." Created just after FDR's death, this picture is one of many hand-crafted posthumous depictions of a heroic leader. The captain firmly in charge of his ship became a powerful metaphor for the active presidential style forged by Roosevelt.

The ambiguity of meaning found in the Roosevelt iconography is certainly part of the appeal of his image. Artists considered Roosevelt to be a difficult subject "whose mobile features never remained in repose long enough for them to capture the expression they sought." His seemingly chameleon nature allowed Americans to impose their hopes and fears onto representations of this larger-than-life political actor. One contemporary of FDR suggested "that Roosevelt as an enigma seems to be a fairly well-founded impression." The historian James MacGregor Burns said of FDR that "bewildering complexity" was his most visible trait. John Milton Cooper, Jr., has pointed out some contradictions of FDR, including that "he was . . . a person of flashy charm but barely disguised deviousness."[24] Roosevelt was a man who could not stand without help yet embodied power and mastery, and a champion of the poor who never had to earn his own living. These contradictions and complexities undoubtedly contributed to the range of representations and interpretations found in the evidence.

Although most of these representations were positive, some were not. Like other powerful figures, FDR's public was peopled with vicious enemies as well as adoring friends. This is reflected in the historical record of both print and material artifacts. There are some cruel portrayals of the president in cartoons, doggerel, and verse, as well as indirect attacks in the form of satires and unflattering caricatures mocking his wife, Eleanor. Anti-Roosevelt humor survives, for example, in such artifacts as business cards. These cards apparently were "everywhere, stuck up over cash registers, along the edges of desk blotters, passed from hand to hand by salesmen calling on customers, and materializing from billfolds wherever men gathered for shop talk and a smoke."[25] A typical example reads: "If you don't give me an order, I'll vote for That Man again." Political buttons argued, "We Don't Want Eleanor Either!" or "Out! Stealing Third." There were anti-Roosevelt poems galore, often distributed by business firms. One example, circulated by the Deluxe Stamp Works of Auburn, Nebraska, stated:

> "Who ploughed up cotton, corn, and wheat,
> Who killed our pigs, destroyed our meat?'
> 'Twas he, the captain of the fleet.
> 'Twas Roosevelt.[26]

Interestingly, much of the anti-Roosevelt material reflects the dominant images of the president, particularly the sea captain imagery, as in the previous poem. But this material is in the minority. The overwhelming tone of the thousands of surviving artifacts commemorates rather than excoriates FDR.

The vast amount of FDR memorabilia is appropriate for a man who was himself an avid collector—"of stamps, coins, stuffed birds, prints and books."[27] The historian Samuel Eliot Morison warned the president "that he was overwhelming his new Presidential library, not with books or files, but with things." The basement of the library was stuffed with the president's favorite carriages, sleighs, farm implements, a 1936 Ford Phaeton automobile, and even two iceboats—the 69-foot *Icicle* and the smaller vessel, *Hawk*. "I know you are the Nation's No. 1 collector," Mr. Morison wrote, "But collecting can be overdone even by No. 1."[28]

The surviving FDR memorabilia, however, is not overdone but is priceless. The collections offer exciting potential for understanding a dimension of how FDR was understood, venerated, and sometimes vilified by ordinary people. Such artifacts as neckties, smoking pipes, trays, political buttons, thermometer plaques, and busts captured representations of the president in a variety of guises that functioned in a variety of ways. Some were made for the purposes of political promotion or commentary. Some were made for commercial reasons. But others reflect a kind of hagiography or veneration of a beloved leader. The iconography of FDR, through such images as sphinx, father, doctor, and ship's captain, interpreted historical actions to build a popular mythology of the president that has survived half a century. This wealth of memorabilia, along with the strong images preserved in the historical literature, helped FDR to attain "the distinction of his predecessors, George Washington and Abraham Lincoln, of being recognizable to Americans of all generations."[29] Indeed, these artifacts of popular political culture both contribute to and reflect FDR's distinctive niche in the collective national memory.

ENDNOTES

1. A "splendid deception" and unspoken code of honor among photographers and reporters kept the extent of his paralysis hidden from the public, but on a few occasions, the president chose to reveal his disability. See Doris Kearns Goodwin, *No Ordinary Time: Franklin and Eleanor Roosevelt: The Home Front in World War II*, p. 586-587 (New York: Simon & Schuster, 1994).

2. Museum of American Political Life, *Hell-Bent for the White House*, p. 36 (Hartford, CT: University of Hartford, 1988).

3. Robert B. Westbrook, "Politicis as Consumption: Managing the Modern American Election," in Richard Wightman Fox and T. J. Jackson Lears, eds., *The Culture of Consumption*, pp. 145-173 (New York: Pantheon Books, 1983).

4. Jonathan H. Mann, "Morsels of History," in Arthur M. Schlesinger, Jr., ed., *Running for President*, p. 452 (New York: Simon and Schuster, 1994).

5. Press Release: "News from the Office of the Governor [of Illinois]" October 30, 1990; "The Jacobs Collection of FDR Memorabilia Donated to the Illinois Historic Preservation Agency," *The Political Bandwagon* (December 1990), 1; both of these are in the Jacobs File, Jacobs Collection, Center for New Deal Studies. The Jacobs Collection was donated to Roosevelt University in 1993. At the same time, Jacobs donated a large collection of print material related to the president to the University of Illinois at Chicago. For an overview of FDR and the world of collectors, see the run of the magazine, *The Roosevelt Collector*, Center for New Deal Studies.

6. "The Joseph M. Jacobs collection of Franklin D. Roosevelt Memorabilia," Undated MS, Jacobs File, Jacobs Collection, Center for New Deal Studies.

7. John Milton Cooper, Jr., "Foreword" in Patrick J. Maney, *The Roosevelt Presence: A Biography of Franklin Delano Roosevelt*, p. xi (New York: Twayne, 1992).

8. On the ranking of FDR and other presidents, see William Pederson and Ann McLaurin, eds., *The Rating Game in American Politics: An Interdisciplinary Approach* (New York: Irvington, 1987).

9. On FDR's use of Lincoln symbolism, see Michael Kammen, *Mystic Chords of Memory: The Transformation of Tradition in American Culture*, p. 452 (New York: Vintage Books, 1993) and Maney, *The Roosevelt Presence*, pp. 193-194.

10. Alan Brinkley, "Legacies of the New Deal," The Chronicle of Higher

Education, May 19, 1995, p. B1. See also James MacGregor Burns, *Roosevelt: The Soldier of Freedom*, pp. 6-7 (New York: Harcourt Brace Jovanovich, 1970).

11. "The Sphinx," note attached to artifact (Hyde Park, NY: Franklin D. Roosevelt Library Museum, n.d.); for the cartoon, see Otis L. Graham, Jr. and Megham Robinson Wander, *Franklin D. Roosevelt: His Life and Times*, p, 120 (Boston: G.K. Hall, 1985).

12. Katie Louchheim, ed. *The Making of the New Deal: The Insiders Speak*, p. 7 (Cambridge: Harvard University Press, 1983).

13. For the cartoon see Burns, *Roosevelt*, p. 423; see also John Gunther, *Roosevelt in Retrospect: A Profile in History*, pp. 415-416, 508 (New York: Harper and Row, 1948). See also Joseph Alsop, *FDR, 1882-1945: A Centenary Remembrance*, p. 206 (New York: Viking, 1982).

14. Graham and Wander, *Franklin D. Roosevelt*, p. 340.

15. Gunther, *Roosevelt in Retrospect*, p. 290.

16. Ibid. See also Samuel I. Rosenman, *Working with Roosevelt*, p. 416 (New York: Harper & Brothers, 1952); Geoffrey Ward, *A First Class Temperament, The Emergence of Franklin Roosevelt*, chap. 16 (New York: Harper & Row, 1989, and George Wolfskill and John Hudson, *All But the People: Franklin D. Roosevelt and His Critics, 1933-39*, p. 225 (London: Macmillan, 1969), p. 225.

17. Graham and Wander, *Franklin D. Roosevelt*, p. 472.

18. Ibid., p. 382.

19. Ibid., p. 383; Frank Freidel, *Franklin D. Roosevelt: A Rendezvous with Destiny*, p. 27 (Boston, Little Brown, 1990).

20. Rosenman, *Working with Roosevelt*, p. 172.

21. Ibid., p. 174.

22. Alsop, *FDR, 1882-1945*, p. 207.

23. Joseph and Esther Jacobs interview by L. Weiner, July 1993, Jacobs File, Jacobs Collection, Center for New Deal Studies.

24. Graham and Wander, *Franklin D. Roosevelt*, p. 333; Noell F. Busch, *What Manner of Man?*, p. 168 (New York: Harper & Brothers, 1944); Burns, *Roosevelt*, p. 9; Maney, *The Roosevelt Presence*, p. xi.

25. George Wolfskill and John Hudson, *All But the People: Franklin D. Roosevelt and His Critics, 1933-39*, p. 26 (London: Macmillan, 1969).

26. Ibid., pp. 26-9. For a discussion of some of the negative material created "in fun and malice," see Jerome K. Wilcox, "Anti-FDR Checklist," *The Roosevelt Collector* (May 1954), pp. 3-18. See also the political buttons in the Jacobs Collection.

27. Goodwin, *No Ordinary Time*, p. 108.

28. *New York Times*, June 6, 1995, p. A12.

29. Graham and Wander, *Franklin D. Roosevelt*, p. 259.

2

The Sun Comes Out Tomorrow
Hollywood's Depiction of Franklin D. Roosevelt and The New Deal, From *Gabriel Over the White House* to *Annie*

Ron Briley

In a May 31, 1995 speech, G.O.P. presidential Senator Bob Dole of Kansas lambasted Hollywood for the "mainstreaming of deviancy," arguing that a "line has been crossed, not just of taste but of human dignity and decency." Dole's political attack echoed the sentiments expressed by conservative film critic Michael Medved in his 1992 best seller *Hollywood vs. America*. Medved wrote, "Tens of millions of Americans now see the entertainment industry as an all-powerful enemy, an alien force that assaults our most cherished values and corrupts our children." In the assertions of Dole and Medved, as well as Vice President Dan Quayle's controversial commentary on television's "Murphy Brown," Hollywood's depiction of sex and violence is linked to an assault upon traditional American institutions and values such as the family, patriotism, religion, free enterprise, and individual responsibility. More liberal defenders of the Hollywood entertainment industry perceive conservative voices such as Dole and Medved as providing rhetorical cover to justify the destruction of government programs to aid those less privileged in American society, those citizens whom president Franklin D. Roosevelt labeled as the one-third of a nation ill-fed, clothed, and housed. Thus, writing in the *Nation*, Michael Eric Dyson asserted, "To be sure, there have been severe assaults on American families and their values, but they have come not from Hollywood but from Washington: cruel cuts in social programs for the neediest, a redistribution of wealth to the rich and a conservative political campaign to demonize poor black mothers and their children."[1]

For those concerned with Hollywood as an institution reflecting and encouraging the decline of traditional American values of individual responsibility and self-reliance, there appears almost a direct line stretching from the politics of current Democratic incumbent Bill Clinton through Lyndon Johnson's Great Society back to its origins in Franklin Roosevelt's New Deal. In this conservative critique, it is government expansion and intrusion into American life, encouraged and abetted by Hollywood's embracing of Roosevelt's New Deal and liberal ideology, which have eroded individual accountability and prepared the way for a decline in American values. One possible approach, proposed by this study, for considering this thesis is to examine Hollywood treatment of the liberal icon and conservative demon Franklin D. Roosevelt and the legacy of the New Deal.

Roosevelt's patrician upbringing in the rural estate of Hyde Park was considerably different from the urban and ethnic environment of the moguls who created the motion picture industry in Hollywood. Described by biographers as a "genteel reformer" whose environment "laid no stress on competitive achievement in business or politics,"[2] Roosevelt, nevertheless, formed many friendships with influential members of the film community, such as Melvyn Douglas and Helen Gahagen Douglas, who served in Congress and suffered defeat at the hands of Richard Nixon in a controversial California senatorial contest. In addition, in a 1941 address to the Annual Awards Dinner of the Academy of Motion Picture Arts and Sciences, Roosevelt demonstrated his understanding of the role played by Hollywood in American life. The president observed, "The American motion picture as a national and international force is a phenomenon of our own generation. Within living memory we have seen the American motion picture become foremost in all the world. We have seen it reflect our civilization throughout the rest of the world—the aims and aspirations and the ideals of a free people and of freedom itself." While praising the industry as a champion of American democratic values, Roosevelt did not ignore the economic influence of the Hollywood product, condemning European dictators for blocking the exhibition of American films.[3] Thus, the origins of World War II as a conflict over access to international markets was certainly part of Hollywood's support for FDR during the war.

However, the Hollywood community was certainly not monolithic in its support for the New Deal. Concern over the perceived radicalization of New Deal policies led some film industry moguls, such as Louis B. Mayer and Irving Thalberg, to use film as a technique to discredit the 1934 California Democratic nominee for governor, novelist Upton Sinclair and his program to End Poverty in California.[4] While Roosevelt's support for Sinclair was somewhat lukewarm, Mayer and Thalberg's fake film footage, portraying legions of the unemployed entering California to take advantage of Sinclair's programs, made certain that a Republican would be elected governor of California. Sinclair advocated that unused factories be turned over to the unemployed, who would produce goods for their use, followed by a barter system between factories ushering in a radical reconstruction of the economy. Mayer and Thalberg perceived this program and the liberalism of the New Deal as threatening their economic interests. Accordingly, Roosevelt, like Bill Clinton, formed an ambiguous relationship with Hollywood voices who simply do not represent a one-dimensional entertainment perspective.

Although some of the roots of the contemporary controversy surrounding politics and the film industry may be found in the political and personal animosities focused upon Roosevelt, most of these associations were unknown to the general public (although the relationship between Roosevelt and the Hollywood Community merits serious scholarly attention in its own right). Therefore, in order to consider how the American people's perception of Roosevelt and New Deal policies were influenced by the Hollywood film industry, it is necessary to examine film depiction of the president and his political legacy. This chapter concentrates on Hollywood commentaries regarding politics during the 1930s, the World War II, and postwar anticommunist paranoia. Most of these films, with a few exceptions such as the controversial *Mission to Moscow* (1943), failed to directly portray Roosevelt and his administration, preferring to work through political allegory, assuming that the audience would be able to make some rather obvious connections, with such films as *Gabriel Over the White House* (1933), *Wild Boys of the Road* (1933), *Our Daily Bread* (1934), *The President Vanishes* (1934), *Confessions of a Nazi Spy* (1939), *Mr. Smith Goes to Washington* (1939), *The Grapes of Wrath* (1940), *Young Mr. Lincoln* (1940), *Meet John Doe* (1941), and *Wilson* (1944).

After retreating before the onslaught of the investigations launched by the House Committee on Un-American Activities, Hollywood liberals appeared ready to embrace the legacy of FDR with the 1960 film adaptation of Dore Schary's play *Sunrise at Campobello*. Although this represented Hollywood's only major effort to deal with the life of FDR, the film often seemed to better reflect an endorsement of John Kennedy's New Frontier. With the civil rights movement and Vietnam War undermining the liberal postwar consensus, Hollywood entertainment and audiences expressed little interest in the legacy of Roosevelt, with the exception of television docu-dramas, which have not found a great audience or the prestige of a theatrical release. Thus, many younger members of the American public have had their perception of Franklin Roosevelt shaped by the 1980s musical *Annie*, in which Eleanor and Franklin Roosevelt offer musical accompaniment to wish the Depression away. This film, which deserves considerable commentary, uses Roosevelt to support the more conservative values of the Reagan years. Although Franklin Roosevelt has not been the subject of a Hollywood theatrical release since 1982 (although current preoccupation with the sex lives of Eleanor and Franklin Roosevelt would seem to make such a project a natural in the Hollywood depicted by Bob Dole), the legacy of New Deal ideology regarding the relationship between the individual and government policies remains a crucial element of the contemporary Hollywood scene from *Apollo 13*, government support of the space program and astronauts with traditional values, to *Kids*, in which young offsprings of a liberal society appear amoral and adrift in a world without individual responsibility and accountability. However, a survey of Hollywood's depiction of Franklin Roosevelt and his New Deal provides little evidence for a concerted Hollywood plot to support government programs that undermine the role of individual responsibility in American society.

If the historical and contemporary Hollywood scene indicates an ambiguity that undercuts the assumption of depravity and rejection of traditional American values, it is not surprising, for the film treatment of FDR lacks a clear focus. As scholar William Leuchtenburg observed, the legacy of Roosevelt and the New Deal is ambiguous. Although the New Deal did not solve the economic causes of the Great Depression, Leuchtenburg wrote, "When recovery did come, it was much more soundly based because of the adoption of the New Deal programs." And as for FDR himself, Leuchtenburg argued his importance "resides in his ability to arouse the country and, more specifically, the men who served under him, by his breezy encouragement of experimentation, by his hopefulness, and—a word that would have embarrassed some of his lieutenants—by his idealism." Perhaps no greater compliment to Roosevelt has been paid than that of his successors who have lived in his shadow. And even such Roosevelt critics as Ronald Reagan and Newt Gingrich have found it prudent to evoke positive memories of Franklin Roosevelt while simultaneously denouncing the idealistic and humanitarian programs of the New Deal.[5]

An examination of Hollywood's depiction of Roosevelt lends credence to this confusing legacy, rather than the film community's embracing of what critics would call the "stateism" inherent in New Deal policies. In films such as *Public Enemy* (1931) and *I Am a Fugitive from a Chain Gang* (1932), made during the nadir of the Depression, Warner Brothers established a reputation for a social consciousness, depicting the despair of the economic crisis and the failure of the American dream. In *Public Enemy*, Tom Powers (James Cagney) turns to a life of crime and, in an inversion of the Horatio Alger mythology, at least temporarily attains the rewards of material success denied to his brother Mike, who attempts to follow the traditional path of patriotic service, education, and the work ethic. Whereas Tom dies a violent death, the audience finds his life more attractive than that of his brother Mike, who seems to have suffered death and loss of spirit in a meaningless existence. In *I Am a Fugitive from a Chain Gang*, James Allen (Paul Muni) serves his country during World War I, but economic conditions blunt his pursuit of the American dream, and he is falsely imprisoned on the chain gang. Escaping from his confinement, Allen is temporarily successful in Chicago. However, when his true identity is revealed, Allen makes a deal with the state and voluntarily returns to serve a portion of his sentence. Allen is betrayed when the state reneges on the deal, and he is returned to the chain gang. Escaping again, Allen becomes a fugitive, and in the chilling last line of the film, he answers his girlfriend's inquiry as to how he will be able to survive by simply stating, "I steal." The American dream has collapsed and, along with it, the social contract. Unable to protect life, liberty, and property, Allen seems justified in his revolt against the established order.[6]

In this environment of fear and despair captured by Warner Brothers with the fictional characters of Tom Powers and James Allen, historian Arthur Schlesinger described a profound political crisis on the eve of Roosevelt's inauguration. Writing in the first volume of his *Age of Roosevelt*, Schlesinger found, "The images of a nation as it approached zero hour: the well-groomed men, baffled and impotent in their double-breasted suit before the Senate Committee; the confusion and dismay in the business office and the university; the fear in the country club; the angry men marching in the silent street; the scramble for the rotting garbage in the dump; the sweet milk trickling down the dusty road; the noose dangling over the barn door; the raw northwest wind blasting its way across the Capitol plaza."[7]

In this milieu of political revolt and uncertainty, Hollywood moguls produced films that advocated strong solutions for America's ills. For example, in Cecil B. DeMille's *This Day and Age* (1933), high school students take the law into their hands and disperse shysters who have hidden behind the cloak of due process, and *Washington Masquerade* (1932) and *Washington Merry-Go-Round* (1933) focus on corruption in the nation's capital. However, the most controversial of early 1930s political films was *Gabriel Over the White House* (1933), released several weeks after Roosevelt's inauguration by William Randolph Hearst's Cosmopolitan Studios, in conjunction with MGM. In *Gabriel*, President Judd Hammond (Walter Huston), sounding a great deal like President Herbert Hoover, meets the challenge of the national economic crisis by espousing political platitudes regarding the democratic spirit of the American people. However, Hammond is transformed by an automobile accident. Apparently on his death bed following the accident, Hammond is revived when the spirit of the Angel Gabriel enters his body. Responding to this second chance at life, Hammond enters into a virtual orgy of action aimed at providing for economic recovery, weeding out political corruption, and ushering in world peace. Accordingly, the president repeals prohibition, ends racketeering through the application of a vigorous martial law, protects the bank accounts of the common people, provides aid for farmers, uses surplus food to feed the starving, enlists the unemployed in an Army of Construction "subject to military discipline," and summons representatives of foreign powers to a disarmament conference where a display of American air power convinces these nations to disarm and pay their war debts. After using Lincoln's quill pen (the Lincoln motif was to prove popular with both writers and filmmakers during the difficult Depression years) to sign the universal disarmament accord, Hammond collapses and dies in the arms of his lover, who assures him that he is "one of the greatest men who ever lived." Yet, Hammond accomplishes his great deeds through authoritarian means, as he forces his cabinet into resigning and coerces Congress into declaring a State of National Emergency providing the president with dictatorial powers.[8] Clearly, Hearst, a Roosevelt supporter at this point, sought to influence the action of the new administration. And, indeed, in the New Deal, there is much of the vigorous action, policy and program ideas, and enhanced executive power suggested by Jeff Hammond and the *Gabriel* script, but missing is the radical application of authoritarian means.

The implications of *Gabriel Over the White House* for Roosevelt and the American form of government were obvious to contemporary critics, who labeled the film as fascist but dismissed the impact of Hearst's political fantasy. In the *Nation*, reviewer William Troy described *Gabriel* as an effort to "convert innocent American movie audiences to a policy of fascist dictatorship in this country." However, Troy concluded that American audiences, not particularly susceptible to the blandishments of Hearst, were "unready or unwilling to sacrifice entertainment for political propaganda." In a similar vein, political columnist Walter Lippmann dismissed the Hearst epic, arguing that the political message would hardly replace the traditional Hollywood romantic genre. Describing the world of *Gabriel* as the "infantile world of irresistible wishes," Lippmann quipped that in contrast with Hearst's President Hammond, the great screen lovers "seem not only more enchanting than ever but more efficient, learned, and profound in their knowledge of what is common to the whole race of men." The *New Republic* labeled *Gabriel* as a "half-hearted plea for Fascism," but observed that Roosevelt's success with Congress "has served to canalize most of the pro-dictatorship sentiment." In agreement with the *New Republic*'s review, film historians Peter Roffman and Jim Purdy argued that whereas Roosevelt's Hundred Days failed to solve the economic problems of the Depression, the president's actions restored hope to the American people and "made the move beyond the law suggested by the right-wing cycle unnecessary."[9]

Thus, the despair of *Public Enemy* and *Fugitive from a Chain Gang* for which DeMille and Hearst prescribed vigilantism and dictatorship was replaced by more benevolent depiction of political leadership and possibilities for regaining the American dream. In the 1933 production *Wild Boys of the Road*, Warner Brothers ostensibly returned to the formula of *Fugitive from a Chain Gang* by focusing on human suffering and discontent brought on by the Depression. However, this film was to provide a much more optimistic conclusion than James Allen's "I steal." The *Nation* praised the producers of *Wild Boys* for a realistic portrayal of the "increasing number of boys and girls in all parts of the country who are leaving their homes, where they can no longer be assured of either food or shelter, to shift for themselves on the road." However, the radical potential of this explosive subject matter was deflected by the film's conclusion, which sought to restore faith in the nation's political establishment. After chronicling the hardships suffered by young Eddie (Frankie Darro), who was forced to leave his family home due to the vicissitudes of the Depression, culminating in an unjust arrest for robbery, director William Wellman opts for an optimistic Hollywood ending. Eddie gives a courtroom speech berating the inequities of the American economic system. The judge, "bearing a reasonable resemblance to FDR" and seated beneath an NRA eagle emblem on the wall, is moved to dismiss the case, assuring Eddie that conditions in the country will improve and that he will personally help the young man and his friends find employment.[10] This rather direct endorsement of Roosevelt and the New Deal was also reflected in the more optimistic mood displayed in musicals (*42nd Street*, 1933), screwball comedies bridging class barriers (*It Happened One Night*, 1935), and gangster pictures such as *G-Men* (1935) in which former Public Enemy James Cagney joins the FBI.

However, not all film productions supported the premise that the Roosevelt style of leadership and New Deal programs were restoring confidence and placing America on the road to recovery. Stepping outside of the Hollywood mainstream, director King Vidor independently financed *Our Daily Bread* (1934), which was awarded a prize by the Moscow film festival. Borrowing from the documentary style of Soviet filmmaker Sergei Eisenstein, Vidor constructs a drama of a collective farm in which the unemployed of urban America seek solace and redemption through the land and the dignity of their labor. The film also appears to endorse authoritarianism as when the members of the collective discuss a form of government, and a Swedish immigrant carries the day with his argument, "We got a big job here and we need a big boss." John Sims (Tom Keene) emerges as that man of destiny, although his strength of purpose is tested by a blond sex symbol, who almost breaks up his marriage and the farm. However, John comes to his senses, returning to his wife and the land, leading the collective in the construction of an irrigation ditch that prevents drought and brings abundance.

Critical response to *Our Daily Bread* was mixed. Whereas some commentators praised the film for dipping into the "profound and basic problems of our everyday life," many others found the plot to be contrived, the acting wooden, and concluded that "directors should not be social propagandists." Despite a fair amount of attention paid in the press to Vidor's film, the independent production never found a wide audience. But certainly the production represented a criticism of Roosevelt and the New Deal with its assertion that a more collective approach, yet one guided by an authoritarian hand, was needed for the economic malaise affecting the nation.[11]

Roosevelt also faced hostility from more conservative members of the Hollywood establishment who were displeased with the Resettlement Administration's venture into filmmaking with Pare Lorentz's *The Plow that Broke the Plains* (1936). According to Lorentz, Will Hays, president of the Motion Picture Producers and Distributors of America, threatened to boycott the Modern Museum of Art Film Library for screening documentary films and prohibited the distribution of *The Plow that Broke the Plains* throughout the film industry. In response to these efforts at censorship, Lorentz pointed out that Hollywood was "the most backward of all our corporate industries, spending nothing for experimental production in its lust for profits."[12]

The animosity engendered within elements of the Hollywood community by the Roosevelt administration's documentary film program was paralleled by the ambivalence to the president portrayed in the work of one of the pillars of the Hollywood establishment in the 1930s, director Frank Capra, who as President of the Academy of Motion Picture Arts and Sciences sought to maintain the industry's control over labor in the film community. During World War II, Capra worked with the Office of War Information and Roosevelt officials in formulating the propaganda film series *Why We Fight*. On meeting FDR, Capra described the president as a man whose "head was the biggest, his face the widest, and his smile the most expansive I have ever seen." In fact, Capra confessed that Roosevelt had almost converted the director into becoming a Democrat.[13] Although Capra found Roosevelt personally charming, he was not about to alter his conservative principles. A Sicilian immigrant who had worked his way up from poverty, Capra failed to understand why those facing economic deprivation in the Depression looked to government rather than individual initiative for salvation. Along with his conservative social philosophy, Capra opposed Roosevelt because he feared that the president was a threat to democracy. Thus, in 1948, he asserted, "I am a Republican. I even voted against FDR right along, because I thought he was getting too big for the country's good. I am passionately against dictatorship in any form."[14]

This conservative slant was apparent in three of Capra's most acclaimed films: *Mr. Deeds Goes to Town* (1936), *Mr. Smith Goes to Washington* (1939), and *Meet John Doe* (1941). In each film, Capra's small-town rural hero is beset by the sinister forces of urban corruption and promises of power, yet in the end, American innocence and individualism emerge triumphant over these temptations. The plot for *Deeds* is disarmingly simple. Longfellow Deeds (Gary Cooper) inherits a fortune and leaves his small-town environment for the greener pastures of New York City. When he begins to give away his fortune to the unemployed, relatives, wanting to deny Deeds the inheritance, attempt to have the eccentric declared mentally incompetent. A distraught Deeds, after becoming convinced that Babe Bennett (Jean Arthur) is in love with him, makes an impassioned plea, convincing the judge that he is competent and offering a sane solution for troubled times. A deconstruction of Capra's message in *Deeds* is that government action is not required to deal with the Depression. Instead, economic relief may be attained through the philanthropy and common sense of wealthy individuals. Herbert Hoover's faith in the rugged individualism of the American people to overcome the Depression seems well personified in the character of Longfellow Deeds.[15]

A more direct assault on government as a source of corruption and threat to the individual is made in *Mr. Smith Goes to Washington.* Jefferson Smith (James Stewart) is appointed to the U.S. Senate by a corrupt political machine that operates under the assumption that the idealistic Smith will be easy to control. The naive young Senator, head of the Boy Rangers, arrives in the nation's capital eager to visit the Lincoln Memorial and make some small contribution to American democracy. For his pet project, Senator Smith selects the establishment of a dam for the Boy Rangers to be paid for out of private donations rather than government funding. However, the political machine plans the boondoggle of constructing a dam on the same land. The forces of corruption, led by Smith's hero, the state's senior senator Joseph Paine (Claude Rains), attempt to discredit and humiliate Smith. Inspired by political icon Abraham Lincoln, whose imagery was used effectively by Roosevelt, Smith fights back, using a filibuster to block the proposed legislation to create a dam. Demonstrating little faith in the power of democracy to triumph, Capra concludes his film by having an exhausted Smith pass out from the strains of his filibuster. However, honesty does prevail when a guilty Senator Paine attempts suicide and exposes the maneuverings of the political machine. It seems that if Senator Paine had simply displayed a little less conscience—then the corrupt scheme would have succeeded.

Capra's lack of faith in politicians in the nation's capital, dominated by the Roosevelt administration, was most evident to a screening of four thousand expectant Washingtonians under the auspices of the National Press Club. On hand were three members of the cabinet, about half of the House, and most U.S. Senators, who charged the film lowered the Senate's dignity. In a *Time* piece, three unidentified senators reviewed the picture, commenting, "Not all Senators are sons of bitches. Punk! It Stinks." However, film audiences and critics loved the film, praising its democratic themes. For example, Franz Hoellering, writing in the *Nation*, extolled the virtues of the film, observing, "The picture has the spirit of true democracy--there is no trace of the fake patriotism which certain business men have been trying to sell in the movie houses."[16]

Although Capra's reservations about the democratic potential of Washington politicians was lost on many observers, there could be little doubt regarding his fears of an American dictatorship in his 1941 offering, *Meet John Doe.* The Capra hero in *Meet John Doe* is a down-and-out minor-league baseball player, Long John Willoughby, whose arm has gone bad. Endeavoring to feed himself, Willoughby agrees to assume the role of John Doe, who is a fictional character created to enhance newspaper circulation. Doe is to represent the common man and threatens to commit suicide because of the sad condition of modern civilization. However, Doe soon begins to develop a political following, and John Doe clubs spring up across the nation. On the eve of a national John Doe convention, Willoughby discovers that newspaper publisher D. B. Norton (Edward Arnold) is manipulating the Doe movement in order to establish a dictatorship in America. When Willoughby attempts to expose Norton's designs, he is denounced as a fake, and the Doe club members turn on their former leader. Seeking to resurrect the John Doe movement, Willoughby plans to carry out the original suicide threat. But he is dissuaded by the love of reporter Anne Mitchell (Barbara Stanwyck) and members of the John Doe clubs, who want to renew the movement. Carrying Anne in his arms, Willoughby and his followers stride into the night determined that the forces of populism will prevail over darkness and dictatorship.

This conclusion, with which Capra struggled, filming several different scenarios, is most ambivalent and underscores the uncertainty of Capra's belief regarding American democracy in 1941, as Roosevelt was embarking on an unprecedented third term. How can the people triumph when they are so easily manipulated by Norton, and they seem helpless without a leader? The members of the John Doe Club insist that they need Willoughby to renew the movement, but what is to keep Willoughby from using his power to corrupt the populist goals of the clubs? The film rests on the powers of the people, yet Capra is persuasive with his message that the people may be misled easily. Where does that leave the American democratic tradition on the eve of a conflict against fascism?

The American people, uncomfortable with this ambiguity, proved lukewarm to *Meet John Doe* and critical commentary was divided. The *Nation* remarked on the film's "muddled thinking and mawkish sentiments," whereas Otis Ferguson in the *New Republic* called John Doe an American hero, "the easy shambling young man, shrewd and confused, rugged, a lovable innocent but don't tread on him."[17] And as the nation moved from the domestic crisis of unemployment and Depression to the threat of international conflict, the individual heroism of Longfellow Deeds, Jefferson Smith, and John Willoughby, even if Capra appeared to have misgivings about the nature of these heroes and American democracy, seemed to be in step with the sacrifices to be asked of the people. Confronted with the rise of foreign dictators, Americans were not prepared to contemplate indigenous totalitarianism. The more radical edges of the New Deal, whether in government policy or film, were trimmed as the Roosevelt administration attempted to wrap itself in more traditional packaging and symbols.

Thus, Alfred Haworth Jones argues that during his second presidential term, Roosevelt moved to identify his administration with the image of Abraham Lincoln. Initially, the goal was to make the Lincoln image serve the "partisan purpose of providing historical justification for New Deal policies," but as Roosevelt began to focus on the hostilities in Europe, Lincoln's example was enlisted in "support of a nonpartisan foreign policy of aid to the allies." Using the Lincoln studies of Carl Sandburg, Stephen Vincent Benet, and Robert Sherwood, the Roosevelt administration endeavored to use the martyred sixteenth president's name to sanction policies and programs.[18]

This effort to connect the images of Roosevelt and Lincoln, by toning down the more divisive aspects of New Deal policies, was also evident in Hollywood treatments of Lincoln such as *Abe Lincoln of Illinois* (1940), featuring Raymond Massey, and director John Ford's *Young Mr. Lincoln* (1940), starring Henry Fonda. Considering himself to be somewhat of a Lincoln scholar, Ford welcomed the opportunity offered by producer Darryl Zanuck to do a film on Lincoln. According to Ford biographer Ronald L. Davis, the director perceived of Lincoln as the "idealized American—quiet, self-reliant, resourceful, pragmatic and honorable."[19] Ford's Lincoln embodied the values of a traditional American hero, and Roosevelt image makers sought to cast the president in a similar light as he championed values of democracy in a world increasingly dominated by injustice. The class divisions of the early Depression years and New Deal were to be bridged in this heroic image.

The downplaying of more radical and collectivist possibilities within the New Deal was further evidenced in Ford's film translation of John Steinbeck's *The Grapes of Wrath* (1940). Film scholar Vivian C. Sobchack asserted that Ford's adaptation is more conservative than the novel as film shots and settings tend to focus on the Joad family, deemphasizing the broader socioeconomic environment of the Depression. Also, Ford's decision to conclude his film with the government camp and its director, who bears a physical resemblance to FDR and uses a cigarette holder like the president, provides an endorsement for Roosevelt and his policies.[20] Ford's vision of Lincoln and the trails of the Joad family focused on the individual striving for justice, whereas the more divisive aspects of class division and calls for authoritarian actions in such early FDR era films as *Gabriel Over the White House* were hushed as the president began to shift from Dr. New Deal to Dr. Win-the-War.

Yet, this change in the president's attention brought new controversies to American politics and Hollywood productions. In 1939, Warner Brothers produced *Confessions of a Nazi Spy* in apparent support of Roosevelt's concern with getting the American people to focus on the European fascist threat to democracy and trade. The selection of film topics that endorsed an interventionist policy set off storms of protest from American isolationists. Montana Senator Burton K. Wheeler wrote film industry czar Will Hays, warning, "The propaganda for war that is being waged by the motion picture companies of this country is reaching a point at which I believe legislation will have to be enacted regulating the industry in this respect unless the industry itself displays a more impartial attitude." On a similar note, North Dakota Senator Gerald P. Nye insisted that Hollywood was under the thumb of the Roosevelt administration. From his Senate pulpit, Nye proclaimed, "In the country the movies are owned by private individuals, but it so happens that these movie companies have been operating as war propaganda machines almost as if they were being directed from a single central bureau." Nye implied that the Roosevelt White House was producing propaganda similar to that of the Soviet Union.[21] Allegations of Soviet influence within Roosevelt's New Deal became a major issue during the early Cold War years, but were placed on the back burner as the United States entered World War II and Hollywood assumed the role of propagandist for the war effort.

The film industry worked closely with the Office of War Information, producing films to explain the war effort to the American people and providing feature films, such as *Bataan* (1943), which instituted a formula based on dehumanizing the enemy and celebrating the melting pot concept of American society.[22] Of the hundreds of Hollywood wartime productions, two films stand out due to their implications for Roosevelt's foreign policy, *Mission to Moscow* (1943) and *Wilson* (1944).

In *Mission to Moscow*, Warner Brothers continued its close association with the Roosevelt White House by producing a film adaptation of U.S. Ambassador Joseph E. Davies's controversial memoirs. In his book and the prologue to the film, Davies describes his activities as a simple businessman until summoned by FDR on a mission to learn more about the enigmatic Soviet Union. Davies, played by Walter Huston, discovers that the Soviet leaders such as Stalin early recognized the menace of Nazi Germany and sought to form a common front with the democracies, but were rebuffed. The businessman turned diplomat for the persuasive FDR stresses the similarities between the American and Soviet peoples as allies during the war. But the wartime alliance and Warner's film were most controversial. The *New York Times* praised the film for coming out "sharply and frankly for an understanding of Russia's point of view, without fear of stepping on toes, such as those of the Trotskyites," with its depiction of the Moscow purge trials. Of course, as we now know, the Stalinist purges effected a great many more people than the followers of Trotsky and much more than toes were crushed by Stalin. Despite this glossing over of the purge trials, the Office of War Information was enthusiastic in its support for the film, congratulating the studio for the "forthright courage and honesty which made its production possible."[23]

Most film critics, however, failed to share the enthusiasm of the OI. In the *Nation*, James Agee referred to most of the film as "shameful rot," and Philip Hartung in *Commonweal* found *Mission to Moscow* to be dull and pedantic, although an impressive gesture toward one of our allies "whom we have been too slow in treating as a neighbor." However, *Life* magazine and the *New Republic* described the film as simplistic. According to *Life*, the complicated history of international diplomacy was reduced by *Mission to Moscow* to "terms of lily-white virtue and blackest villains," and the *New Republic* labeled the film a "mishmash" of Hollywood politics. The *New Republic* review concluded, "A while ago it was Red-baiting, now it is Red-praising in the same sense—ignorantly. To a democratic intelligence it is repulsive and insulting."[24] This critical response indicates that *Mission to Moscow* was not a piece of successful propaganda through which the Roosevelt administration and Warner Brothers duped the American public as later congressional investigations into Hollywood sought to prove.

On the other hand, Darryl Zanuck's venture into the realm of politics and propaganda with *Wilson* in 1944 met with more popular support and acknowledgment (including ten Oscar nominations) than that of Warner Brothers with *Moscow*. *Wilson* was made to teach the American people a history lesson. The United States was involved in the World War II because the nation, specifically the Senate, had failed to support Woodrow Wilson's vision of collective security contained in the 14 Points, the League of Nations, and the Treaty of Versailles. Although a Republican, Zanuck was advocating the internationalism of Franklin Roosevelt as contained in the Atlantic Charter and United Nations. The parallels between Roosevelt and his political mentor Wilson were obvious to James Agee, who described *Wilson* as an "extremely powerful campaigner" for FDR's fourth term in 1944. Nor was the film's martyrdom of President Wilson lost on Roosevelt, who, when screening the film in the White House, suffered an unhealthy rise in blood pressure and was visibly upset. *Wilson* was a box office success and surely must have had some impact on American support for postwar collective security, but critical commentary was divided, indicating that within the film community there was dissent regarding the policies pursued by the Roosevelt administration. In *Commonweal*, the film was praised as positive propaganda for "world understanding and world peace," but Manny Farber in the *New Republic* questioned Zanuck's history, observing that the film sought to demonize the German nation, perpetuating "the lie that the United States' career in the First World War contained only the highest moral aims and actions."[25]

Whether or not *Wilson* played any role, Roosevelt was elected to a fourth term in 1944. Yet, if he could have fared better than Wilson in managing the postwar world remains unknown, as on April 12, 1945, Roosevelt died from a cerebral hemorrhage. The internationalism championed by the president was a casualty of the Cold War as was, indeed, the New Deal. Opponents of Roosevelt used the milieu of the Cold War as a background against which to challenge the policies and philosophy of the New Deal, arguing that the collectivism of government programs to aid the victims of the Depression undermined individualism while encouraging the growth of socialism within the United States.

Americans had ended World War II confident that they were entering what publisher Henry Luce called the American century. However, as the wartime alliance with the Soviets evaporated into the Cold War, complete with a hostile force, equipped with atomic energy, in control of Eastern

Europe and China, Americans lost their confidence in victory culture and searched for scapegoats. It was this search that led the House Committee on Un-American Activities (HUAC) to Hollywood in 1947 to look for communists who were using the film industry to undermine American values. Besides an investigation into the Hollywood community guaranteed considerable publicity for politicians serving on the committee. The 1947 foray into Hollywood resulted in the infamous case of the Hollywood Ten, which sent ten actors, writers, and directors to jail for contempt of Congress by refusing to recognize the right of the congressional body to investigate the political beliefs of American citizens. After serving a prison term, film director Edward Dmytryk admitted that he had, indeed, been a member of the Communist Party, but recanted his former political beliefs. In a *Saturday Evening Post* interview, Dmytryk, in an effort to renew his career, defined communism as similar to the "waxy console that protects the tubercle—dissolve that waxy covering and you could kill tuberculosis in no time. And that's what you have to do with communism. I know. I've been there. I know now that you can't aid a communist front in any way without hurting your own country."[26]

The story of Dmytryk and the Hollywood Ten was only the beginning of Hollywood's Cold War, for, following the outbreak of the Korean War in 1950, HUAC was back in the film community making headlines. In this second round of hearings, the committee focused on the failure of Hollywood to take "positive and determined steps to eliminate communists," calling such witnesses as actors Sterling Hayden, Larry Parks, Will Geer, Jose Ferrer, and Edward G. Robinson; as well as writers Richard G. Collins and Budd Schulberg. As usual, the hearing generated a great deal of press interest, expanded industry blacklists, and led to boycotts organized by such groups as the American Legion. The film industry's response to these investigations was a timid one symbolized by Frank Freman, vice-president and chief of operations at Paramount Pictures, who described American Legion picketing of motion pictures as in the spirit of "friendly co-operation." Producers, directors, actors, and writers became afraid to directly confront controversial issues during the 1950s, and the Hollywood social problem film was dropped in favor of science fiction and Western allegories. Hollywood also produced such vapid anticommunist pictures as *My Son John* (1952) in which Robert Walker plays a brilliant young diplomat who has betrayed his nation to the Communist Party. His father, portrayed by Dean Jagger, tries to knock some sense into his son by literally thumping him on the head with a Bible, but to no avail. In this climate of opinion, the film industry was too intimidated to deal with a depiction of FDR and the New Deal, except to insinuate that New Deal types might be susceptible to communist infiltration.[27]

However, in 1960 with the emergence of energetic, young, liberal, and photogenic Democratic President John F. Kennedy and the New Frontier,

Hollywood resurrected the Roosevelt image in a film production of Dore Schary's successful Broadway play *Sunrise at Campobello*. The play concentrates on a thirty-four-month period in the life of Franklin Roosevelt when he is stricken by paralysis, but Roosevelt emerges triumphant when, with the love and support of his mother, Eleanor, and Louis Howe, he reenters politics with his nominating speech for Al Smith before the 1924 Democratic National Convention. Premiering on Broadway in January 1958, the play garnered five Tony awards, and Hollywood offers began pouring in for Schary. The playwright agreed to serve as a producer of the film for Warner Brothers, hiring play director Vincent J. Donehue to assist with the production in which Ralph Bellamy reprised his Broadway role as FDR and Greer Garson was added to the cast to portray Eleanor Roosevelt. The film opened on September 28, 1960, in the midst of the presidential contest between Kennedy and Richard Nixon. Schary insisted that his work had nothing to do with contemporary politics. *Sunrise at Campobello* was simply a "contained story about a man struck down by a crippling disease, and the effect it had upon his immediate family. He was a man who happened to be a political figure."[28] However, the evidence regarding the film seems to suggest otherwise.

Schary was a well-known Democratic political activist in both the New York and Hollywood artistic communities. According to William Leuchtenburg, John Kennedy was present at the theatrical premiere of *Sunrise* and met with the playwright, discussing in particular the scene in which Roosevelt defends the right of Catholic Al Smith to seek the presidency. In addition, the Democratic National Committee, meeting in Los Angeles, was invited by Schary to attend the filming of the climatic scene in which Roosevelt ascends the podium and nominates Smith. Finally, Schary was in attendance at the 1960 Democratic National Convention, which nominated Kennedy, presenting a short campaign film, *The Paper Curtain*. Perhaps the most significant aspect of Schary's political activism, as suggested by Martin F. Norden in an article for *Film & History*, was that after the era of the blacklist "Hollywood denizens may express their opinions publicly without fear of reprisal."[29]

The film opened to mixed, but generally positive, reviews. Philip T. Hartung in *Commonweal* wrote enthusiastically about *Sunrise at Campobello*, proclaiming that the film had "appeal for all moviegoers, regardless of their political affiliations and fixed ideas about 'that man in the White House." Praising the performance of Bellamy as FDR, an almost unanimous reaction, Hollis Alpert found Schary's production to be one that "everyone should see." Other reviewers, in publications such as the *New Republic* and *Time*, described the film as overly sentimental and characterized by "cornball domestic comedy." In a more sophisticated commentary, Brendan Gill of the *New Yorker*, although an admirer of FDR, questioned the historical accuracy of *Sunrise at Campobello*, asserting that Schary loved Roosevelt too much, investing the picture with too much sentimentality that caused the "screen to go soft, run at the edges and sometimes at the center."[30] Contemporary historiography of Roosevelt lends credence to some of the points raised by Gill in his commentary. Although some biographers would agree with Schary that Roosevelt's paralysis was crucial in formulating his liberal political philosophy, the domestic tranquillity of the Roosevelt household (almost akin to the situation comedy families of the television era of *Leave it to Beaver, Father Knows Best,* and *The Adventures of Ozzie and Harriet*) portrayed in Schary's production fails to accurately reflect the troubled relationship between Eleanor and Franklin.[31]

Despite its political timeliness and a great deal of positive commentary, the film version of *Sunrise at Campobello* failed to find much of an audience. With the assassination of Kennedy and the decline of liberalism under the strains of the Vietnam War, civil rights movement, and growth of a counterculture, Hollywood in the 1960s and 1970s was more likely to tackle a film biography of 1930s outlaws Bonnie and Clyde than a film depiction of Franklin Roosevelt and his New Deal. However, in 1982, as Ronald Reagan sought to implement the conservative agenda of the so-called Reagan Revolution, Hollywood returned to the topic of FDR and The Depression with a film adaptation of the hit Broadway musical *Annie.*

Based on the Depression-era comic strip, *Annie* tells the story of billionaire Daddy Warbucks (Albert Finney), who takes orphan Annie into his home for a week. She ends up spreading sunshine into the life of the dour Warbucks and inspires Roosevelt to launch New Deal legislation in a version of the hit song "Tomorrow," performed by Annie along with Eleanor (Lois de Banzie) and Franklin (Edward Herrmann) Roosevelt. Much attention was focused on the astronomical figure of nine and one-half million dollars that producer Ray Stark paid for the film rights to the stage production. Bringing in veteran film director John Huston, Stark spent approximately sixty million dollars bringing the project to the screen, which he planned to recoup with ticket sales, video rentals, television rights, and merchandising of the *Annie* image with dolls, clothes, toys, and lunch boxes.[32] This commercialization of *Annie* was representative of the early 1980s business expansion characterized by corporate mergers and raiding.

Indeed, the ideological implications of *Annie* were apparent to many observers. For example, in an astute piece for *Vogue,* Molly Haskell commented, "The musicalization of *Annie* has always struck me as an odd proposition: a cranky right-wing Depression-era cartoon transformed into a sticky liberal Recession-era lollipop. The naked greed of the kiddie rags-to-riches fantasy is only partially concealed in the pseudo-Dickensian saga of orphanage horrors, on the one hand, and, on the other, the redemption of the unregenerate capitalist Daddy Warbucks by the combined forces of Annie and FDR."[33] In this partnership of Roosevelt and Warbucks, we see the class antagonisms of the 1930s erased in favor of government and big business cooperation that culminated in the 1980s orgy of greed called the savings-and-loan scandal.

Critical commentary on the film was primarily negative, and John Huston totally disavowed the film. Pauline Kael in the *New Yorker* referred to *Annie* as a "manufactured romp," and in the *New Republic*, Stanley Kaufmann observed, "Genuine sentimentality has a certain self-respect, this film insults it." *Time* criticized Stark and Huston for removing the Broadway "Hooverville" number, along with any consideration of the Depression Era. Nevertheless, some reviewers enjoyed the Eleanor, Franklin, and Annie rendition of "Tomorrow," leading Judith Crist to call the musical number "a sweet encounter."[34] Despite such familiar songs and a marketing blitz, the film never found the anticipated blockbuster audience, yet through the magic of video, many young people's initial visual image of FDR is formed through the lens of *Annie* and its distorted image of the New Deal and the 1930s.

Since *Annie*, Hollywood has not returned to a film depiction of Franklin D. Roosevelt, but perhaps the time is ripe for a cinematic reevaluation of the Roosevelt legacy. But what might we expect from a contemporary Hollywood account of FDR, a source on which all too many Americans depend for their history? This general survey of Hollywood as commentator on the legacy of Franklin Roosevelt and the New Deal suggests that the film industry's depiction of FDR has been ambiguous rather than the embracing of liberal dogma by a sympathetic film community. From the 1930s social consciousness films of Warner Brothers, to World War II propaganda pictures, and to Dore Schary's *Sunrise at Campobello*, there is cinematic endorsement of Roosevelt and his legacy. However, there is a considerable volume of Hollywood conservative dissent from this liberal interpretation, ranging from Frank Capra, to the anticommunist films of the 1950s, to the antiestablishment films of the 1960s and 1970s, and, finally, to the banal *Annie* of the 1980s. This study fails to find any conspiracy or pattern, argued by conservative critics of Hollywood, through which Hollywood has consistently portrayed, in a positive fashion, a liberal ideology of big government intent on undermining traditional values of American individualism.

Yet, FDR remains very much with us. As conservative politicians such as Ronald Reagan and Newt Gingrich attempt to dismantle the New Deal, they continue to revere and evoke the memory of FDR. In such a confusing time, a cinematic reexamination of the life of the colorful and controversial FDR might prove relevant, entertaining, and, of greatest significance to Hollywood executives, profitable. On the other hand, perhaps Bob Dole has a point. A contemporary film treatment of Roosevelt might degenerate into the subtlety of such television programs as *Hard Copy* and a *Current Affair*, and audiences would be introduced to an exploitation of the Roosevelt family's sex life, complete with lesbianism, extramarital affairs, and consideration of how the president could function sexually through his paralysis. The historical context of the Depression and the effort to formulate programs to aid those unemployed and in danger of starvation could well get lost in the sensationalism. FDR and the New Deal deserve much better.

ENDNOTES

1. For the contemporary debate on Hollywood and American values, see Dan Balz and Thomas B. Edrall, "There's Big Presidential Box-Office in Banking Hollywood," *Washington Post National Weekly Edition*, 12 (June 12-18, 1995), p. 12; Michael Medved, *Hollywood vs. America*, p. 3 (New York: Harper Perennial, 1992; and Michael Eric Dyson, "Dole's Rap," *Nation*, 260 (June 26, 1995), p. 909.

2. Frank Freidel, *Franklin D. Roosevelt: A Rendezvous with Destiny*, pp. 3-15 (Boston: Little, Brown, 1990); and James MacGregor Burns, *Roosevelt: The Lion and the Fox*, 1882-1940, pp. 3-5 (New York: Harcourt Brace & World, 1956).

3. Fanklin D. Roosevelt, "Our Own Problem of Defense Involves the Future Democracy Wherever It Is Imperiled by Force of Terror," address to Annual Awards Dinner of Academy of Motion Picture Arts and Sciences, February 27, 1941, as cited in Samuel Rosenman, *The Public Papers and Addresses of Franklin Roosevelt*, vol. 10, pp. 40-44 (New York: Russell and Russell, 1950).

4. For the 1934 Sinclair campaign see Greg Mitchell, *The Campaign of the Century: Upton Sinclair's Race for Governor of California and the Birth of Media Politics* (New York: Random House, 1992).

5. William E. Leuchtenbeurg, *Franklin D. Roosevelt and the New Deal*, pp. 346-347 (New York: Harper & Row, 1963); William E. Leuchtenburg, *In the Shadow of FDR: From Harry Truman to Ronald Reagan* (Ithaca: Cornell University Press, 1983); Garry Wills, *Reagan's America: Innocents at Home* (Garden City, NY: Doubleday, 1987); and Robert Kuttner, "Caution: New Deal Wrecking Crew Celebrating FDR," *Boston Globe*, July 20, 1995.

6. Nick Riddick, *A New Deal in Entertainment: Warner Brothers in the 1930s*, pp. 64-70 (London: British Film Institute, 1983); John E. O'Connor, *I Am A Fugitive from a Chain Gang: Wisconsin/Warner Brothers Screenplay Series* (Madison: University of Wisconsin Press, 1981); and Henry Cohen, ed., *The Public Enemy: Wisconsin/Warner Brothers Screenplay Series* (Madison: University of Wisconsin Press, 1981).

7. Arthur M. Schlesinger, Jr., *The Crisis of the Old Order, 1919-1933*, p. 5 (Boston: Houghton Mifflin, 1957).

8. For historical discussion of *Gabriel Over the White House*, see "Film Images During the Great Depression," in Lawrence W. Levine, *Unpredictable Past: Explorations in American Cultural History*, pp. 135-239 (New York: Oxford University Press, 1993); Andrew Bergman, *We're in the Money: Depression American and Its Films*, pp. 115-120 (New York: Harper & Row, 1972); and Peter Roffman and Jim Purdy, *The Hollywood Social Problem Film: Madness, Despair, and Politics from the Depression to the Fifties*, pp. 68-73 (Bloomington: Indiana University Press, 1981).

9. William Troy, "Fascism Over Hollywood," *Nation*, 136 (April 26, 1933), pp. 482-483; "A President After Hollywood's Heart," *Literary Digest*, 115 (April 22, 1933), p. 13; "Four Films: Art and Propaganda," *New Republic*, 74 (April 19, 1933), p. 282; and Roffman and Purdy, *Hollywood Social Problem Film*, pp. 72-73.

10. For *Wild Boys of the Road*, see: William Troy, "Forgotten Children," *Nation*, 137 (October 18, 1933), p. 458; Roffman and Purdy, *Hollywood Social Problem Film*,

pp. 92-94; and Bergman, *We're In the Money*, pp. 100-103. A copy of the *Wild Boys of the Road* film script may be found in United Artists Collection, State Historical Society of Wisconsin, Madison. Another film which generally seemed to support Roosevelt was *The President Vanishes* (1934), in which a president beset by munitions makers, international bankers, and native fascists, seeking to perpetuate another war, are foiled by the nation's leader who fakes his own kidnapping to bring these sinister forces under control.

11. For a discussion of *Our Daily Bread*, see Bergman, *We're in the Money*, pp. 74-82; and for critical commentary on the film, see Andre Sennewald, "King Vidor and *Our Daily Bread*," *New York Times*, October 7, 1934; "On the Current Screen," *Literary Digest*, 118 (October 20, 1934), p. 31; Otis Ferguson, "Some Films That Failed," *New Republic* 80 (August 29, 1934), pp. 75-76; and *Motion Picture Herald*, August 18, 1934, p. 38.

12. For the documentary film movement and the New Deal, see Robert L. Snyder, *Pare Lorentz and the Documentary Film* (Norman: University of Oklahoma Press, 1968); and John E. O'Connor, *Guide to the Image as Artifact* (Washington, DC: American Historical Association, 1988).

13. Frank Capra, *The Name Above the Title*, pp. 344-366 (New York: Vintage Books, 1985).

14. For a discussion of Capra's political beliefs, see Joseph McBride, *Frank Capra: The Catastrophe of Success*, pp. 239-263 (New York: Simon and Schuster, 1992). For additional background information on Capra and his work, see: Raymond Carney, *American Vision: The Films of Frank Capra* (New York: Cambridge University Press, 1986); Leland A. Pogue, *The Cinema of Frank Capra: An Approach to Film Comedy* (South Brunswick, NJ: A.J. Barnes, 1975); Victor Scherle and William Turner Levy, *The Films of Frank Capra* (Secaucus, NJ: Citadel Press, 1977); James R. Silke, *Frank Capra: One Man-One Film* (Washington, DC: American Film Institute, 1971); and Richard Glatzer and John Raeburn, eds., *Frank Capra: The Man and His Films* (Ann Arbor: University of Michigan Press, 1975).

15. For *Mr. Deeds Goes to Town*, see Donald C. Willis, *The Films of Frank Capra* (Metuchen, NJ: Scarecrow Press, 1974); Mark Van Doren, "Second Comings," *Nation*, 142 (May 13, 1936), pp. 623-624; "On the Current Screen," *Literary Digest*, 121 (April 11, 1936), p. 19; and "Mr. Capra Goes to Town," *New Republic*, 86 (April 22, 1936), pp. 315-316; and Patrick Gerster, "The Ideological Project of Mr. Deeds Goes to Town," *Film Criticism* (Winter, 1981), pp. 35-48.

16. For *Mr. Smith Goes to Washington*, see Willis, *The Films of Frank Capra*; "Mr. Smith Riles Washington," *Time*, 34 (October 30, 1939), p. 49; Otis Ferguson, "Mr. Capra Goes Someplace," *New Republic*, 100 (November 1, 1939), pp. 363-370; Philip T. Hartung, "Mr. Capra Goes To Town," *Commonweal*, 31 (October 27, 1939), p. 14; and Frank Hoellering, "Films," *Nation*, 149 (October 28, 1939), pp. 476-477.

17. For *Meet John Doe*, see Willis, *The Films of Frank Capra*; Charles Wolfe, ed., *Meet John Doe* (New Brunswick, NJ: Rutgers University Press, 1989); Richard Glatzer, "Meet John Doe: An End to Social Mythmaking," in Glatzer and Raeburn, *Frank Capra*, pp. 139-148; Philip T. Hartung, "Capra and Doe's Little Punks," *Commonweal*, 33 (March 28, 1941), pp. 575-6; Anthony Bower, "Recent Films," *Nation*, 152 (March 29, 1941), p. 390; and Otis Ferguson, "Democracy at the Box Office," *New Republic*, 104 (March 24, 1941), pp. 405-406.

18. Alfred Haworth Jones, *Roosevelt's Image Brokers: Poets, Playwrights, and the Use of the Lincoln Symbol* (Port Washington, NY: Kennikat Press, 1974), pp. 3-6.

19. Ronald L. Davis, *John Ford: Hollywood's Old Master*, pp. 102-109 (Norman: University of Oklahoma Press, 1995).

20. Vivian C. Sobchack, "The Grapes of Wrath: Thematic Emphasis through Visual Style," in Peter C. Rollins, ed., *Hollywood as Historian: American Film in a Cultural Context*, pp. 68-87 (Lexington: The University Press of Kentucky, 1983).

21. For *Confessions of a Nazi Spy*, see: Roffman and Purdy, *Hollywood Social Problem Film*, pp. 212-3; *Confessions of a Nazi Spy*, Script, 1939, State Historical Society of Wisconsin, Madison; and Pare Lorentz, "*Confessions of a Nazi Spy*," in *Lorentz on Film*, pp. 168-169 (New York: Hopkinson and Blake, 1975). For the isolationist response to films such as *Confessions of a Nazi Spy*, see: Burton K. Wheeler to Will Hays, January 13, 1941 in United Artists Collection, State Historical Society of Wisconsin, Madison; and Gerald P. Nye, "Our Madness Increases as Our Energy Shrinks," August 4, 1941, in Gerald P. Nye Papers, Herbert Hoover Presidential Library, West Branch, Iowa.

22. For Hollywood during World War II, see Joe Morella, Edward Z. Epstein, and John Griggs, *The Films of World War II* (Secaucus, NJ: The Citadel Press, 1973); Clayton R. Koppes and Gregory D. Black, *Hollywood Goes to War: How Politics, Profits, & Propaganda Shaped World War II Movies* (New York: The Free Press, 1987); and Bernard F. Dick, *The Star-Spangled Screen: The American World War II Film* (Lexington: University Press of Kentucky, 1985).

23. Joseph Davies, *Mission to Moscow* (New York: Simon and Schuster, 1941); David Culbert, ed., *Mission to Moscow* (Madison: University of Wisconsin Press, 1980); and Bosley Crowther, "Mission to Moscow," *New York Times*, April. 30, 1943.

24. James Agee, "Films," *Nation*, 156 (May 22, 1943), p. 749; Philip Hartung, "Hollywood's Mission," *Commonweal*, 38 (May 21, 1943), pp. 124-132; "Mishmash," *New Republic*, 108 (May 10, 1943), p. 636; and "*Mission to Moscow*: Davies Movie Whitewashes Russia," *Life*, 14 (May 10, 1943), p. 30.

25. For a detailed discussion of *Wilson*, see Thomas J. Knock, "History with Lighting: The Forgotten Film *Wilson*," in Rollins, *Hollywood as Historian*, pp. 88-108; Doris Kearns Goodwin, *No Ordinary Time: Franklin and Eleanor Roosevelt: The Home Front in World War II*, (New York: Simon and Schuster, 1994); p. 545. James Agee, "Films," *Nation*, 159 (August 19, 1944), p. 221; Philip T. Hartung, "14 Points and More," *Commonweal*, 40 (August 18, 1944), pp. 424-425; and Manny Farber, "For He's a Jolly, Good, Fellow," *New Republic*, 111 (August 14, 1944), pp. 187-188.

26. Edward Dmytryk with Richard English, "What Makes a Hollywood Communist," *Saturday Evening Post*, 223 (May 19, 1951), pp. 30-31.

27. On the Hollywood Red Scare, see Larry Ceplair and Steven Englund, *The Inquisition in Hollywood: Politics in the Film Community, 1930-1960* (Berkeley: University of California Press, 1979); William Bledsoe, "Revolution Come to Hollywood," *American Mercury*, 49 (February, 1940), pp. 152-160; "More Hollywood Reds," *Newsweek*, 37 (April 23, 1951), pp. 36-38; William V. Shannon, "Hollywood Returns to the Stand," *New Republic*, 124 (June 25, 1951), pp. 21-22; Hannah Bloom, "The Hollywood Hearings," *Nation*, 173 (October 13, 1951), p. 304; Phil Kirby, "The Legion Blacklist," *New Republic*, 126 (June 16, 1952), pp. 14-15; Roffman and Purdy, *Hollywood Social Problem Film*, pp. 284-319; and Nora Sayre, *Running Time: Films of the Cold War* (New York: The Dial Press, 1982).

28. Dore Schary, *Sunrise at Campobello: A Play in Three Acts* (New York: Dramatists Play Service, 1958); Dore Schary, *Heyday: An Autobiography* (Boston: Little, Brown, 1979); and Dore Schary, "The Road to Campobello," *New York Times*, September 25, 1960.

29. Leuchtenburg, *In the Shadow of FDR*, p. 82; and Martin F. Norden, "*Sunrise at Campobello* and 1960 Presidential Politics," *Film & History*, 16 (February, 1986), pp. 2-8.

30. Philip T. Hartung, "Casting Shadows Before," *Commonweal*, 73 (October 7, 1960), pp. 47-48; Hollis Alpert, "The Twenties Revisited," *Saturday Review*, 43

(September 24, 1960), p. 30; *New Republic*, 143 (October 10,1960), p. 75; and Brendan Gill, "The Current Cinema," *New Yorker*, 106 (October 8, 1960), pp. 106-107.

31. For a historical interpretation that emphasizes the role of Roosevelt's paralysis see Ted Morgan, *FDR: A Biography* (New York: Simon & Schuster, 1985). Morgan writes, "His illness made it possible for him to identify with the humiliations and defeats of depression America. It was a suffering land, but it had the capacity to change and to grow, as he did. Indeed, this capacity for growth became the core of his character" (p. 3). For historical accounts of the Eleanor—Franklin relationship and the illness contracted at Campobello, see Joseph P. Lash, *Eleanor and Franklin*, pp. 359-392 (New York: W. W. Norton, 1971); Kenneth S. Davis, *FDR: The Beckoning of Destiny*, pp. 647-675 (New York: G. P. Putnam's Sons, 1971); and Blanche Wiesen Cook, *Eleanor Roosevelt: Volume One, 1884-1933*, pp. 302-337 (New York: Viking, 1992).

32. For the economics of *Annie*, see Harlan Jacobson, *"Annie," Film Comment*, 18 (July-August, 1982), pp. 47-48; Kenneth Turan, *"Annie," New York Times Magazine* (May 3, 1982), pp. 40-43, 65-70; Pauline Kael, "The Current Cinema," *New Yorker*, 58 (May 31, 1982), pp. 82-84; and "The Last Tycoon: Marketing a Freckle-Faced Orphan," *Commonweal*, 109 (June 18, 1982), p. 372.

33. Molly Haskell, "The Cranky Charm of Annie," *Vogue*, 172 (June, 1982), p. 42.

34. Lawrence Grobel, *The Hustons* (New York: Charles Scribner's Sons, 1989), pp. 724-729; Pauline Kael, "Current Cinema," pp. 82-84; Stanley Kaufmann, "Creepin' Lizzards," *New Republic*, 186 (June 9, 1982), pp. 22-23; "Here Comes *Annie* Again," *Time*, 99 (May 27, 1982), pp. 84-85; Colen L. Werterbeck, Jr., "Small Pleasures," *Commonweal*, 109 (June 4, 1982), pp. 338-339; and Judith Crist, "Better Than on Broadway," *Saturday Review*, 9 (June, 1982), pp. 64-65.

II

Art, Architecture, and Music of the 1930s

3

Federal Arts Policy and Political Legitimation

Graham Barnfield

Arthur M. Schlesinger Jr.'s *Age of Roosevelt* trilogy opens with a volume entitled *Crisis of the Old Order*,[1] reflecting a period when "the specter of cataclysmic disorder" stalked the land.[2] The dislocation caused by the social conflicts of the interwar years has generated an acute sensitivity to the threat of social breakdown that still resonates in contemporary affairs. This makes it easy to generalize about the 1930s as a period of crisis, leading numerous commentators to draw simplistic parallels with the present.[3] What is more difficult is to assess how different themes, practices, and discourses were mobilized in order to navigate a way out of this crisis.

The pages that follow attempt to reconstruct three distinctive trends. First of all, key problems of political legitimation are summarized, drawing on a number of European theorists. The difficulties facing the federal government in its attempts to secure the loyalties of the population as a whole receives consideration. The social crisis, originating in the nativism of the early 1920s, acquired a predominantly ethnic form of expression. It was further compounded by the emergence of full-blown recessionary trends in the late 1920s. Taken together, such pressures encouraged the nation-state to reorganize its relationship with U.S. citizens. On the national political plane, this led to the New Deal coalition. The present chapter confines itself to one aspect of this reorganization, namely, its impact in the sphere of cultural policy.

The second strand of argument concerns the tensions between various departments of government as these changes unfolded. The Commission of Fine Arts, discussed at length in what follows, was regarded by its appointees as embodying all that was best in culture, a position that in their eyes conferred exclusive authority in matters of aesthetic judgment. Given its explicit appeal to tradition as a source of legitimacy, the commission became disconcerted by new arts funding arrangements based on a direct appeal to "the People."

The closing pages of this chapter examine the discourses through which government officials—including President Roosevelt himself—sought to link their arts policies to a distinctive national identity. Federal art both exemplified the outlook of the New Deal and further modified it through public discussion of a democratized culture. This suggests that historical forces also impacted on the forms of cultural patronage generated by the New Deal. Indeed, the strategies of arts funding catalyzed by Franklin D. Roosevelt in response to the Depression highlight the broader relationships between cultural institutions and their age.

At the same time, it is often important to take a step back from the web of connections between such bodies and particular historical moments, as surface appearances do not fully express underlying trends. Consider, for instance, the contested readings of the Works Progress Administration Federal Project Number One (aka Federal One). It has become one of the best known arts programs developed under the New Deal. Its murals still adorn many public buildings, and its state guidebooks are widely respected, by John Steinbeck among others.[4] However, not all of the commentary on Federal One has been so sympathetic to its component projects. On one hand, they are remembered as pragmatic welfare relief, ensuring that "at least no-one starved." On the other, they have been vilified for a litany of sins, from operating a fraudulent "boondoggle" by setting new levels for "big government" largesse to foisting a "red nest" of tax-funded subversion on the nation as a whole.[5]

Such assessments represent a wide-ranging conflict of interpretation. Too often, the concerns of the 1950s, or the 1970s, have been incorporated into historical analysis purporting to interpret the New Deal and its broader context. As Richard Pells reminded us, "any effort to re-examine the conflicts and passions of the 1930s becomes, inevitably, a commentary on contemporary problems as well."[6] Consequently, care must be exercised to unravel the concrete problems that faced the initiators of Federal One's arts patronage from the preoccupations of later years. Failure to do so carries the risk of reading history backwards.

The Old Order Changes

The Commission of Fine Arts, an institution that suffered a decline in stature under the New Deal, well illustrates the wide-ranging forms of the legitimation crisis—and is hence the focus of this chapter. The commission's diminishing influence throws into sharp relief some of the tensions that resulted from a major policy shift regarding state intervention in the arts. Moreover, such discourses are themselves infused with the question of political legitimacy. Hence, a common assumption of the commission and its modernizing New Deal antagonists: Both thought that they could derive authority by claiming the mantle of tradition. Writing about the Federal Art Project, its coordinator Holger Cahill declared that the prerequisite for art was "the stored up environment of the past."[7] As seen in what follows, this emphasis on tradition was a sentiment shared by the commission.

The category "tradition" has been defined as a "semiconscious process of selective remembering and forgetting," which "means in practice a demand to alter the conduct of contemporary society."[8] However, this immediately begs the question as to why a demand for such tradition exists. While commission attempts to define tradition differed as to when precisely "modernity" nullifies artistic value, they agreed on the importance of heritage—in whatever form—as an indicator of the worth of cultural production in its particular forms.

It is possible to locate this demand within the broader crisis of cultural authority that prevailed during the interwar period. Dissatisfaction and alienation were widespread in the aftermath of the 1914-1918 conflict, despite the boom that cushioned the United States from the type of upheavals shaking Europe.[9] Significantly, the mechanisms through which major disruption was offset included a mixture of nativism, Puritanism, and repression, exemplified by warnings against "Rum, Romanism, and Rebellion"[10] in the 1928 presidential campaign. The main legacy of such politics was the resultant loss of social cohesion, expressed in a failure to integrate the masses into political life and a tangible threat of society unraveling. Whereas a confrontational approach was effective between the end of the war (via the passage of the 1924 National Origins Act and the defeat of Al Smith), within five years it posed more problems than it solved.

Galvanizing national politics against Catholicism and immigrants established a point of connection between the federal government and small-town America. However, as the decade drew to a close, the cities and their inhabitants constituted the most productive segment of American society. Urban populations, identified in the 1920 census as those living in towns of more than 25,000, were temporarily criminalized out of national life as a result of immigration control and Prohibition.

Under Roosevelt's leadership, such concerns were pushed aside, the so-called "undesirables" of the 1920s transformed into the bedrock of the New Deal coalition.[11] Although space does not permit a more detailed discussion, these trends also influenced the documentary orientation of Federal One.[12] In effect, the form of nativism originating in the 1920s and its potentially destabilizing consequences were sidelined as Roosevelt assumed power. The decline of this nativism, visible in the electoral arena, is also apparent in its near total exclusion from publicly funded art. Hence, it would be a mistake to focus entirely on the ethnic aspects of the "crisis of the old order." That would be to substitute a part for the whole. Indeed, economic slump changed utterly the character of that crisis.

In expanding this interpretation of crisis, a further hypothesis develops, concerning its relationship to the experimental mechanisms of cultural patronage that developed under the New Deal. By concentrating on slump and tradition, an effort can be made to interpret the mediations linking the crisis and state support for the arts. Logically, this procedure demands that the nature of the state itself be considered.

The State as Patron

Elmar Altvater, a state theorist of the "derivation" school, argued that the state has four key social functions. It should support the general conditions of production, such as infrastructure; it should create and enforce the legal order; it should regulate conflicts between labor and capital; and it should promote the national economic interest in the world market.[13] Whereas certain New Deal "alphabet agencies" can be identified as performing these roles, it is by no means obvious that state-sponsored arts projects made such a contribution. In part, this results from working at two analytical levels, abstract state theory, and a more concrete concern with the cultural politics of the New Deal.

This is further complicated because the execution of state functions in the manner described is by no means unproblematic. The economic crises that are the starting point of this analysis are susceptible to partial modification through government intervention. Yet although the state may "steer" society against forces that deny it part of its normal sovereignty, there are objective limitations to this process. A central tension occurs between the restoration of conditions favoring accumulation and the procurement of popular support, mediated through the separation of state activity into discrete "economic" and "political" spheres, often in the form of separate, seemingly autonomous, public institutions. On this basis, argued Claus Offe, the forms of intervention can undermine their economic utility; greater numbers participating in the political process can increase the potential for people to pursue their economic interests by using the democratic arena to demand economic change.[14]

In such conditions, state intervention assumes contradictory forms. Interactions between material conditions and the prevailing political outlook are conducted indirectly. On the one hand, the state can modify some of the social and economic problems it faces, eliciting mass loyalty in the process. On the other, such arrangements highlight the artificiality and fragility of the state itself by encouraging aspirations it cannot fulfill. Regardless of the institutional separation of politics and culture, these contradictory influences meant that the government's program was widely experienced as a series of moral imperatives that drew attention to the necessity for structural change.[15] Provided separation is maintained in "the analysis of the institutional ensemble which constitutes the capitalist state's apparatus with the evaluation of the historically specific regime,"[16] this is a useful starting point for thinking about the integration of the American populace into political life, and the role of the state in this process during the interwar period. It was within these contradictory spaces that New Deal arts policies developed and, conversely, such contradictory tren were institutionalized in the form of government-sponsored arts pro cts.

A Slump Sensibility

Insofar as the Roosevelt administration outlined a popular program, resolving mass unemployment was a key concern. The slump undermined the certainties of the previous decade, while posing the necessity for state intervention. This had two main components: relief—sometimes aligned to the notion of "pump-priming" the economy—and the conservation of skills. Both of these objectives were compatible with supporting the general needs of the economy. They were embraced as part of the pragmatism that characterized the Roosevelt administration, led by "the most complete devotee of playing by ear the White House had ever known . . . a patrician reformer whose mind was a potpourri of the three major programs which had emerged in the previous century."[17] Two factors fueled such possibilities, the declining prestige of American business and the widespread belief that increased consumer expenditure could regenerate the economy. On the former, "Roosevelt himself believed that liberty in America was imperiled more by the agglomerations of private business than by the state. The New Dealers were convinced that the depression was the result not simply of an economic breakdown but of a political collapse; hence, they sought new political instrumentalities."[18] The ad hoc character of the New Deal meant that the general properties of the state, as identified by Elmar Altvater, often found expression in an eclectic political vocabulary. Authorities ranging from the Brookings Institution to Utah banker Marriner Eccles identified underconsumption as the cause of the Depression, to be resolved through increasing mass purchasing power.[19] Their reflationary approach was all but ignored, despite the development of numerous public works program during the First Hundred Days.[20] Controversy focused instead on the appropriateness of state intervention as an economic instrument. This reinstituted complaints similar to those against which John Maynard Keynes defended the Hoover administration through comparisons between the Depression and the 1914-1918 war.[21] Advocating raising the spending power of unemployed Americans also proved problematic because of widespread belief that handouts promoted idleness and dependency. Regardless of the debates among economists, pump priming, demand management, and reflation played second fiddle in public discourse to the notion of preserving the skills of the unemployed. Although some still claim that FDR "smuggled" Keynesian measures into an ostensibly Progressive program,[22] a more satisfactory approach would identify descriptive similarities between Keynesianism and the New Deal at its height. Insofar as it pertains to the premise of this work, the moral imperative toward maintaining skills is central to understanding why cultural practitioners were integrated into WPA.

While proponents of such measures insisted that their programs would not compete with employees in the private sector, they also had to find something for their relief recipients to do. Norms that held for skilled workers applied equally to cultural practitioners. Prior to the inception of the Federal Theater Project as part of Federal One, unemployed actors had performed *The Taming of the Shrew*, watched by Civilian Conservation Corps workers. This became something of a model for New Deal administrator Harry L. Hopkins, who explained such developments by claiming that "people get a sense of respectability by working instead of getting relief."[23] Likewise, an important influence on the transition between the Commission of Fine Arts and Federal One was the College Art Association's Emergency Work Bureau (later the Emergency Relief Board), first privately financed then funded by New York state's Temporary Emergency Relief Administration, which was supervised by Hopkins and director Audrey McMahon.[24] The same pragmatic spirit is encapsulated in Hopkins' comments on unemployed cultural practitioners: "Hell! They have to eat just like other people."[25] In practice this meant a willingness to adopt the methods of local and state forms of "art as relief."

Those administering the institutional mechanisms that developed to ameliorate recessionary trends became ideologically committed to the form of response to the slump that they were implementing, a development itself contemporaneous to the proliferation of new forms of arts patronage. As the government adopted experimental methods, existing cultural institutions like the commission became increasingly unsettled by the process.

Such factors also influenced the content of many of Federal One's undertakings. Thus, numerous projects attempted to convey notions of American heritage, whether to attendees at art classes or to the viewers of murals adorning public buildings. A less nostalgic vision also appeared under the agency's auspices, where sympathetic portrayals of ethnic minorities emerged, as did documentary representations of the industrial work force in which "white ethnics" played a significant role.[26] In effect, the destabilizing consequences of nativism during the 1920s were vacating the national political stage once the election of Franklin D. Roosevelt was secure. Although such trends were most significant within the electoral arena, nativist sentiments directed at the "new immigrants" were largely excluded from public art under the Roosevelt administration.

Given this process of rehabilitation, to focus entirely on the ethnic aspects of the "crisis of the old order" would be to miss the big picture. Expanded interpretation of this crisis beyond a simple urban/rural split permits further development of a hypothesis concerning the relationship of legitimation crisis to the experimental mechanisms of cultural patronage that emerged under the New Deal.

Tradition Under Pressure: FDR and the Commission of Fine Arts

Trends associated with crisis impacted on the changing strategies of

Federal Arts patronage. Beginning in 1933, Roosevelt endorsed a wide range of arts patronage structures, including the Public Works of Art Project (PWAP), the Treasury Relief Art Project, the Section of Fine Arts (widely known as the Section), and WPA Federal One's Federal Art Project. As noted in what follows, such institutions promoted a self-conscious promoted discussion about national artistic traditions, within which the nation as a whole could participate, both as consumers and as subjects. However, it is perhaps in relation to an older, precrisis state-cultural formation that the public, presidentially endorsed criteria for good art become clear.

In dealing with President Roosevelt's directives to the art world, both formal and informal, it is important to consider the politics of art. Logically, this implies an investigation of the relationship between artistic production and external political life. However, this does not preclude any assessment of the internal politics of art, that is, "the specific historical conditions of the production of art; the social relations within which that production is carried out; the functions of art critics, audiences, the institutional structures (museums, galleries), and the patrons and purchasers of art."[27] The interaction of New Deal agencies with the insecure art world was informed by such considerations, in addition to the interventionist policies and pump-priming economic objectives discussed previously. One such relationship was that between the Roosevelt administration and the Commission of Fine Arts.

The Commission of Fine Arts was established by Congress in 1910. It followed the failed "Council of Fine Arts," appointed the previous year by Theodore Roosevelt. It consisted of some thirty artists and ceased to exist after one meeting. Even that short existence proved a source of tension between the executive and legislative branches of government.[28] Moreover, the council's successor had a closer relationship with Congress than with the White House, which explains in part its objections to the innovative sources of arts patronage that accompanied the New Deal. Franklin D. Roosevelt's conciliatory gestures toward this body, coupled with a number of attempts to moderate its influence, allow the historian an insight into the official aesthetic visions deemed appropriate for the Democratic majority.

The commission's advisory status brought it into close proximity to the nation-state. It was chaired by Charles Moore, a Doctor of the Arts awarded an honorary degree at Harvard University. Moore himself was praised as "a citizen who labored unremittingly for the orderly development of our national capital."[29] This assessment reflected the commission's responsibilities, allowing it to decide whether coins, public buildings, monuments, and official emblems were of sufficient artistic quality. Presidents Taft, Wilson, and Harding all used executive orders to request commission advice on a wide range of artifacts produced under government auspices, most notably in relation to the architecture of the

District of Columbia. Committee members, drawn from a number of creative disciplines, significantly architecture and the fine arts, were presidential appointees for a four-year term, with a realistic possibility of renewing each appointment. On retirement, a member joined the commission alumni, "whose counsel is available when decisions of high importance are to be made and policies to be decided upon."[30]

Administrators Interpret the President's Aesthetics

Friction between the president and the commission developed almost immediately. Charles Moore wrote to Roosevelt in April 1933 stressing the need for the commission to "retain its status as an independent advisory body."[31] The growing perception that the New Deal meant an unparalleled extension of federal power prompted committee members to seek assurance that their position of influence was secure. They became increasingly aware that figures in the Roosevelt administration had begun to consider the demands of arts administrators Edward Bruce and George Biddle for new arts policies. In part, such demands were encouraged by the hidebound outlook of the committee, which "saw art as noble and scholarly, and, if it were good, slightly mystical." According to Richard McKinzie, it "opposed all that smacked of the twentieth century, and a good part of that which belonged to the nineteenth."[32]

This assessment of the commission underlines its opposition to "modernism" on principle. Given its close links with the authorities, its advisory status boded ill for artistic innovation. Indeed, when in July 1933, Roosevelt sent Biddle a copy of the latest commission report, he opined that it "did not sound very promising for mural paintings."[33] Within three days, Moore had contacted the president, quoting a colleague's interpretation of these remarks and requesting the president clarify his views on such matters.[34]

Bruce was quick to explore alternatives to art's conventional relations with officialdom, as mediated through the commission. After an intensive period of lobbying, most notably within the Department of Justice, he staged one of a number of "working dinners" in October 1933. He expounded his vision of a new arts policy for America to the assembled dignitaries. Among those present was the Assistant Secretary to the Treasury, Lawrence Robert, who recommended that Bruce "ignore the Commission of Fine Arts and place mural decorations in public buildings if he had a sponsoring committee representing 'a sufficient variety of art interests so that he would be protected in acting on their advice.'"[35] Finding new sources of patronage allowed Bruce and his fellow administrators to bypass the commission as a source of credibility in the public arena. This process also established new channels of communication between artists and Roosevelt, while undermining the commission's cultural authority.

A factor further diminishing the commission's significance was the combination of Bruce and George Biddle overseeing relations between Washington and the arts projects. In an astute tactical move, commission chair Charles Moore was incorporated into the advisory committee appointed to oversee the Public Works of Art Project. An appendage of the Treasury Department, funded by the Public Works Administration, and administered by the Civil Works Administration, executive power in PWAP was vested in Bruce. *De facto*, the commission lost its monopoly on setting aesthetic standards. The commission-appointed PWAP advisors were rendered powerless by Bruce's position of strength.

With the preliminary signs of the commission's declining influence, a number of its critics began raising their complaints with Roosevelt directly. Primarily, such criticisms concerned personnel and aesthetic matters. Both types of complaint expressed discomfort with the commission's conservative antimodernism. For example, the architect Rossell Edward Mitchell felt that Moore, a former art gallery director, was an inappropriate chair, given that "about 95 percent of the time of the Commission is taken up with buildings." He went on to claim that "many deplorable things, architecturally, would not have passed, especially if a trained and learned man had been on the job all the time."[36]

Mitchell's letter expressed the breakdown of the commission's professional division of labor. The highlighting of its administrative failures could also fuel allegations of aesthetic incoherence. Thus, while Mitchell claimed that "there can be little objection . . . to designing these great structures in the very ancient styles of Greece and Rome," he also complained of "such monstrosities as the Washington auditorium." Corrective action was needed so that "the 'Approval of the Fine Arts Commission' would not continue to bring forth regretful smiles from those who know what is going on."[37] Mitchell's call for action echoed the sentiment of an increasingly significant section of the art world.

Other critics attempted to draw the president's attention to the commission's irrelevance to contemporary life. Count Rudolphe de Zapp of the White House press room suggested a drive to Americanize public buildings, "and to eliminate those Greek and Roman decorative schemes which have absolutely no connection with the American mentality."[38] A vigorous emphasis on innovation caused much discomfort in the traditionalist camp.

For two years, the commission attempted to obstruct modernist initiatives. This created constant friction with the Section of Fine Arts, which was regarded as more credible artistically than any of the arts projects concerned primarily with unemployment relief. Thus, in addition to Bruce's difficulties with the Treasury bureaucracy, the Commission "seemed determined to thwart any but the most formal and traditional art in Washington."[39] However, by this time, Bruce was securely ensconced amid "first rank New-Dealers," having far greater influence in the government than his conservative antagonists, which he further extended through frantic lobbying.

Roosevelt's role in this debate was as a conciliator, treating the art institutions on their own merits and standing aloof from controversies over aesthetic issues. Hence, in congratulating commission retiree John Mead Howells, the president paid tribute to his "ability and wide experience as an architect, and knowledge of the history and traditions of American architecture . . . the great tradition established by Washington and Jefferson for the National Capital."[40] Sculptor and commission member Lee Laurie was also acknowledged for providing advice that was "helpful and inspiring to the artists, stimulating them to do their very best work for the Government. In this way you have served your country and at the same time have advanced the cause of the fine arts."[41]

Moreover, presidential relations with the commission appeared smooth and its counsel was sought on a number of occasions. For example, when New York artist Louise H. Orchard contacted Eleanor Roosevelt for comments as to whether caricatures of the latter and her spouse could be included in a mural, the matter was referred to the Commission by Stephen Early, the White House press secretary.[42] The previous year Early had made a similar decision himself on a request to produce a cartoon biography of FDR.[43] Taken together, this devolution of responsibilities was symptomatic of the commission's changing status. Although Roosevelt remained cordial toward it, many of its traditional tasks were passing into other hands.

Indeed, the commission's obsessive hostility toward "modernism" encouraged federal authorities to seek alternative institutions through which to seek counsel, most notably within the Section and in the Treasury Relief Art Project, which was dubbed the "Ritz" of the art projects by *Time* magazine. In May 1938, $40,000 was set aside for a Section-sponsored competition to design a Smithsonian gallery of art. The commission supported a number of conservative architects opposed to Eliel and Eero Saarinen's entry, "gratuitously announcing that when the design was submitted to them that they would reject it and any other which exhibited a 'similar flavor of modernism."[44]

Such judgments were consistent with an outlook that was self-consciously derived from classical antiquity. However, this traditionalism was not the sole antimodernist and implicitly anti-European approach to American art. The development of urban and rural regionalism since the 1920s had engendered diverse styles and practices "only unified by [a] philosophy that all European modernistic art and all elitist art should be rejected in favor of representational art which was easily accessible to the ordinary American and which reflected the life style in the United States."[45] The inception of PWAP, most significantly in its support for mural painting, led to official embracing of these schools, helping to validate their claims of being authentically American. Moreover, the institutional realignment behind this shift undermined and marginalized a number of commission preoccupations. The growth of state-subsidized realist art in the 1930s curtailed much of the normative influence of pre-industrial cultural styles.

Little of this was to occur without conferring political advantages on the Roosevelt administration. Following five years of haggling and controversy, the president confided in Frederic Delano that "just for once I would like to put on the Commission a 100 percent New Deal Democrat . . . . do not care whether the individual is a resident of the District of Columbia or not—but I do want someone who will not 'lie down' or oppose if we seek, in the future, to honor Monroe or Madison or Cleveland or Wilson."[46] Departmental reorganization offered Roosevelt the opportunities he sought.

The Commission of Fine Arts had been subject to restructuring before. In June 1933, under Executive Order No. 6166, administration of commission expenditure was delegated to the Department of the Interior. A number of administrative functions were also consolidated in this department, including the bodies responsible for administering the Capital, significantly the Public Buildings Commission. The responsibility for disbursing was placed under Treasury control, replacing the 2,200 commissions previously responsible.[47] Such centralization increased presidential leverage in matters of cultural patronage.

Further reorganizations of the executive branch occurred in the waning years of the 1930s. The Public Buildings Administration and the Section were both transplanted to the new Federal Works Agency. Bruce's fears that this would render his own agency obsolete seemed well-founded; it was now forced into cohabitation with another, the WPA Federal Arts Project.[48] In the same process, the Section lost a number of its influential friends and guardians, and wartime procurement threatened further its role as an embellisher of government offices.

Temporarily, Roosevelt offset the Section's predicament by making it part of the Public Building Administration and guaranteeing that 1 percent of each building's cost be set aside for decoration. Moreover, despite widespread concern about Bruce's health,[49] he was appointed to replace Charles Moore as head of the commission when the latter retired. This represented Bruce's final triumph over the commission's inflexibility.

Substantial changes were in motion. Bruce had secured the appointment in spite of "his opinion of several of the Fine Arts Commission [which meant that] undoubtedly there would be an A-1 row if he were put on it."[50] Accompanying Bruce's temporary ascendancy in the commission was an increased acceptance of his criteria for aesthetic quality. For example, in 1942, its members demonstrated sympathy with Bruce, attacking Archibald MacLeish's Office of Facts and Figures for producing graphic propaganda based on "cold mechanical airbrush competence."[51] Unfortunately, Bruce's triumph was to prove brief, and his death in 1943 and the closure of the Section of Fine Arts virtually coincided with each other.

Roosevelt's interventions in debates over aesthetics appear even-handed and nonpartisan. However, it is clear that he was quite prepared to work toward undermining the orthodoxies of the Commission of Fine Arts through administrative means. Roosevelt seldom intervened in artistic disputes himself. Instead, he experimented with appointees and advisory bodies in a manner that ensured a shift away from the inflexible traditions of the commission and toward the latent national realist movements in American art.

The president's proximity to such trends can be deduced from his public forays into "art criticism." This marks the movement from the internal politics of art, based on its production and its institutional relations, to an external expression, namely, the place of art within the emerging Democratic majority. In the public promotion of a government-funded national art, how such "external" politics operate is visible, projecting a desire for both national unity and a particular relationship between government and cultural practitioner. Without wishing to ignore these themes in their own terms, the extent to which such initiatives were a product of the Oval Office merits investigation. If art, as Alain Jouffroy said some three decades later, "is the armchair in which the state sits for its own pleasure,"[52] then it is necessary to examine why the head of state should choose to identify armchair and occupant so closely.

Roosevelt and National Identity in Art

Franklin D. Roosevelt made few explicit endeavors to establish the aesthetic criteria by which the value of the new government-sponsored art could be assessed. He was reluctant to become embroiled in many of the broader controversies associated with the projects, with the exception of the debate over the employment of communists on Federal One. In public, Roosevelt emphasized the universal eligibility of unemployed artists for relief funds. In private, he echoed Bruce who, in response to San Francisco's Coit Tower mural affair, hoped that artists "don't fool around with this Socialistic thing any longer."[53]

In such instances, Roosevelt's emphasis on the political was primarily a pragmatic response to the New Deal's critics, to whom the arts projects presented an easy target. And substantial controversies over communism frequently overshadowed the various federal projects during their final years. However, this should not prevent noting the president's overall political trajectory in matters of cultural patronage, namely, an emphasis on the synonymous nature of New Deal art, the Democratic majority, and the nation-state. His specific aesthetic commentary was subordinate to this.

Both official and personal correspondence over time suggest that a number of arts lobbyists adopted a strategy of alerting Roosevelt to the political potential of government art projects. Initially, this took the form of suggesting that, subject to obvious financial constraints, the projects go beyond the basic provision of unemployment relief for artists. These contacts keyed into FDR's frustration with some of the schemes, most poignantly expressed when he wrote to Bruce, claiming "I should like to find some way of employing a better type of artist at more than relief compensation, but I do not see how we could do it out of present relief funds."[54] The inadequacies of organizing art through unemployment assistance were becoming increasingly apparent, most notably due to a shortage of suitably talented artists eligible for relief funds.[55] Advocates of federally funded arts programs seeking to address these frustrations began by offering their services, and implicitly the services of an artistic community, to the nation-state itself.

The initiatives of George Biddle, himself a school acquaintance of Franklin Roosevelt, are instructive to the study of such a strategy. Indeed, Biddle is seen today as the "father of Federal Arts" thanks to his widely publicized "conviction that American art could blossom by finding expression in the great social adjustments of the depression and the New Deal."[56] Whereas several of his contemporaries justified arts patronage with vague reference to European arrangements, Biddle lobbied FDR from the more concrete vantage point of the experience of the Mexican muralists. The general problem was posed thus:

> The younger artists of America are conscious as they never have been of the social revolution that our country and civilization is going through and they would be very eager to express their ideals in a permanent mural art if they were given the government's co-operation.[57]

Biddle conveyed a sense of the overlap between the crisis and its accompanying government responses, and the cultural practitioner's growing social awareness. Moreover, he presented a rudimentary policy option for institutionalizing this situation through emulation of Mexico, "home of the greatest national school of mural painting since the Italian renascence [sic]." As if to confirm his hypothesis, he echoed Diego Rivera's suggestion that this renaissance "was only possible because Obregon allowed Mexican artists to work at plumbers' wages in order to express on the walls of government buildings the social ideals of the Mexican revolution."[58]

In short, Biddle suggested the scope to bring forth artistic greatness from national adversity, conditional on the pragmatic emphasis on relief being matched by aesthetic dedication to the mural form. In a later letter, to Eleanor Roosevelt, Biddle spelled this out more explicitly: "mural art can never be important unless it is interpreting a great social and collective idea."[59] Such assertions, coupled with his enthusiasm for the Mexican muralists, become ironic in light of subsequent controversies.

Running through the personal correspondence of both Biddle and Bruce is a strand of respect for the president and loyalty to the vision of the New Deal. The former was expressed in a stream of greetings cards, Christmas presents, and other gifts.[60] As arts lobbyists and administrators, Bruce and Biddle combined flattery and gratitude in order to remind the president of their innovation's potential rewards. As Bruce wrote to Roosevelt:

> I hope that in my small way, I have been able to convince you of my devotion to you and the things you stand for and that you will allow me to make a suggestion, which I feel is needed in this country. . . . I genuinely believe that an appeal on your part to the best side of human nature would bring an instant response and would ring around the world.[61]

Bruce's gushing prose suggests his belief in the president's capacity to translate popular support, derived from political loyalty, into widespread and participatory arts appreciation. Moreover, such correspondence is indicative of the extent to which federal arts administrators saw their successes and future prospects as bound up with the development of the New Deal.

Such sentiments were echoed by George Biddle. Although acting in a professional capacity, the fierce personal loyalty to FDR was clearly visible when he stated that, "as President of the Mural Painters of America, I should like to tell him personally on behalf of American artists how greatful [sic] they are to his administration."[62] Correspondence between Roosevelt and his arts lieutenants illustrates the range of relationships connecting artists to the administration. With characteristic flattery, Bruce presented his own successes in such terms: "obviously, the award of the [Columbia] University Medal of Excellence, although described as a personal award for my work as an artist, has been given to me as a tribute to your art program."[63]

A combination of friendship and politicking continued throughout the decade. As the years passed, the clamor for personal attention remained, albeit mediated by an awareness of external events. An example was Biddle's comments that accompanied a copy of his autobiography sent to the White House: "I had hesitated at this moment in our country and the world's history to bring to your attention the record of so slight an achievement."[64] Such attention was all the more important given the threat that wartime reorganization posed to existing government art projects.

Roosevelt himself attempted to stand above the various aesthetic controversies, paying close attention instead to matters of personnel. Although on one occasion he expressed doubts over the historical accuracy of a Poughkeepsie post office mural depicting eighteenth-century white settlers with horses,[65] such interventions were exceptional. In retrospect, much of his official correspondence appears preoccupied with staffing issues and deflecting criticisms made by Congress and by members of the public. In contrast, the necessity of distinctly national art forms was a theme reserved for public consumption.

In many respects, FDR took his cue in such matters from Bruce. In opening the First Municipal Art Exhibition, Bruce summarized cogently Federal Art's congruence with mass appeal: "the Public Works of Art Project is, I believe the first genuinely democratic movement which has ever been started for the employment of the artist and the support of the arts."[66] This opening speech is instructive in that it allows us to identify the different elements, which meant that such art could be presented as democratic:

> A great Democracy has accepted the artist as a useful member of the body politic, and his art as a service to the state. It has taken the snobbery out of Art, and made it part of the daily food of the average citizen. It is, I believe, a distinct setting up of our civilization, a new conception and definition of public works—a recognition that things of culture and of the spirit contribute to the well-being of the nation.
>
> It has elevated the artist to the rank of artisan—has recognized him as a laborer worthy of his hire.
>
> It has been made possible by our well beloved President. It is part and parcel of the New Deal. It is a significant example of the motivating force behind the President's whole policy—to give all the people of our country a more abundant life. [67]

Politically, the speech established a new role for art in a democratic society. Aesthetically, it projected a number of challenges to the conventional status of the artist within American society, hence, the attempts of both Bruce and Roosevelt to demystify and defend the artist, now elevated "to the rank of artisan."

Art became available to all as the output of a state industry, albeit one supported by popular mandate. The arts were treated explicitly as a resource with which to offset the ravages of the slump. Bruce's lavish praise of his presidential mentor did not divert the emerging consensus in Washington, namely, that the connection between the New Deal coalition and the embellishments on public buildings conferred aesthetic worth on the latter. What developed was the peculiar moralization of art through political means. Conversely, the fact of having any cultural policy became "a sign of the civilized time we are living in through [Roosevelt's] leadership."[68] The president himself led something of a double life in public arts, which combined adjudicating on appointments matters with officially sanctioning public buildings and their attendant embellishments.

The leading pioneers of government arts patronage operated with a degree of autonomy in aesthetic matters, provided their political credentials were compatible with those of the government. However, such conditions did not preclude the direct innovations of the president himself. An example of Roosevelt's willingness to modify long-standing New Deal themes could be seen when he opened the Museum of Modern Art (MOMA) in New York. In keeping with the prevailing ethics, he argued that the "conditions for art and democracy are one and the same."[69] Indeed, "in encouraging the creation and enjoyment of beautiful things we are furthering democracy itself."[70] Such a democratic conception was not exclusively based on political democracy, hence, the argument that the traveling exhibit was the ideal form to "extend the perspective of the general public which too often has been accustomed to think of the fine arts as painting, and possibly sculpture."[71] Here, the definition of art is broadened to include contemporary industrial design, architecture (including "the great social art"—housing), photography, the printed book, illustration, the advertising poster and the moving picture. The accepted conception of the high arts, coupled with their implicit alienation from a popular audience, was being challenged by some of the highest authorities in the land.

A second strand of this approach was the projection of contemporary proclivities for popular participation in the arts backwards into history. Striking a populist note, Roosevelt claimed that American art had "always belonged to the people and has never been the property of an academy or a class."[72] In effect, the urban and rural regionalisms of the "American scene" were being accorded an eternal position in an emerging nationalist historiography.

Finally, with the benefits of hindsight, Roosevelt's MOMA radio address permits detection of a presentiment of the arguments that later devastated the credibility of federal art, and the regionalist traditions it coopted. Roosevelt ended his speech: "as in our democracy we enjoy the right to believe in different religious creeds or none, so can American artists express themselves with complete freedom from the strictures of dead artistic tradition and political ideology."[73] This division, between tradition and ideology, and between form and content, was often more imagined than real. In later years, the two were subject to further conflation by the new Cold War ideology, which called into question the orthodoxies of the New Deal.[74] As the normative influence of Democratic hegemony began to unravel, the critical assessment of that hegemony was informed by new conventions.

Conclusion

How can state cultural policy develop in a fashion that is both effective and internally consistent? How can it both procure popular consent and enthusiasm while avoiding the pitfalls of appearing to be bidding opportunistically for such support? This chapter argued that the state itself was negotiating these difficulties, a process reflected on a smaller scale in official arts bodies. On one hand, the Commission of Fine Arts presented itself as part of an idealized classical tradition, drawing its appeal from the past and [was] thereby unaccountable to public tastes and artistic fashions. On the other hand, the various arts agencies that emerged from the New Deal pitched their appeal more directly, to notions of relevance, "the people," and the nation's heritage. All sought to vindicate their activities with reference to some external authority, beyond the simple allocation of federal resources to cultural practitioners. As already noted, subsequent interpretations of these processes were refracted through the concerns of later years.

Initial reactions against the New Deal's legislative packages engendered a public discussion about what role government should play. In this climate, some commentators felt that the administration missed opportunities for effective communication with its constituencies. Leading literary critic Malcolm Cowley remarked:

> I do not think the first New Deal lost heavily by not engaging the interest of writers, except possibly in one respect. If a few writers had been part of it, they might have explained it better to the public. The New Dealers themselves were inspired talkers, but they didn't write English; they wrote in the different jargons of economists, sociologists, lawyers, or administrators, or in that mixture of all four to which Harold Ickes, I think it was, later gave the name of gobbledygook . . . Good writers in Washington might have helped the Brains Trust to project a less sinister image of itself; in that one respect the projects of those early days might have suffered from their absence.

Despite Cowley's frustration, over time the administration came to realize the importance of engagement with cultural practitioners in order to cement its relationship with broader social currents.

The Depression increased state intervention, notably under the Roosevelt administration. This created a framework with which to overcome some of the problems of political legitimacy. Such a process was not free of contradictions, and to certain sections of society it proved somewhat disturbing. It also helped to foster a climate in which the New Deal was often cloaked in the language of the past, as innovation was presented as an extension of established traditions.[76] Those state institutions that supervised cultural production embodied the both the elements of presentational continuity as well as expressions of change.

The Depression prompted a reorganization of the relationship between the state and the arts. In some quarters, it was experienced as a new period of creativity, which both allowed residents in less-developed areas of the United States to see murals while it liberated realist art from its exclusive association with illustration in the newspaper and graphics industries.[77] Such energies were also used in mass communications, hence, the penultimate section of this chapter, which considered the way that Roosevelt centered a discussion of artistic development around the question of national identity.

This trend was itself subject to further modification. Federal One itself faced expenditure cuts between 1937 and 1939, commencing with the closure of the Federal Theater Project and ending in the subordination of its remaining appendages to the U.S. war effort.[78] Although this process was insufficiently developed to transform New Deal arts patronage into a political mouthpiece, it did allow for the disassociation of Federal One from the sensibility of crisis that had first engendered it. This trend was accelerated by the growing chorus decrying "big government," boondoggles, and communist affiliations that assailed the very notion of arts patronage in the late 1930s.

Insofar as such sentiments suggest a rudimentary form of Cold War demonology, they functioned as a distorted mirror image of the New Deal. In contrast to the latter, which attempted to overcome the legitimacy crisis, the attack on the New Deal was itself a reaction to the changing demands of the 1930s. Given the centrality of state intervention to the war effort, its outright abolition was not practical. However, cultural patronage for forms of craft production was a relatively peripheral component of state intervention, making it an easier target. On this basis, Roosevelt was denied the opportunity to institute a national artistic tradition in his own image.

ENDNOTES

1. Arthur M. Schlesinger, Jr., *The Age of Roosevelt: The Crisis of the Old Order, 1919-1933* (Boston: Houghton Mifflin, 1957)

2. Anthony J. Badger, *The New Deal: The Depression Decade, 1933-1940*, p. 38 (London: Macmillan, 1989).

3. Ed Vuilliamy, "For whom does the bell toll now?" *London Guardian* (July 15-16, 1995), p. 1; Martin Walker, "The Lost and Lasting Legacies of FDR," *Guardian* (April 11, 1995), p. 10; David C. Wheelock, "Monetary Policy in the Great Depression: What the Fed Did, and Why," *Federal Reserve Board of St. Louis* (March/April 1992), pp. 3-28; Garry Willis, "What Makes a Good Leader," *Atlantic Monthly* (April 1994), pp. 63-80.

4. In *Travels With Charley*, 1962, John Steinbeck praises the State Guide series as "the most comprehensive account of the United States ever got together," p. 122 (London: Mandarin, 1990).

5. On the etymology of "boondoggle," see Margaret Marshall, "Art on Relief," *Nation* (September 5, 1936), p. 271n.

6. Richard H. Pells, *Radical Visions and American Dreams: Culture and Social Thought in the Depression Years*, p. ix (New York: Harper & Row, 1973).

7. Holger Cahill, "Foreword: American Resources in the Arts," in Francis V. O'Connor, ed., *Art for the Millions: Essays from the 1930s and Administrators of the WPA Federal Art Project*, p. 34 (Greenwich, CT: New York Graphic Society, 1973).

8. Frank Füredi, *Mythical Past, Elusive Future: History and Society in an Anxious Age*, pp. 60-61 (London: Pluto, 1992).

9. See William E. Leuchtenburg, *Perils of Prosperity* (Chicago: University of Chicago, 1958).

10. George Marsden, *Fundamentalism and American Culture: The Shaping of Twentieth Century Evangelism*, pp. 70-71 (New York: Oxford University Press, 1980. This slogan was first used in 1884, albeit attached to popular Protestant movements.

11. See Bernard H. Sternsher, "The New Deal Party System: A Reappraisal," *Journal of Interdisciplinary History* (Summer 1984); pp. 53-81; Kristi Anderson, *The Creation of a Democratic Majority 1928-1936* (Chicago: University of Chicago Press, 1979).

12. This theme is explored at greater length in Graham Barnfield, *Addressing Estrangement: Federal Arts Patronage and National Identity Under the New Deal* (Sheffield, Communications, Media and Communities Research Centre Occasional Papers, 1993). This is not to suggest that the preoccupations of the 1920s were forgotten entirely; in 1933, Mississippi high school students listed strong drink, illicit sex, idleness, gambling, narcotics, and pornography as pressing national issues, far more important than poverty (Badger, *The New Deal*, p. 57).

13. Bob Jessop, *The Capitalist State: Marxist Theories and Methods*, p. 91 (Oxford: Martin Robertson, 1982). Further information on the "state derivation" school and its forerunner, Evgeny B. Pashukanis, can be obtained in Jessop's *State Theory: Putting Capitalist States in Their Place*, esp. pp. 53-58 (Cambridge: Polity, 1990).

14. See Jessop, *The Capitalist State*, p. 127.

15. The discussion on the relationship between state form and political legitimacy is based on a critical reading of Jurgen Habermas, *Legitimation Crisis* (trans. T. McCarthy), (London: Heinemann, 1976); David Held, "Crisis Tendencies, Legitimation and the State," in John B. Thompson and David Held, eds., *Habermas: Critical Debates* (London: Macmillan, 1982); Philip K. Lawrence, "The State and Legitimation in the Work of Jurgen Habermas," in Graeme Duncan, ed., *Democracy and the Capitalist State* (Cambridge: Cambridge University Press, 1989), and Istvan Mezsaros, *The Power of Ideology* (Sussex: Harvester Wheatsheaf, 1989). I am indebted to James Heartfield for the multitude of insights he has shared regarding these issues.

16. Rhonda F. Levine, *Class Struggle and the New Deal: Industrial Capital, Industrial Labor and the State*, pp. 10-12 (Lawrence: KS: University Press of Kansas, 1988).

17. Eric F. Goldman, *Rendezvous With Destiny: A History of Modern American Reform*, pp. 251-254 (New York: Vintage Books, 1955).

18. William E. Leuchtenburg, *Franklin D. Roosevelt and the New Deal, 1932-1940*, p. 333 (New York: Harper & Row, 1963).

19. Patrick Renshaw, "Organised Labour and the Keynesian Revolution," in Stephen Baskerville and Ralph Willet, eds., *Nothing Else to Fear: New Perspectives on America in the Thirties*, pp. 220, 218 (Manchester: Manchester University Press, 1985).

20. John Gunther, *Roosevelt in Retrospect: A Profile in History*, pp. 308-311 (London: Hamish Hamilton, 1950).

21. Albert U. Romasco, *The Poverty of Abundance: Hoover, the Nation and the Depression*, pp. 176-177 (New York: Oxford University Press, 1965).

22. Alonzo L. Hanby, *Liberalism and its Challengers: FDR to Reagan*, p. 13 (New York: Oxford University Press, 1984).

23. Katie Loucheim, ed., *The Making of the New Deal: The Insiders Speak*, p. 193 (Cambridge: Harvard University Press, 1983).

24. Patricia Hills, *Social Concern and Urban Realism: American Painting of the*

1930s, p. 10 (Boston: Boston University Art Gallery, 1983).

25. Cited in Robert Sherwood, *Roosevelt and Hopkins*, p. 57 (New York: Harper, 1948).

26. Barnfield, *Addressing Estrangement*, passim.

27. Marx W. Wartofsky, "The Politics of Art: The Domination of Style and the Crisis in Contemporary Art," *Journal of Aesthetics and Art Criticism*, 51 (Spring 1993), p. 221.

28. See "Thirtieth Anniversary Meeting of the National Commission of Fine Arts," Report of May 17, 1940, Meeting, p. 4; Commission of Fine Arts Box, Official Files 187; Commission of Fine Arts 1933-1938 file; Franklin D. Roosevelt Library, Hyde Park, New York. Future references to this and many other collections appear by collection type, number and file name, followed by location, e.g., OF 187, FDRL.

29. See press cutting, M. H. McIntyre to Mrs. F. E. Farrington, July 2, 1937, OF 187, Commission of Fine Arts 1933-36 file, FDRL.

30. Franklin D. Roosevelt to John Mead Howells, January 22, 1937, OF 187, Commission of Fine Arts 1933-38 file, FDRL.

31. Charles Moore to Franklin D. Roosevelt, April 3, 1933, OF 187, Commission of Fine Arts 1933-38 file, FDRL.

32. Richard D. McKinzie, *A New Deal for Artists*, pp. 6-7 (Princeton NJ: Princeton University Press, 1973).

33. Ibid., p. 6.

34. Moore to Roosevelt, July 31, 1933, OF 187, Commission of Fine Arts 1933-1938 file, FDRL.

35. McKinzie, *New Deal for Artists*, p. 8.

36. Mitchell to Roosevelt, December 21, 1933, OF 187, Commission of Fine Arts 1933-38 file, FDRL.

37. Ibid.

38. de Zapp to Roosevelt, September 8, 1934, OF 187, Commission of Fine Arts 1933-38 file, FDRL.

39. McKinzie, *New Deal for Artists*, p. 38.

40. Roosevelt to Howells, January 22, 1937.

41. Roosevelt to Lawrie, January 22, 1937, OF 187, Commission of Fine Arts 1933-38 file, FDRL.

42. See Louise Orchard to Eleanor Roosevelt, October 17, 1938, OF 187, Commission of Fine Arts 1933-38 file, and Reference 116-0, FDRL. The Commission ruled against the caricature.

43. T. Scott to Stephen Early, November 10, 1936, Presidential Personal File 1 (PPF): 487 (Art and Artists), FDRL. Initially, the venture was acceptable to Early, within the boundaries of taste, decency, and partisanship.

44. McKinzie, *New Deal for Artists*, p. 45.

45. Maria Caudhill, "Introduction," in *The American Scene, Urban and Rural Regionalists of the '30s and 40s, Exhibition Program*, April 1 to May 13, 1976, University Gallery, University of Minnesota, p. 6.

46. Roosevelt to Frederick A. Delano, April 17, 1939, OF 187, Commission of Fine Arts, 1933-38 file, FDRL.

47. See *The Presidential Papers and Addresses of Franklin Delano Roosevelt, Volume 2: The Year of Crisis 1933*, pp. 223-228 (Random House, 1938).

48. See Barnfield, *Addressing Estrangement*, p. 20n.

49. See Delano to Roosevelt, January 15, 1940, OF 187; Memorandum, James Rowe Jr. to Roosevelt, January 15, 1940, OF 187A; McKinzie, p. 50.

50. Memorandum, James Rowe Jr. to Roosevelt, January 15, 1940.

51. McKinzie, *New Deal for Artists*, p. 50.

52. Cited in Richard Gilman, "The Idea of the Avant-Garde," in Edith Kurzweil and William Phillips, eds., *Writers and Politics: A Partisan Review Reader* (Boston: Routledge and Kegan Paul, 1983), p. 78.

53. McKinzie, *New Deal for Artists*, p. 25; based on telegram, Rowan to Heil, July 21, 1934. The document was housed at Record Group 121, Preliminary Inventory Entry 105, National Archives, Washington, DC.

54. Roosevelt to Bruce, December 13, 1934, PPF 2577, FDRL.

55. McKinzie, *New Deal for Artists*, p. 39.

56. Ibid., p. 5.

57. Biddle to Roosevelt, May 9, 1933, PPF 458, FDRL, p. 3.

58. Ibid., p. 2.

59. Biddle to Eleanor Roosevelt, June 28, 1933, PPF 458, FDRL.

60. For example, see M. A. Lehand to Mr. and Mrs. Edward Bruce, January 9, 1939. Roosevelt to Edward Bruce, January 2, 1941, PPF 2577, FDRL.

61. Bruce to Roosevelt, August 28, 1935, PPF 2577, FDRL.

62. Biddle to Roosevelt, January 20, 1936, PPF 458, FDRL.

63. Bruce to Roosevelt, March 6, 1937, PPF 2577, FDRL.

64. Biddle to Roosevelt, October 3, 1939, PPF 458, FDRL.

65. Roosevelt to Bruce, December 8, 1938, PPF 457; see also OF 400; New York "P", FDRL.

66. Edward Bruce, "Address at the first Municipal Art Exhibition of City of New York," February 27, 1934, PPF 2577, FDRL.

67. Ibid.

68. Bruce Roosevelt via McIntyre, February 26, 1938, PPF 2577; see also OF 10, FDRL..

69. Franklin D. Roosevelt, "Only Where Men are Free Can the Arts Flourish, the Civilization of National Culture Reach Full Flower," Radio Dedication to the Museum of Modern Art, New York City, May 10, 1939. Reprinted in *The Presidential Papers and Addresses of Franklin Delano Roosevelt*, Volume 2: The Year of Crisis 1933, pp. 335-338.

70. Ibid, p. 337.

71. Ibid, p. 337.

72. Ibid, p. 337.

73. Ibid, pp. 337-338.

74. See Serge Guilbault, *How New York Stole the Idea of Modern Art: Abstract Expressionism, Freedom and the Cold War* (Chicago: University of Chicago Press, 1983).

75. Malcolm Cowley, *The Dream of Golden Mountains: Remembering the 1930s*, p. 184. (New York: Penguin, 1980).

76. Thus the New Deal's supporters often packaged their new-found legislative power in the language of the previous half-century's anti-trust, populist politics. See Schlesinger, *Age of Roosevelt: The Crisis of the Old Order*.

77. Suzanne La Follette, "Toward an American Art," *Nation* (October 10, 1936, p. 430); Milton W. Brown, *American Painting from the Armory Show to the Depression*, p. 220 (Princeton, NJ: Princeton University Press, 1955).

78. The 1939 cuts in arts funding are described in Belisario Contreras, *Tradition and Innovation in New Deal Art*, p. 220 (NJ: Associated University Presses, 1983)

4

A Reassessment of New Deal Art: Examining the Mural Program in Texas

Francine Carraro

On December 8, 1933, U.S. Treasury official Edward Bruce invited several of his New Deal associates, eight directors of art museums across the nation and special guest Eleanor Roosevelt to discuss the economic plight of thousands of artists and to convince the group of the efficacy of his plan for a government-supported art project.[1] Over lunch in Bruce's living room, a new federal agency called the Public Works of Art Project (PWAP) was formed,[2] PWAP was dedicated to providing emergency aid to needy artists. By December 13, 1933, newspapers across the nation began making startling announcements about an unprecedented government program for artists. In Texas, the *Dallas Times Herald* announced in headlines, "Texas Creative Artists Will Be Employed at Wages for Craftsmen—Paintings, Murals and Statuary to Decorate Public Buildings at Government Expense" and "Artists Plan Decoration. City Hall and Schools to Be Adorned by Jobless Painters."[3] The *Dallas Morning News* announced, "Artists to Redecorate Municipal Buildings as Government Pays Wage," with an editorial entitled "Emergency Use of the Arts."[4] These articles outlined a simple, yet unprecedented, project: The federal government would pay visual artists to create art that would then become government property. As announced by the press, the artwork would "include the decoration and embellishment of public schools, prisons, State structures and . . . may be mural decorations, paintings, sculptures and similar undertakings of an esthetic nature."[5]

Without elaborate explanation, the Dallas newspapers urged artists to begin work at once and to submit proposals for large-scale projects to decorate public schools, courthouses, post offices, and prisons. The articles did not specify how artists could apply for these unusual commissions, but the message was clear—artists in Texas and across the nation in need of work had the opportunity to produce works of art for government wages.

The hastily formed and short-lived PWAP, the first formal agency in the United States for government support of the visual arts, was based on the premise that artworks paid for by public dollars would remain in the public domain. The 1995 conference, "FDR After 50 Years: Politics and Culture of the 1930s and 1940s," presented the opportunity to reassess those fifty-year-old works of art that were paid for by New Deal dollars and remain on public walls. Today, there is new scholarly and popular interest in the origins and issues surrounding those New Deal works of art, although in the half century since the program, many of the works have been destroyed, painted over, or removed and their significance and the reputations of many of the artists have been forgotten. This is a reassessment of the successes and failures of the PWAP and subsequent New Deal art programs formed to provide needed relief for unemployed artists in the midst of the Great Depression as well as a critique of a body of artworks produced in Texas under those programs that reflect the aesthetic and stylistic concerns of that era.

John Ankeney, director of the Dallas Museum of Fine Arts, attended the luncheon that founded the PWAP. He came to Washington, DC, as a kind of cultural ambassador from one of the nation's vibrant regional art centers of artistic activity. Texas artists had been spotlighted in the press as major exponents of realism and regionalism. Ideas expressed at the meeting about the emergence of a national art made up of regional schools were not new to Ankeney nor to Texas artists. Plans for the PWAP were based solidly on the values and aesthetics of regionalism and the American Scene movement in that the new federal agency was to operate on the premise that art should be accessible and meaningful to all Americans regardless of locality and that art is necessary and of vital interest to the nation. These ideas were very dear to Texas artists.[6]

Museum director Ankeney returned to Dallas as director of PWAP Region 12, which included Texas and Oklahoma. He immediately formed a committee of museum professionals and university art professors from across the region. A publicity campaign was launched to inform regional artists of new opportunities for government commissions and to persuade the doubting public of the importance of government supported art in public places. Ankeney believed that the PWAP was an important step toward reaching a golden age in American art. Seeking public support for this new governmental project, Ankeney wrote a newspaper article that relied heavily on historical justification for art patronage and mural painting by evoking the memory and grandeur of the Italian Renaissance to convince the skeptical that art was a necessary and vital force "to keep our national consciousness alive," rather than a luxury that the nation could ill afford. Ankeney pronounced in grand and eloquent tones that "Texas artists are offered the chance to recreate salient and socially significant events taken from our actual existence and environment . . . to relive the bravery and hardihood of our pioneer forefathers."[7] Ankeney was instrumental in establishing Texas as one of the first states under the new federal program to receive works of art for tax-supported buildings.

The early months of the New Deal were charged with that kind of optimism and urgency bolstered by high-toned rhetoric as new bureaucracies sprang into existence. In the election campaign of 1932, Franklin Roosevelt promised a New Deal in which government would take immediate and decisive action to solve the pressing economic and social problems of a country staggering from four years of economic depression. By the winter of 1933-1934, work relief programs for the fifteen million unemployed were a well-established part of the New Deal. The primary objective of the PWAP was relief, but the founders envisioned that artwork would serve also to educate, delight, and enlighten the American people. Because the PWAP's parent organization was the Treasury Department, art produced by PWAP-funded artists would be displayed in tax-supported buildings. Theoretically, the opportunity for government art commissions existed in every state for every needy artist.[8]

As director of Region 12, Ankeney urged artists to "come up to the high standard of excellence," and he reiterated the PWAP founders' belief that art for the public must be understandable and accessible.[9] He admonished artists to paint scenes of regional and topical nature such as historic events, folklore, and themes supportive of American ideals.[10] Artists in Texas readily accepted Ankeney's challenge to paint the American scene because they considered the federal project as a means to broaden their artistic careers. Artists, both professionals and amateurs, welcomed the opportunity to earn a PWAP paycheck and to place a work of art permanently in a public place. Texas artists saw their art as part of a national movement, a positive force that would further both the acceptance and availability of art in America. Artists were aware that the American public feared that a government-sponsored art program could become the voice of a monolithic government, and the artists themselves were wary of a program that could potentially force a stylistic straitjacket on them. Stylistically, artists in Texas and the vast majority of American artists in 1933 were realists who viewed art as a nonpolitical medium. The charge to paint subjects of local, regional and historical nature was accepted without question by artists who, by training and practice, painted portraits, landscapes, still-lifes, and history paintings. Most artists were discovering America through art concerned with depicting scenes of local and regional, interest in a realistic style called the "American Scene." Although occasionally abstract compositions by artists were accepted by the New Deal officials, the accessible style of didactic realism was officially sanctioned by the founders of the federal art programs, and artists readily complied.[11]

Ankeney delegated projects to artists of his region as quickly as he could secure the permissions for the public spaces. Just two weeks after the PWAP was founded, artists in Dallas who did not have a full-time job were busy painting works for schools, hospitals, and courthouses. The largest PWAP commission in Dallas county, a series of panels at Old City Hall, was completed by Jerry Bywaters and Alexandre Hogue. The two young artists, ready to prove their artistic abilities, were only commissioned and paid for work on four panels. However, with energetic zeal, they finished twelve panels that chronicled the history of the settlement and development of the City of Dallas. The artists' efforts were praised publicly by PWAP Chief Edward Bruce and the famous regionalist artist Thomas Hart Benton.[12]

The PWAP created a whirl of artistic activity across the nation that lasted only seven months. Artists chosen by the regional committees were given two months to complete their works at a pay scale of $26.50 to $42.50 per week, based on the Civil Works Administration's wage scale for skilled labor. By the time the nationwide program ended on June 30, 1934, forty-four artists in Texas had received much needed paychecks from Uncle Sam, and across the nation 3,749 artists had been supported by the government at a price of $1.3 million, with 90.3 percent of the total going directly to artists for 15,633 works of art.[13] While PWAP production was impressive in numerical terms, the vast majority of the PWAP paintings and sculptures were not impressive in artistic terms.

From the outset and throughout the PWAP's short tenure, issues concerning government patronage of art and questions concerning government support of professional versus needy artists remained unquestioned and unresolved. Professional artists vied for the same commissions as novices, which accounts for the uneven quality of art-works produced for the PWAP in Texas and across the nation. It became evident to many that mural painting, like any art form, is redeemed or condemned by the ability of the artist. Bywaters voiced his concern that the "better artists" and not the "hack painters" be given the commissions.[14] The evaluation of the artworks, however, became a separate issue from the evaluation of the government program.

In its own day, the PWAP was deemed a success by the New Deal administration for its delivery of artworks to the public and for its distribution of relief funds directly to artists throughout the nation. The artists who received PWAP commissions were not only gratified to receive government funds, but also were encouraged by what they perceived as a national commitment to the arts. Bywaters asserted, "that there [were] probably more pictorial *faux pas* than profound manifestations uncovered by the PWAP, but this project gave despairing artists new courage, showed the public that art might have some interest for them and definitely proved that Gotham's art dictatorship was undeserved and false."[15] Artists like Bywaters, ready to prove themselves on a national level, seized the opportunity of a national program that promised to decentralize and democratize the art world. Both the founders of the PWAP and the artists who participated believed that art should not remain the exclusive purview of the privileged few. The prospect of art commissions in every city and hamlet was confirmation for artists that American art was poised for a renaissance.

Viewed from a distance of fifty years, the PWAP must be judged on the basis of the objectives of the federal program in contrast and in concert with the aspirations of the artists and the response of the public. The PWAP was a success or a failure to the extent that the program balanced or fumbled the divergent needs and interests of the patron, the artists, and the audience. The government, as art patron, was concerned with supplying necessary economic relief for a specific segment of the population, that is, artists. While remaining accountable for the use of tax dollars, the government as patron purchased artworks for the edification of the public. Economic circumstances induced artists to accept public employment to produce works of art accommodating public taste. The balance of mutual interests of the government, artists, and the public involved a compromise in the quality of the art, however unwilling the participants were to admit that.

Twenty years after the last PWAP commission, the Dallas Old City Hall murals by Bywaters and Hogue were destroyed when the building was renovated. The praise by Bruce and Benton was forgotten and the New Deal murals were considered old-fashioned in the postwar era of economic boom. Public taste in art had changed; modern viewers were uncomfortable with the simplistic, didactic realism of these old pictures. The fate of the Dallas City Hall murals is indicative of a government agency that was formed to provide immediate relief and was never intended to be a permanent program. It was only assumed that the PWAP works of art would remain in the public domain, although no long-range funds or perpetual mechanism were provided to ensure that. The art objects—good or bad, deserving or undeserving of preservation—were not the primary concern of the government program.

The PWAP was the first of several New Deal programs aimed at putting artists to work as artists.[16] The administration's objective was to put people to work with jobs that were in keeping with their skills. In October 1934, a new federal agency was formed in an attempt to solve some of PWAP's problems. Administered by the same folks in Washington, including Edward Bruce, Forbes Watson, and Edward Rowan, the Section of Painting and Sculpture of the Treasury Department had a new focus and a new structure. Under a new funding arrangement, artworks for public buildings were obtained through open, anonymous competitions. The Section held just over 200 competitions nationwide and awarded more than 1,300 commissions. Artworks under Section rules were financed by 1 percent of the funds allocated for construction of new or remodeled public buildings. From 1934 to 1943, the business of obtaining original paintings and sculptures for the public domain and the support of artists continued despite bureaucratic rivalries and a few disagreements between artists and the public about the stylistic possibilities of presenting the American Scene. The Section returned a large number of artworks to the taxpayer, including more than 2,500 murals, 18,000 sculptures, 108,000 easel paintings, and 11,000 designs nationwide.

The process of commissioning artists for Section projects was democratic and handled with dispatch. New projects were announced with specifics about the location, size, and placement of the artwork in a call for entries that was posted nationwide. Artists entering competitions for murals for new government buildings were required to submit a completed design for the mural in color on a scale of one inch equaling one foot along with a full-sized two-foot square detail of the mural. After regional committees juried the entries and made their selection, the winning entry was sent to Washington, DC, for final approval. The commission was then announced publicly and the artist began work under the supervision of the Section's federal and regional authorities. These open and anonymous competitions brought local audiences in contact with a wider, and largely heretofore alien, world of art.

The partnership between the federal government and artists to bring art to the public was demonstrated at its best when murals were installed above the postmaster's door without offending anyone. The presentation of a new work of art as a gift of the government to the community did not automatically ease any mistrust or uncertainty about the presumptive strangeness of artists by local citizens. The value of art was determined locally as the new murals were scrutinized by a receptive, but reservedly skeptical, local audience.

In Texas, most of the mural commissions granted from competitions under the Treasury Section were completed between 1939 and 1943. Both large cities and small towns in Texas benefited from the program. For some rural communities, the new post office mural was the first and only original painting on public display. Bringing art to hometown people involved introducing them to a larger and unfamiliar work of images and ideas. For example, in 1939, Russian-born Victor Arnautoff received a commission for the small east Texas town of Linden. His mural for the Linden post office entitled *Cotton Pickers* is stylistically indebted to the work of Mexican muralist Diego Rivera, whom Arnautoff once assisted. Arnautoff's mural was accepted by the citizens of Linden without comment or incident, which was remarkably different from the scandal caused by Arnautoff's earlier PWAP mural for the Coit Tower in San Francisco. The public's reaction to Arnautoff's blatant use of symbolic references to Communism in his Coit Tower murals threatened to end New Deal patronage of the arts. The citizens of remote Linden, Texas, were unaware of the scandal.

For the post office in Giddings, Texas, Dallas artist Otis Dozier painted *Cowboys Receiving the Mail,* after local judges rejected his original composition, which depicted, in gruesome detail, the local industry of chicken processing. Dozier revised the subject to tell the story of a cowboy opening a new pair of mail-order boots. The mural may have appealed to New Deal administrators and to local patrons receiving packages from the postmaster, but the cowboy story and far west Texas setting have little to do with the town of Giddings located east of Austin in farm land of rolling hills. In Arlington, Texas, Dozier pictured a farm family gathering pecans. A new red pickup truck in the picture served as convincing evidence that the New Deal farm policies brought success. These works by Dozier are examples of the partnership of interests among the patron, painter, and public expressed in Section commissions. In the democratic spirit of compromise and cooperation, the government as patron commissioned and supervised the artist, the artist presented a readable and accessible image, and the public responded by deeming the mural acceptable in the court of public opinion.

Several Dallas artists completed commissions for the Section. Among the most successful were the works of Tom Stell and Lloyd Goff. Stell's mural for the Longview, Texas, post office, which documents farm animals and contemporary farm machinery, remains vibrant in color and composition. When Lloyd Goff completed a mural picturing tanned, burly cowboys for the *Before the Fencing of Delta County* for the Cooper, Texas, post office, local residents were so happy with the mural that they honored the artist with a formal reception.

Because the Section competitions were anonymous and based on quality of work, women artists were afforded unprejudiced opportunities for commissions. Jeanne Magafan painted the community's traditional Christmas dance for the post office at Anson, Texas. The threat of scandal erupted, however, when the painting was unveiled; the residents of a dry county complained about the "obnoxious liqueur jug" that was pictured in the lower right corner of the composition. Sculptor Allie Tennant completed a triptych in plaster relief entitled *Oil, Cattle and Wheat* for the Electra, Texas, post office. These examples and others support the assertion that the New Deal art programs proved to be a significant factor in the promotion and development of the professional careers of women artists in Texas and across the nation.

Occasionally, Section commissions were obtained as a result of an honorable mention or runner-up status on an important competition. For example, in June 1938, Dallas artists Jerry Bywaters and Alexandre Hogue were awarded a large mural commission for the Houston Parcel Post Building on the basis of competent designs that they had submitted for a Dallas project but had been rejected. One hundred forty-four artists from across the nation had submitted designs for the Dallas Post Office Terminal Annex, but New Mexico artist Peter Hurd won the competition and the $7,200 commission for a series of murals. Thirty-one other appointments were awarded from this competition, including three murals each by Bywaters and Hogue.

For the Houston Parcel Post Building, Bywaters and Hogue chose to paint the history of the Houston Ship Channel. Hogue depicted the early river boat traffic and the actual surveying, clearing, dredging, and building of the canal. Bywaters portrayed contemporary workmen on the wharf loading an oil tanker and loading cotton bales onto a freighter. The artists worked for two years researching the subject and painting the murals, which were six feet high and eighteen feet long. A highly publicized dedication ceremony for the mural was held on July 6, 1941.

Sometime in the mid-1950s, the Houston murals by Bywaters and Hogue were quietly removed from the walls. Bywaters' paintings of dock workers, which represented purposeful, productive work and embodied such hope during an era of joblessness, were viewed with suspicion in the Cold War era of labor union disputes. The murals were lost until 1976, when they were rediscovered rolled up in the basement of the Houston Parcel Post Building. The artworks were cleaned by the General Service Administration and installed in the Federal Building in Houston, where they remain on exhibit.

The government-sponsored art program played an important role in the financial and artistic survival of individual artists in Texas. In an article that Bywaters wrote for the *Southwest Review*, he commented, "These Federal projects offer a small but steady income and encourage the regional artist to paint what he knows best—the life and history of his own community."[17] For Bywaters and other artists, the New Deal art programs were a clear expression of the promotion of regionalism. The government projects confirmed for many the continued progress of American art.

Today, of the 125 works of art for public buildings that were commissioned by the New Deal federal art programs in Texas, 76 still exist, but many of the murals have been moved to new locations; 17 have been destroyed, usually as a result of building new post offices or renovating old ones; 32 are unaccounted for or lost. Works of art have disappeared from the walls of post offices, courthouses, and schools because records of allocation were inadequately maintained. The care of artworks was neglected over time from lack of expertise, interest, and funds. In the years since 1943 when the last Section project was completed, the New Deal artworks have become the wards of the General Service Administration and many have been victims of lowered ceilings, obstructing light fixtures, and other obtrusive renovations.

When viewing the New Deal murals today, the evaluation of the art-work is obscured by the evaluation of the government program. Martin Kalfatovic, in his 1994 comprehensive bibliography and chronology of the New Deal fine arts projects, soberly acknowledges the quality of the artworks: "Perhaps no Michelangelos or da Vincis were discovered by the New Deal art projects. No Sistine ceilings were created to adorn the Federal Buildings in Washington or the thousands of post offices and courthouses across America."[18] However, Kalfatovic forgives the faults of the artwork and praises the virtues of the program: "In that time many thousands of artists were employed, many tens of thousands of works of art were created, a number of which even the most virulent critic must admit to be, if not the greatest expression of the creative spirit, at least a document of the creative spirit of American art at a particular time in the nation's history."[19] As Kalfatovic suggests and cultural historian Karal Ann Marling asserts,[20] the mural paintings have lost their status as unique art objects and have become cultural artifacts or documents of an historic social program. They remain pictures in the post offices encased in history unable to transcend the confines of a particular time and place. The New Deal murals take on importance only as material evidence of an unprecedented art project with a story that is a large and complicated one of social, political, economic, and cultural interest.

The historic legacy of the New Deal art programs is more complicated than the warehousing of old paintings. With ramifications unforeseen by its founders, the New Deal art programs significantly altered the relationship of art and the artist to the art audience and American society. The government as art patron, with its own set of iconographic, stylistic, and ideological concerns, served to politicize art. Issues of aesthetics, freedom of expression, and standards of excellence, which doggedly troubled the various art programs of the New Deal, continue to weigh in the balance of today's judgment of contemporary public support of the arts, although there are great differences in the battlefield and the combatants. References to these issues surface with glib statements that link the New Deal art programs philosophically and historically with the National Endowment for the Arts in a battle cry to continue government funding of the arts. Viewed from the distance of time, New Deal art programs serve as a model to remind us that art, chosen on sociological grounds in the name of cultural egalitarianism, will not long remain art, and questions will linger about art in a democratic society, elitism in a populist culture, and individual expression in a multicultural setting.

ENDNOTES

1. In May 1933, American social realist artist George Biddle wrote President Roosevelt and urged him to initiate a government program of art patronage to employ artists. As a former classmate of FDR at Groton, Biddle became a close adviser to the president concerning New Deal art programs.

2. The Civil Works Administration allocated $1,039,000 to fund the PWAP, and the Treasury Department, which had experience with large architectural commissions, was designated to administer the program.

3. *Dallas Times Herald*, December 13, 1933.

4. "Artists to Redecorate Municipal Buildings as Government Pays Wage," *Dallas Morning News*, December 13, 1933; "Emergency Use of the Arts," *Dallas Morning News*, December 14, 1933.

5. *Dallas Morning News*, December 13, 1933.

6. For information about regionalist art of the 1930s and 1940s in Texas, see Francine Carraro, *Jerry Bywaters: A Life in Art* (Austin: University of Texas Press, 1994); and Rick Stewart, *Lone Star Regionalism: the Dallas Nine and Their Circle* (Dallas: The Dallas Museum of Fine Art, 1985).

7. John Ankeney, "Ankeney Explains Plan of Government Public Works of Art Project; Chance for Texas Artists," *Dallas Times Herald*, January 14, 1934.

8. For sources of information on New Deal art projects, see Martin R. Kalfatovic, *The New Deal Fine Arts Projects: A Bibliography, 1933-1992* (Metuchen, N.J.: Scarecrow Press, 1994).

9. *Dallas Times Herald*, January 14, 1934.

10. Ankeney, the founders of the PWAP, and the artists of Texas believed in an American renaissance in art. The Mexican mural renaissance of the art of Diego Rivera, Jose Clemente Orozco, and David Alfaro Siqueiros subsidized by the Mexican government served as confirmation of the idea of a mural renaissance for a national art. The founders and participants in the New Deal art program were mindful of the success

of the Mexican mural project. The Marxist ideology of the Mexican muralists notwithstanding, American artists found the Mexican experiment a viable resource as a model for a government-supported art program.

11. The government projects were not, however, without controversy about style and subject, as Karal Ann Marling eloquently describes in her work *Wall to Wall America: A Cultural History of Post-Office Murals in the Great Depression* (Minneapolis: University of Minnesota press, 1982).

12. Elisabeth Crocker, "Benton Praise for City Hall Mural Recalled," *Dallas Morning News*, February 9, 1940.

13. Public Works of Art Project, *Report of the Assistant Secretary of the Treasury to Federal Emergency Relief Administrator*, pp. 5-8 (Washington DC: U.S. Government Printing Office, 1934).

14. Jerry Bywaters, "El Paso Panels Show History of Mining," *Dallas Morning News*, July 15, 1934.

15. *Dallas Morning News*, August 15, 1937.

16. The New Deal created four art programs: The Public Works of Art Project (PWAP), the Works Progress Administration Federal Art Project (WPA/FAP), the Treasury Section of Painting and Sculpture (the Section), and the Treasury Relief Project (TRAP).

17. Jerry Bywaters, "Art Comes Back Home," *Southwest Review*, 23, no. 1 (October 1937), p.80.

18. Kalfatovic, *The New Deal Fine Arts Projects*, p. xvii.

19. Ibid.

20. See Marling, *Wall to Wall America*.

5

Pioneers, Bad Men, Rangers, and Indians:
Heroes in Texas Post Office Murals

Philip Parisi

In his famous first inaugural address, FDR admonished Americans that they had only fear to fear; then he launched the New Deal to lead them out of their economic and spiritual malaise. One of the many ideas that Roosevelt pursued was initiating a public art patronage program to provide both relief for needy artists and art for the people. Under one of the many federal art projects, the walls of newly constructed post offices became canvases for a didactic mural art that was expected to help bolster public confidence and restore faith in the American Dream.[1] But, what images were chosen for post office murals, and how were they expected to achieve the government's objectives?

Since ancient times, stories of heroes have inspired people and reinforced cultural values. A hero is a courageous being, physically and spiritually superior, who possesses extraordinary, culturally revered qualities. Heroes personify ideals and are powerful vehicles that help define a people. In Texas, pioneers, Indians, Texas Rangers, and even outlaws were perceived to be among the key figures that embodied the region's identity. In the Texas post office murals, these Texas icons were elevated to heroes to advance New Deal goals.

In 1933, more than $1 million was allocated from Civil Works Administration funds to put unemployed artists to work under the Public Works of Art Project (PWAP). Six months later, in 1934, this successful pilot project ended, and soon was followed by the U. S. Treasury's Section of Fine Arts. Under the Section hundreds of murals were created around the country, paid for using 1 percent of construction funds allotted for decoration. The Section was headed by Edward Bruce, an accomplished painter and expert in international business who worked for the Treasury Department. His administrative staff included Edward Rowan as chief assistant. Formed in part to continue the work of PWAP, the Section sought to provide more than relief for artists. Unlike other federal art programs, it sought the best available artists to decorate the walls above the postmaster's door. To accomplish this, artists were required to compete anonymously for mural commissions.

Murals were painted on post offices where the public would see them each day as they conducted their postal business. Historical themes were among those suggested to artists by the Section. Among other historical subjects, artists chose images of prominent local persons and types. Because of their roots in the state's cultural identity, such figures became the icons to be emulated during the turmoil and uncertainty of the Depression. Many of the figures are portrayed nobly in moments of triumph over difficulty. They became powerful visual reminders to mural viewers that the country's greatness was made possible by the undaunted efforts of their ancestors. For the contemporary generation as inheritors of that tradition, the murals posed an unspoken challenge to measure up to previous achievements.[2]

The Section's mural program originally was inspired by the Mexican mural movement of the 1920s, especially the work of Diego Rivera. His murals featured heroes of the Mexican revolution and themes of workers and indigenous people. However, unlike the Mexican murals, subjects with political content were screened out of the competition for post office murals; such subjects, it was feared, would remind people of the economic and social crisis of the Depression.[3] The historic figures idealized in post office murals emphasized positive values such as hard work, unity, courage, and resourcefulness. Further, because the selection of post office mural subjects was made with public input, this often gave added significance to the figures.

The style favored by Section leaders for murals was that of the American Scene movement in painting popularized in the 1920s and 1930s by the work of Thomas Hart Benton, Stuart Curry, and Grant Wood.[4] These artists led the way to the rediscovery of regional American subjects, such as small town life, American landscapes, and American characters as worthy of subjects for painting. Art of the American Scene was more accessible to the people than abstract art of the dominant European modernism of the time, and it spoke directly to the people in a simple, representational style.

The epic of exploration and settlement of Texas and the Southwest presented several kinds of colorful characters for portrayal as heroes. For example, the frontier hero appears strikingly in a romantic rendering of pioneer settlers by José Aceves for the post office of the Central Texas farming community of Mart. Titled *McLennan Looking for a Home*, the mural depicts the towering pioneer in buckskin, patriarchal Neil McLennan, an early settler of the region, as the central figure and hero. McLennan's handsome expression and his erect stance render him the strong image of a self-assured hero, imbued with appropriate frontier traits of a courageous family leader. A Section press release about the mural calls "the story of McLennan's wanderings in Texas as celebrated in Mr. Aceves' portrayal . . . a symbol of all the heroic struggles of the First Americans to settle the Lone Star Republic."[5] His presence in the painting's foreground looms larger than life and suggests that he is the apotheosis of the Texas pioneer.

Other clues in the painting point to McLennan as the hero figure. All eyes are on him. His handsome wife, who dutifully sits in the wagon in the background with the children, looks expectantly to her husband. Also under the mother's gaze is the son and future hero who stands by the father and carries a stick resembling his father's musket. McLennan's central role in the painting makes his role as protector and visionary who leads his people to their dreams seem obvious. He is a figure that Mart residents looked up to; the county is named after him. The mural seems to invoke all his heroic qualities and bring them before present viewers for emulation.

Tom Lea's mural for the El Paso, Texas, federal building, titled *O Pass of the North*, depicts a historical sequence of character types representative of the region's settlement period, including aboriginal Indian, conquistador, missionary, adventurer, Texas Ranger, farmer, rancher, miner, and sheriff. The various figures all have one salient thing in common—their fierce resolve to conquer the hostile desert and establish the social order in a frontier environment. Their dream was to create a better life, each in his and her own way. But, they all were willing to undergo extraordinary hardships. Lea was well aware of the inspirational effects that these early settlers might have on local mural viewers. "I hold two hopes for this work just completed," he said in a newspaper interview on completion of the mural. "One, that it may bring to life in a few minds that vivid history of the Pass to the North. And the other, that the point of view I have taken as a creative artist may help to demonstrate that the function of a mural painting in a community is to deepen and enrich a people's perception of its own tradition and the characters of its own land."[6]

Lea's heroic mural characters, the forerunners of El Pasoans, are taken from different aspects of the region's early settlement and placed side by side. With their erect posture and self-assured looks, they appear in their moment of triumph. All figures share the same intensity of purpose that is reflected in their gaze. Their eyes seem transfixed confidently toward a distant point, suspending them timelessly beyond the picture's frame.

But Lea had no illusions about the true character of New World heroes in armor or buckskin. He understood clearly that heroes have a less than noble side also, and that efforts to portray them as icons inevitably must overlook their negative aspects. Lea observed: "Of course, the first wanderers and 'pioneers' were not heroes in real life any more than old cut-throat Odysseus was." He called his mural characters "undisciplined Missouri frontier rascals . . . who made great fighters and foragers."[7] But, he added, because of their toughness and endurance, they also were beyond "real life."

The underlying visual message of this mural, and many other Texas post office murals with historical figures, seems to be that just as people of the past struggled to establish the greatness of America, which had momentarily faltered, the current generation will overcome the hardships of the Depression and will succeed in making a better life for its descendants. Marling observes that to the extent the murals express this, "they become an emotive, mystical act of faith in America's capacity to survive."[8] The El Paso mural's inspirational inscription over the doorway separating the two panels reads: "O Pass of the North, Now the Old Giants Are Gone, We Little Men Live Where Heroes Once Walked the Inviolate Earth."

Lea's inscription, however, seemed overzealous and a distortion of their own ideas of a hero and viable role model for a contemporary generation that seemed to have lost its way. The Section feared that, instead of inspiring mural viewers, the inscription would work to discourage people by presenting ideals too high for the people to emulate. This is clear in the comments by assistant Section chief Edward Rowan to Lea.

"We would prefer, if possible, for you to use another inscription that would not disparage the individuals of the present time who occupy the land that your are depicting. . . . It is our opinion that as much strength of character and volubility of purpose is required to live a simple life of a good citizen today as was required of the pioneers."[9] However, Lea, who is from El Paso, reassured Rowan that everyone was enthusiastic about the inscription and that El Pasoans fully understood the difficulties of living in that arid region. They maintained a strong sense of "pride in the courage and strength of forebears who conquered it. None of them find the implication that their own modern lives cannot or do not use that heritage."[10] Lea's conviction was persuasive, and Section officials took him at his word. The inscription remained intact.

Peter Hurd's fresco for Big Spring, titled *O, Pioneers*, also uses an inscription to enhance the mural's messages. This one, however, received a different reaction from the Section. In the mural, the heroic qualities of family are stressed. It presents an image of the hero poised with his family in a moment of self-assurance at the end of a hard workday. Clearly evident is the self-reliance of the isolated family thrown on its own resources and is able to overcome the great obstacles to survival on the desolate landscape. The self-assured look of the centrally positioned figure, the patriarch, expresses traits that both Section officials and artists often recognized as necessary to lead people out of the Depression—independence, responsibility, and courage.[11]

Hurd's inscription, which stretches across the bottom of the mural, reads: "O Pioneers, Democracy Rests Finally Upon Us, and Our Visions Sweep Through Eternity." Like Tom Lea's inscription, the idealism here projects an elevated view of the individual as embodied in each member of the pioneer family. But, unlike Lea's inscription, Hurd's offers a goal that seems more attainable to the people. Section leaders did not object to this inscription possibly because the words include the mural viewer in the dream. The words unequivocally place responsibility for democracy's success on "us." Viewers, thus, become more than passive participants; they become part of the pioneer family's success.

In Hurd's mural, the hero leads his family into a very dangerous, difficult frontier; but, he also leads it out, which is clearly a necessary completion of action. Likewise, following the family's lead of hard work, the painting seems to say, any Texas farm family with its feet firmly planted in the soil, together, can actually attain the sublime vision. It is up to the current generation to continue the struggle to secure the idyllic future. Contemporary mural viewers, then, were reminded that America became great because of the successful efforts of these humble pioneers, despite the present interruption of the Depression.[12]

Did contemporary people get Hurd's message? The artist seemed to think so. In a letter to Rowan, Hurd said: "The comments of the people showed they were emotionally aware, through the painting, of the fortitude and determination of these early settlers and of the character and mettle it took to be among those first to settle West Texas. And that those qualities must not die in the face of today's problems."[13] The people, too, loved it. According to the Big Spring postmaster, Nat Schick, people came from miles around to see the mural, and they praised what they saw.[14] Further, to the extent that Hurd, through his art, delivers the message of hope to the people and successfully leads them out of their depression, the artist himself can also be seen as a hero.

In a time when there was fear of a revolution in the face of the apparent failure of capitalism, only positive images were favored for post office murals.[15] This can be seen in murals that portray a particularly important Texas hero, the Texas Ranger. Artists were careful to avoid scenes that seemed to advocate violence, which they understood would be unacceptable to the Section.[16] The Texas Ranger earned wide respect as the protector of citizens against Indians, bandits, and bank robbers. The rendition of Texas Rangers offered by Minette Teichmueller in her mural for Smithville plays up that ideal. Titled *The Law—Texas Rangers*, it portrays a Ranger who single-handedly gets the drop on two thieves dividing their loot after a robbery. The outlaws stand beneath a tree in a wooded area; their hands are up high and an open money box sits at their feet. A Federal Works Agency press release about the mural informed citizens that "Texas Rangers are still known throughout the world for their cool courage and deadly aim."[17] Neither the mural nor the press release indicates the violence associated with Texas Rangers' activities. The artist portrays the myth of the Ranger as hero who saves the day, and the people's savings, and does so with finesse, that is, without a violent struggle.

Another, more complex portrayal of Texas Rangers appears in Frank Mechau's pair of murals appearing in the downtown Fort Worth Federal Courthouse. The murals are placed side by side across the back wall of a courtroom. One of the murals portrays Texas Rangers working at camp as they are alerted that bank robber Sam Bass plans to ply his trade at a bank in Round Rock, Texas, a small town about 170 miles south of Fort Worth. The second mural portrays the encounter of the Rangers and Bass with his men. The action is frozen at the moment just before the bloody battle that led to Sam Bass's death in a gunfight. Together, the murals juxtapose rangers with folk hero Sam Bass, the good/bad guy, the Robin Hood of legend who was revered by Texans despite his outlaw status.

The mystique of the traditional hero surrounded Sam Bass, who gained a reputation as a bank robber who freely gave out $20 gold pieces to pay for whatever he took from honest people. Bass's acts of popular charity and fairness turned toward the common folks were legendary. One story, for example, relates how Bass, who was persecuted by law men, stopped uninvited for a meal and a night's sleep at a rural household, causing considerable trepidation in the unwilling hostess. However, he paid her generously in $20 gold pieces for the meal and hospitality and insisted that his men treat her politely and respectfully. Another legend tells how, when Bass needed changes of horses during his flights from the law, he confiscated them from hapless travelers whom he encountered; but, he paid well beyond the going rate for securing these fresh mounts.[18] Bass's status as a regional folk hero is understandable, especially in a time of economic need. In his own way, Bass redistributed wealth to help the poor, which is what Roosevelt was trying to do, too.

Although Sam Bass and his gang in the mural are about to be riddled with bullets as they attempt an escape, it is significant that the actual gunfight is not part of the picture. For, in playing down the violent aspect of both Bass and the Rangers, the artist preserves the gentlemanly quality and the dignity of each. Thus, it is not the violence that viewers are encouraged to remember about each icon, but the noble and heroic qualities. The juxtaposition of the two types in the two adjacent murals seems to assert the equality of both heroes as worthy adversaries. (Note also that the mural's title, *The Taking of Sam Bass*, euphemistically avoids suggestions of the violent struggle that ensued.)

Both Sam Bass and the Texas Rangers are appropriate New Deal heroes and reflect its values. The Rangers, on the one hand, uphold law and order, whereas Sam Bass, on the other, represents generosity and paternalism. Together, the pair of mural panels presents a fable to reinforce the concept of social order, while allowing the artist to subtly pay tribute to the popular legend of Sam Bass and his kind of justice.

If the two heroes in Fort Worth present a suppressed violent antagonism of heroes, the antagonism between white settlers and Indians is resolved in the heroic Indian figure of Quanah Parker, who is legendary as the last great chief of the Comanches and respected for his role as peacemaker.

Attitudes toward Quanah as a hero are evident in the mural *The Naming of Quanah* by Jerry Bywaters for the post office of the Texas Panhandle town of Quanah. Parker was the son of chief Peta Nakoni and white settler Cynthia Anne Parker, who was captured by Indians in Central Texas when she was a child. A brave and cunning warrior who led his Comanche band in countless raids and battles against the white intruders, Quanah was never captured and never surrendered. But, he was wise enough eventually to see the inevitability of the white man's influence. He convinced his people to move to Indian Territory in Oklahoma and live in peace, sparing many lives on both sides.

In Bywaters's mural, Quanah is placed squarely in the picture's center, facing the viewer. His hand is raised in a peace sign as he faces a white man, whose back is to the viewer. The painting stresses Quanah as peace-making hero. It is as an event of major importance leading to the settlement of the region and, subsequently, its prosperity. The symbols of progress are seen in the painting's prominent portrayal of the railroad, cowboys driving cattle, agricultural workers busy at harvest, high-tension power lines leading across the landscape in the background, and a modern mineral processing plant. Obviously, this is a fitting subject for a New Deal mural that delivered the message that cooperation with the federal government leads to economic rewards.

Quanah becomes an appropriate New Deal hero, also because he acts as a catalyst to end conflict among antagonists. He also is a catalyst of progress and prosperity. Another of his heroic qualities was his adaptability that enabled him to thrive in a white man's world, a fact that also gained him great respect from both races. Through initiative and good judgment under unfavorable odds, he managed to emerge as a successful tribal leader, as well as a prosperous cattleman. At home in both tribal and white cultures, he often traveled to Washington, and he won the personal friendship of Theodore Roosevelt. As one who brings good to humanity and demonstrates virtues of patience, cunning, and discipline, he is the hero who leads the land to prosperity and fame.

The parade of heroes selected in the painted scenes of Texas post office murals represents some of the historical highlights that helped make Texas regionally unique, but, at the same time, reflects generally accepted democratic values that New Deal leaders sought. All the heroes in the murals seem to have a great love of personal freedom, self-confidence, and a sense of responsibility to a group. They represented these enduring qualities, and they served as silent role-models imprinted on the minds of a generation of Americans who turned their gaze upward above the postmaster's door and learned once more how to dream.

ENDNOTES

1. Forbes Watson, "A Perspective of American Murals," in Edward Bruce and Forbes Watson, *Art in Federal Buildings: An Illustrated Record of the Treasury's New Program in Painting and Sculpture*, p. 4 (Washington, DC: 1936); Marlene Park and Gerald E. Markowitz, *Democratic Vistas: Post Office Murals and Public Art in the*

New Deal, p. 5 (Philadelphia: Temple University Press, 1984).

2. Karal Ann Marling, *Wall-to-Wall America: A Cultural History of Post-Office Murals in the Great Depression*, p. 219 (Minneapolis: University of Minnesota Press, 1982).

3. Ibid., p. 218.

4. Matthew Baigell, *The American Scene: American Painting of the 1930s*, p. 55 (New York: Praeger,1974).

5. Press release, Federal Works Agency, Public Buildings Administration, PBA-FA-23, National Archives, RG 121, n.d..

6. Tom Lea quoted in "Lea Steps Down From Scaffold, Court House Mural Completed," *El Paso Herald Post*, June 24, 1938.

7. Tom Lea to Edward Rowan, May 2, 1937, National Archives, Record Group 121.

8. Marling, *Wall-to-Wall America*, p.219.

9. Rowan to Lea, April 26, 1937, National Archives, Record Group 121.

10. Lea to Rowan, May 2, 1937, National Archives, Record Group 121.

11. Marling, *Wall-to-Wall America*, pp. 21-22; 93-94; 107-108; 228-232.

12. Ibid., p. 22.

13. Hurd to Rowan, n. d., National Archives, Record Group 121.

14. Nat Schick to Rowan, September 7, 1938, , National Archives, Record Group 121.

15. Ibid.

16. Richard McKinzie, *The New Deal for Artists*, pp. 57-65 (Princeton: Princeton University Press, 1973).

17. National Archives, n.d.

18. Richard M. Dorson, *America in Legend: Folklore from the Colonial Period to the Present*, pp.137-138 (New York: Pantheon Books, 1973).

6

WPA Frescoes:
Louisiana's Depression Era Economy

Mary R. Zimmerman

The four fresco panels at the Louisiana State Exhibit Museum in Shreveport are monumental works of art depicting the agriculture, industry, and commerce that contributed to the state's economic growth in the 1930s. These frescoes, like others across the state—and the nation—received their funding from federal programs implemented during Franklin Roosevelt's administration, commonly known as the New Deal. In this legislation, the federal government included programs to fund art projects, giving artists who had lost their jobs during the Depression an opportunity to rejoin the nation's work force.

Government-sponsored art programs however, were often highly criticized. Political analyst Russell Lynes wrote that many conservative members of Congress considered art, for the most part, to be a "frivolous" expenditure.[1] Lynes also noted that frequently artists registered with the programs were under attack, and the removal of their funding was a constant threat. One major criticism was the themes chosen for this form of public art. Usually, labor activities common to local regions dominated the works, and the critics in Congress argued that a public expression of labor activities encouraged negative ideas of the era, such as lost jobs and reduced incomes. Lynes adds that congressional conservatives, viewing the art programs as havens for liberals, voiced strong objections to posting the labor-oriented panels in public buildings. The critics in Washington failed to understand that American laborers viewed the paintings that celebrated the value of their skills with honor and high regard. Because their theme documents the labor skills of America's work force, these 1930s fresco murals, hanging in foyers and decorating the facades of the nation's public buildings, are valuable contributions to our nation's art deposit.

Moreover, frescoes sponsored by the New Deal are of great value because the medium is no longer produced with the popularity that it enjoyed in the 1930s. Today's modern architectural designs use space more conservatively. No longer do large fresco murals illustrate the skills of America's work force as a reminder of the roles these workers played in our nation's economy during the Depression era. These works of art are now prized as a valuable source of historical documentation and a major part of our cultural heritage.

The New Deal legislation had a variety of programs that funded public art. Marlene Park and Gerald E. Markowitz, students of the New Deal projects, record that the Works Progress Administration's Federal Art Project was active from 1935 through 1943.[2] This program funded art projects for artists registered on the relief roles, and their works, often exhibited in competition, generally decorated nonfederal buildings. The Treasury Department established two other programs that provided artworks as embellishment for the large number of federal buildings being constructed in this period. One program, created in 1935, was the Treasury Relief Art Project, which, according to Park and Markowitz, funded projects for nonprofessional artists from the relief roles. Another program was the Treasury Department's Section of Painting and Sculpture, later called the Section of Fine Arts. Park and Markowitz explain that artists working under this program "competed for individual commissions and signed contracts for the completion of particular murals or sculptures" to adorn public buildings. These competitions were anonymous, eliminating possible favoritism, and unknown artists had an equal chance to compete. Artists in these programs were usually professionals.

Another way that public art received funding through the New Deal was to include the expenses for art decoration as part of the grant or loan funding for a public building. New Deal programs financed a percentage of the construction cost for thousands of buildings nationwide, and most had prospective wall space and niches designated for art. By the end of the decade, murals and other art forms became accepted decoration for these spaces. It was a common practice for the building contractor to subcontract the artwork just as he subcontracted other portions of the construction project. This was the case with the fresco panels at the Louisiana State Exhibit Museum. The building's contractor, A. J. Rife, of Dallas, Texas, subcontracted the frescoes when the building was constructed.[3] Although the paintings were not drawn into the original blueprints, they were financed by the Federal Emergency Administration of Public Works funds allocated for the building's construction, making the murals a part of the New Deal legacy.

Mounted on the museum's north portico, the murals, considered in 1938 to be "one of the most important mural paintings in the South," have, for the past fifty-seven years, added a classic feature to the museum's facade. The building's design, a superb example of modern architecture, makes an admirable setting for the frescoes. The works stand above massive sheets of hand-finished, pink Texas granite, flanked by walls of Indiana limestone. Prefabricated doors and windows with bronze and aluminum grills adorn the central part of the monumental facade of the circular structure, separating the mural planes. One cannot view the frescoes without having their interpretation influenced by the formal richness of the portico.

As owners of the building, the department of Agriculture and Immigration of the State of Louisiana made the final decision on a theme for the frescoes. The department chose to use the murals outside to reflect themes common to the exhibits inside. Originally, the displays were designed to spotlight the technology used to produce Louisiana's agricultural and natural resources as some of the nation's most advanced and economically productive. The mural presentations also illustrate the laborer's role in the retrieval of these products and his value to the state's economy. Before entering the building, a visitor can examine the frescoes and gain some understanding of what to expect from the exhibits inside.

A visitor can begin by viewing the painting to the left of the building's front door, which features a mammoth male figure personifying North Louisiana. This lumberjack stands near a felled tree that represents North Louisiana's rich timber industry. The complementary piece to the featured panel illustrates activities and labor forces necessary to process products and natural resources indigenous to North Louisiana. The nineteen human figures in this work are dwarfed by the lumberjack as they bend under the burden of their labor. These figures, earnestly pursuing their work, have intense expressions of concentration outlined on their faces. The lower half of this mural shows the production of timber products—whole logs are cut and split for processing, laborers are removing strips of lumber from the factory line, and paper is rolled onto cylinders for distribution. In the foreground is a large oil rig with a gusher of black liquid flowing up through its frame and across the plane of the work. The scene includes the Red River meandering around plantations near the upper portion of the piece. By using this panel and the lumberjack work, with their larger-than-life figures and prominent location, high above the viewer's eye, the artist idealizes North Louisiana's labor force and its industrial and agricultural production, placing emphasis on their value to the region's economy.

The fresco mounted to the left of the front door contains a female figure personifying South Louisiana. She appears to symbolize the nurturing spirit of the agricultural industry that was the base for the state's economy during the early settlement period in the Mississippi River Delta. To the left of this piece on the portico's east wall, a panel complementary to the female motif that illustrates agriculture common to South Louisiana supports this thesis. This panel depicts men of smaller stature than that of the female figure working diligently. These workers, exhibiting the same earnest expressions as their counterparts on the west wall, are bailing cotton, harvesting sugar cane with cane knives, and combining rice with a primitive combine. Also shown is a Catholic bishop performing a ceremony unique to the region. Each year a week-long festival precedes the opening of Louisiana's shrimp fishing season. At the completion of the festival, a church dignitary blesses the shrimp boats before their departure so that they will have a safe journey and an abundant harvest.

The State's Department of Agriculture and Immigration also gave the final nod for the fresco artist. Conrad Alfred Albrizio (1894-1973), who was born in New York to Italian immigrant parents, received the contract. Albrizio came to New Orleans as an architect, a profession that proved to be a valuable asset during his later ventures. The *Louisiana Leader* records that after studying the fresco medium in Italy and France Albrizio abandoned his profession in 1938 to pursue an art career as a professor in the Department of Fine Arts at Louisiana State University.[4] The *Louisiana Leader* continues by saying that Albrizio, who introduced the fresco medium to the South, envisioned this section of the nation as "a rich nucleus" for what he believed would "ultimately constitute true American art" and wanted the people of Louisiana to lead the South in this field. He had definite feelings about Louisiana's role in Southern culture. Albrizio found New Orleans to be a city with a rich cultural blend of many ethnic groups. This environment, situated in the humid atmosphere of the Mississippi Delta, coupled with the city's unusual and historical architecture, created a setting that he perceived as unique, different from any in the South. *The Louisiana Leader* quoted Albrizio: "Louisiana's culture and natural advantages, together with the inherent temperament of her people, should enable the state to play a leading role in the evolution of a distinct and interpretative type of southern art." Albrizio believed that South Louisiana had the complex social and cultural conditions to be the inspiration for southern art, and he spent the remainder of his life working to make this a reality.

Albrizio created frescoes on buildings across the state. He painted murals in Louisiana's original Supreme Court offices and in the Governor's Office and Court of Appeal rooms in the State Capitol. One of his larger murals is in New Orleans's Union Station. He completed New Deal-sponsored frescoes for the post office in Deridder, Louisiana, and another in Louisiana's New Iberia Parish Court House. Four of his murals also decorate the foyer of Louisiana's Capitol Annex building. Today, these works, viewed by thousands of visitors as they enter these public buildings, document a period in Louisiana's history when physical labor was the major force in agriculture and natural resource production.

Albrizio's talent brought him national recognition, and he exhibited in many prestigious museums and art shows. Alberta Collier, writer for the *Times Picayune*, included among Albrizio's accomplishments honors from the Whitney Museum of Modern Art and the Golden Gate International Exposition at San Francisco's World Fair.[5] Collier added that Albrizio, honored for his work, was the Rosenwald Fellowship recipient in 1946. This New York-based foundation financed a year's leave of absence from his teaching duties and gave him the freedom to experiment with various types of art. Because of his large number of major works and his national recognition, Albrizio is an important figure in the nation's art heritage.

Albrizio brought two of his graduate students from Louisiana State

University with him as art assistants to create the frescoes at the museum. One was Ralph McKenzie, who, after graduation, studied for two years with American artist Thomas Hart Benton and later became an art instructor with the Section of Fine Arts of Louisiana in Baton Rouge.[6] The second student was Roy Buchanan Henderson, later an instructor at Northeast Technical School in Monroe, Louisiana.[7] Through the classroom and hands-on field exercises, Albrizio passed his knowledge of creating frescoes to the next generation of Louisiana artists.

Albrizio had a special technique for creating the frescoes. He combined Italian fresco methods, Mexican art planes, and American regionalism. His studies in Italy exposed him to Renaissance art in which muscular bodies were commonplace. Sketches of muscle in various positions in the artist's files confirm that Albrizio spent much of his time sketching human anatomy.[8] A notation in his "Sketch Book" beside one drawing of human muscular limbs recorded that he was "trying to get rhythm" with the rippling flow of muscle indention.[9] In the museum pieces, the artist placed an emphasis on muscular bodies and limbs. The central figure in each of the panels on the north wall of the building's portico has massive proportions. The "gigantic man is more than fifteen feet tall," and his "high torso" is bare, with his "muscular figure standing boldly."[10] The lumberjack's accented muscle structure was a part of Albrizio's development of rhythm. These features are evident in the female figure on the opposite side of the door as well. The large scale of the two figures, along with their contrapposto pose, raised the characters to monumental status, reminiscent of classic fresco traditions. Albrizio appears to have stylized his characters from studies made during his trips to Italy, suggesting perspectives of early Italian artists who immortalized their heroes in larger-than-life art forms.

Albrizio's style in creating frescoes could have been influenced by Mexican muralist Diego Rivera. Rivera, who used the fresco medium as an embellishment on public buildings in Mexico to document the nation's history, experienced a brief popularity in the United States from 1931 through 1941.[11] It is possible that Albrizio patterned his use of montage space planes from the contemporary artist.[12] This stylistic device incorporated multigroupings of scenes within the painting and, in this case, focused on the productivity of Louisiana's rural and urban work force. In these works, the technique was designed to place the focus on physical activity, accenting labor's role in productivity, hoping to build self-esteem and return dignity to the workers' lives. The combination of Italian and Mexican elements in Albrizio's work illustrated a diffusion of international design and layout.

Another influence was Albrizio's use of American Regionalism, a style common to his peers. To win commissions, period artists looked to "landscape, the architecture, the agriculture or industry" to find images to illustrate "place" instead of capturing the "energy, the diversity, the homespun quality" of a region.[13] Albrizio was no exception. He divided his four pieces into two distinct categories—North and South Louisiana. The lumber man, standing over a felled tree and holding his axe close by, has obviously cut down a tree. This image represents all aspects of the timber industry, a major economic factor in this period across the north section of the state. To confirm the identity of the region, Albrizio surrounds the lumberjack with architecture symbolic of North Louisiana—the Long-Allen Bridge spanning the Red River at Shreveport, Shreveport's Slattery Building, and the Caddo Parish Court House. These familiar landmarks leave little doubt as to the "place" referenced by the artist.

Continuing the Regionalism theme, Albrizio uses architecture from the southern section of the state to identify the location suggested by the works on the opposite walls. To the female's left is the Saint Louis Cathedral from New Orleans' Jackson Square; in the background are warehouses from the banks of the Mississippi River; and the Cabildo, also found near Jackson Square, is on her right. By her feet are rows of sugar cane grown only in the southern part of the state.

Unlike some New Deal murals, there is little designation of place suggested by the ethnology in the works. The workers seem to encompass ethnic groups, African America, Cajun French, and Caucasian workers. There has been over the years a fairly common assumption by viewers that the figures in the murals identify only with African Americans. A close analysis discourages this interpretation because the blue eyes on both of the central figures make it impossible to identify them "as to race and meaning."[14] In the two adjacent panels, there appear to be African American workers laboring alongside men with blue eyes and figures with both dark and light complexions. With little designation as to ethnic groups represented, an analysis as to race and color is difficult for the viewer to make.

Standing as stately as the building itself, the frescoes' oversized figures relay a message to the viewer as to the significance of the laborer's work at a time when American pride had fallen. In the Federal Emergency Administration of Public Works-funded paintings, Albrizio personifies North Louisiana as a male figure representing industry essential to area economy and South Louisiana as a female figure standing for agriculture, the financial base of this region. These forces, simultaneously in progress in the two companion panels, are common to the north and south regions. If the viewer steps away from the works, out into the museum's lawn, the two central figures, separate but mounted side by side, seem to come together, suggesting a union, or marriage, between the two economic forces that breathe life into the State of Louisiana.

ENDNOTES

1. Russell Lynes, "Poverty, Politics, and Artists, 1930-1945," *Art in America*

(August-September 1965), p. 88.

2. Marlene Park and Gerald E. Markowitz, *Democratic Vistas: Post Offices and Public Art in the New Deal*, p. 6 (Philadelphia: Temple University Press, 1984).

3. Specification for a Fresco Painting: P.W.A. Project LA. 1049-D State Exhibit Bldg., Shreveport, La." TD [photocopy], p. 4 (F), Somdal Associates, Shreveport.

4. "Louisiana Artist Appointed on Staff" (Louisiana State University) *Louisiana Leader* 6 (February 1936): n.p.

5. Alberta Collier, "Career of Mural Artist Reviewed," *New Orleans Times Picayune*, August 28, 1966, n.p.

6. Public Classes to Begin Here," *Baton Rouge State Times*, August 14, 1949, p. 11.

7. Roy Buchanan Henderson, *A Execution of a Mural in Fresco*, p. 10 (Master's thesis, Louisiana State University Baton Rouge), 1939.

8. Conrad Alfred Albrizio Papers, 1894-1972, Manuscript Group 3349, Louisiana and Lower Mississippi Valley Collections, Louisiana State University, Baton Rouge.

9. Ibid., Sketch Book, Box 2, Folder 48.

10. Mary Willis Shuey, "Murals in New State Exhibits Buildings at Shreveport," *Hammond (Louisiana) Progress* (September 9, 1938), p. 10.

11. Lawrence Gowing, *A Biographical Dictionary of Artists, Vol. II, The Encyclopedia of Visual Arts*, p. 580 (Englewood Cliff, NJ: Prentice Hall 1983).

12. Francis V. O'Conner, ed., *Art for the Millions: Essays from the 1930s by Artists and Administrators of the WPA*, Introduction, p. 22 (Boston: New York Graphic Society, 1975).

13. Park and Markowitz, *Democratic Vistas*, pp. 140-141.

14. Shuey, "Murals in New State Exhibits Buildings at Shreveport."

7

WPA Buildings in Northwest Louisiana:
A Comprehensive Analysis

Mary R. Zimmerman

The New Deal of Franklin Delano Roosevelt's administration granted funding toward the construction of buildings in Northwest Louisiana. By the 1930s, the region's five parishes—Bossier, Caddo, DeSoto, Red River, and Sabine—consisted of a large number of small communities and towns and one city, Shreveport, located in Caddo Parish, with a population of approximately 100,000. Each parish seat had an impressive courthouse, but business districts in this section of the state had few, if any, other large public buildings. There was little hope of financing new construction because the Great Depression had taken its toll on the area's economy, leaving no funds for public improvements. The state had its own problems and was unable to offer assistance.

The economic outlook differed little nationally. With no funding for public improvements, unemployment was at an all time high. Harry Lloyd Hopkins, Roosevelt's federal relief administrator, recorded in his *Spending to Save: The Complete Story of Relief* that in March of 1929 there were 2,860,000 unemployed adults in the United States, and this figure rose to 8,000,000 by spring of the following year.[1] This disaster developed during the presidency of Herbert Hoover, and near the end of his administration, it affected almost every American household. Once Roosevelt took office, the federal government responded to this national emergency by creating the work relief programs of the New Deal. The programs served a dual purpose. They assisted in financing public improvements and funded wages for labor to complete the projects, a combination that helped to begin the nation's economic recovery.

On April 8, 1935, according to Hopkins, the federal government compiled all public works programs under the Federal Emergency Administration of Public Works, and Congress passed the Emergency Relief Appropriation Act of 1935. The portion of this program dedicated to the construction of federal and nonfederal buildings was $767,997,960. Arthur Macmahon, the congressional appointee selected to evaluate administration efforts of the national programs, wrote that the Federal Emergency Relief Administration of Public Works was an intensified process of eliminating the dole system and rerouted 45 percent of the nation's relief to work relief.[2] Macmahon added that by combining the skills of unemployed workers and a national need for public works projects, the federal government reached a "higher level of efficiency and social value" as it preserved labor skills and financed the construction of buildings in nearly every community. Through grants and loans, the federal government funded a mammoth construction operation encompassing the entire nation and laid the groundwork for the building frenzy of the New Deal.

This increase in building activity at the national level encouraged industry to produce new architectural materials. Willard B. Robinson, who researched public buildings in Texas, noted that fluorescent electrical units provided better lighting for the workplace; new shapes for glass panels made architectural designs more flexible; metal materials such as aluminum and stainless steel introduced prefabricated doors and windows; and marble walls and floors received slick machine finishes.[3] These new products gave industry a direct influence on architectural designs. Architects incorporated the new concepts to create architectural forms known as modern architecture.

Although modern architecture could not have evolved without the industrial products, its artistic forms have their roots in Europe's art culture of the 1920s. The mathematical shapes of Holland's De Stijl School and the German Bauhaus' discord of most decoration influenced European architectural designs.[4]

Robinson explained that these components, along with "simplicity, articulation, [and] unbroken lines," were major forms presented in the 1925 L'Exposition Internationale des Arts Decoratifs et Industriels Modernes in Paris. The diffusion of these styles into America's architectural designs became evident when Chicago's World Fair in 1933 and 1934 featured a "steel and glass house" in its Century of Progress Exposition. America's architects developed the European designs with the use of the new industrial materials and produced new architectural forms. There were three aspects working together to influence the changes taking place: the speed in which the federally sponsored structures were financed, the large quantity of new materials available, and the massive number of buildings built. One can appreciate how modern architecture, springing up across the nation, became an American movement.

For the first time in its short history, America had a national architecture not rooted in the past. Robinson described the developed concept of architectural beauty as "line, proportion, and composition" with "circles, triangles, squares, and borders." These designs made it possible for architects to lay out forms that conserved space and served greater functions. New interior designs focused on efficiency by avoiding wasted space. Public buildings constructed in this manner suggested to the American people that the government placed a greater value on the services offered within the structures than on exterior ornamentation. At a time when the nation's morale was at an all time low, these new forms encouraged the working man to renew his confidence in all levels of government.

The construction of buildings with the new architectural designs combined with the New Deal programs gave immediate relief to the unemployed. However, one benefit of the programs often overlooked was the contributions that they made to culture in local communities. There were more than sixty-nine buildings constructed in the parishes of Northwest Louisiana under the New Deal programs, and a review of nine of these structure types confirms their impact on the lifestyle of area citizens. One of the earliest government projects in the region resulted from cooperation among the federal government, the City of Shreveport, and a private institution, Centenary College. The college wanted to rebuild a wooden amphitheater on its campus, and its Executive Committee applied to the Civil Works Administration for assistance with the funding.[5] Because the college was a private institution, there was difficulty in getting approval for the project. After researching New Deal regulations, the committee applied for and received funds from the program for labor to complete the project. In order to qualify for the grant, the committee's minutes show that on September 9, 1933, the college had to lease "the ground to the City [of Shreveport] for amphitheater purposes" for ninety-nine years. The minutes also record that on May 26, 1936, renovation to enlarge the stage with federal funds began following the completion of the "open-air theater."

The architect for the amphitheater disregarded modern trends and used a classical architectural form of the ancient Greeks. The bench-type seats, made of modern-styled reinforced concrete, form a semicircle. Each row of seats is lower than the previous row, ending at the bottom with the stage in the center front. This typical Greek amphitheater layout suited the purpose for which the theater was designed.

The cooperation among the three organizations, federal and city governments and Centenary College, is an example of the programs' versatility and their success in assisting all areas of the community. Shreveport's then Mayor George Hardy confirmed the amphitheater's value to the city by acclaiming that the facility was a major cultural asset.[6] The college began hosting public theater presentations and outdoor music performances. Today, community organizations hold meetings at the facility, and the college frequently sponsors summer community concerts by the Shreveport Symphony Orchestra. This joint venture has, through the years, made the city culturally richer.

Moreover, Shreveport's Public Works Department received a large grant that included buildings for the city. One was the Farmers' Market, or

Municipal Market, located at 2139 Greenwood Road. The new market was, at the time, in an outlying area of the city, away from downtown, where farmers had ample parking and space to exhibit their produce. Earlier markets, placed in the center of town at the parish courthouse, were unsuitable.

The cost for the market building, completed in July of 1935, was $47,775, according to researchers C. W. Short and R. Stanley-Brown, with an overall project figure of $50,344.[7] Originally, there were four buildings planned. Short and Stanley-Brown relayed that buildings "A" and "B" were completed; "C" and "D" were to be completed as needed. The identical structures were open-styled sheds with exposed steel beams. Under each metal roof was an elevated, reinforced concrete dock running the entire length of the building, an elevation that gave the farmers easy access to the stalls. Both sheds were both approximately 37 feet wide and 182 feet long, and together they provided seventy-two stalls. The open design was utilitarian, making it convenient for farmers to sell from their trucks and to load and unload their produce. Further, the buildings' prominent facades stood as monumental fronts for the open sheds. Their modern designs featured light-brown brick with horizontal bands of darker brick, all spaced in designated orders, and this horizontal pattern continued on the brick canopies mounted over the doorway of each structure.

The modern conveniences offered by the Farmers' Market made marked changes in city commerce. Two years after the market opened, the Chamber of Commerce recorded that the expanded market tied the city to a national network of interstate trade. Commerce increased in the first six months of 1938, over that of 1936, with more than 35,000 trucks bringing approximately 25,566,090 pounds of produce to the market for shipment to such cities as Saint Louis, Missouri; Denver, Colorado; and Tampa, Florida.[8] This surge in trade confirmed the market's value. Today, sixty years after increasing in the city's commerce, the buildings continue to serve Shreveport's Public Works Department as an office, shop, and dispatching headquarters.

Another building funded by the grant was Shreveport's Municipal Incinerator, completed in July 1935.[9] The project, with a construction cost of $170,763 and a project price of $183,008,[10] employed fifty workers from the relief rolls.[11] The building's architect was Samuel Wiener of Jones, Roessle, Olschner. He previously studied architectural design in Europe. He returned to Northwest Louisiana and introduced architectural forms that later became known as the International Style. Designated as a pioneer in this field, Wiener received international recognition for his use of International Style. He exhibited the building's architectural design with its ribbon-styled windows and unusual use of overhang in the United States' Pavilion at Paris's International Exposition in 1937.[12] And the building's architecture, the topic of many magazine articles, was also exhibited in New York at the Architectural League and the Museum of

Modern Art. Lewis Mumford, contemporary architect authority, praised the work, noting that "if [he] had any gold medals to distribute, [he] would quickly pin one on Jones, Roessle, Olschner and Wiener for their municipal incinerator at Shreveport, Louisiana."[13] Weiner made significant contributions in establishing the International Style as an architectural form in the United States and gave Northwest Louisiana an important role in creating that trend.

Wiener used his professional expertise as an architect to make a civic contribution with the incinerator design. The necessity of the new incinerator became apparent when "depositing garbage and rubbish on dumping grounds" created "a serious menace to health" and contributed to a decline in property values.[14] The installation of the building helped to raise property values and improve health standards for citizens in the area. The incinerator was also functional. This was one of the first structures in the United States where an architect and industry collaborated to complete a project. Its first floor received the garbage, and its machinery raised concrete bins to the next floor where the burning equipment completed the process.[15] The facility's 150-tons-per-day capacity, combined with an advantage of being located within the city where it was easily accessible, made the incinerator an asset to city residents. Funding for these public works improvements would have been impossible for the city with the given economic times, but financed by the New Deal grants, Wiener's talents helped to improve the quality of life for Shreveport's citizens.

The town of Many in Sabine Parish also requested and received grants from New Deal programs. This community applied for money to build a combination town hall and fire station under the Public Works Administration program. Town leaders held groundbreaking ceremonies for the new building on January 19, 1939.[16] The building's physical location, on State Highway 171, in the heart of the parish, made it accessible to the entire area. Typical of modern architectural designs, the two-story building served to centralize local government with a compact floor plan. The front portion of the ground floor housed the town's two fire trucks, and directly behind this area, the fire department's personnel often met in a conference room provided for this purpose.[17] Toward the back of the building were lodging facilities for one fireman and his family. The second floor, accessible by an indoor stairway, gave ample space for the town's administration offices. The Sabine newspaper explained that the area behind the offices was an auditorium with a seating capacity of two hundred that accommodated city council meetings and civil court sessions. The building, used today for city administration offices and the police department, remains in its original state with only a small amount of renovations to the front section. The New Deal program made it possible for the town of Many to centralize its government services.

Further, Northwest Louisiana parish governments gained buildings from the New Deal programs. Most of these buildings were for the school systems, and their cultural influence touched the entire community. An example is Bossier High School in Bossier Parish. The innovative layout of the school's design had a major impact on the educational system. Designed by Wiener, this building differed from older-type school designs where all school activities were contained in one building. Bossier High School had "a group of buildings [for] different uses, . . . [a] classroom building, gymnasium, auditorium, cafeteria, and manual-training shop."[18] Reflecting an integration of modern styles, this school was the first in Northwest Louisiana designed with a building for each discipline.

The addition of an auditorium began a revolution in local education. In earlier periods, it was customary for a mother to teach the arts to her children at home. If a student's mother was unable to instruct her child to play the piano, for example, then piano lessons were afforded after school. Lemuel Marshall, a former student and current principal in Bossier Parish's school system, relayed that the addition of auditoriums introduced band as part of Bossier High School's curriculum and made music lessons available to all students as part of their formal education.[19] Marshall noted that one of the band's early members returned to direct Bossier Parish's Airline High School band, continuing the tradition of teaching the arts to the next generation.

Moreover, auditoriums made other cultural contributions. Although Bossier High School was the first area school built with an auditorium, many schools added auditoriums funded with assistance from a New Deal program. Caddo Parish schools received seven auditoriums at elementary school sites.[20] Through the years, most of these buildings, although still used today for theatrical presentations and assemblies, served multiple purposes by having the permanent seats removed so that they could be used as gymnasiums when needed.

Like the auditoriums, the addition of school gymnasiums funded by the federal programs changed lifestyles of those in the area. This building type not only added physical education and health to the curriculum, but also introduced competitive sports into the school system by establishing a network of basketball teams. Schools in all five parishes received gymnasiums—Benton High School and Rocky Mount High School in Bossier Parish;[21] Mooringsport High School in Caddo;[22] Pelican High School, Stanley High School, and Longstreet School in DeSoto Parish;[23] Coushatta High School and Hall Summit High School in Red River;[24] and Many High School in Sabine.[25] These additions across the entire Northwest Louisiana region gave students, for the first time, a place to practice basketball and compete with teams from other schools. The games created a bond among the people in the region and brought them closer together in a competitive atmosphere that built self-esteem and community pride at a time when so many people had so little.

The gymnasiums often substituted as auditoriums. Frequently, there was a stage built within the wall behind one of the basketball goals, usually complete with draw curtains. This area doubled as a theater for art performances and assemblies, and the gymnasium floor held folding chairs for the audience. The addition of this large building type for the first time allowed most schools to assemble the entire student body. The meetings that resulted with the addition of the new modern parish buildings brought the community together and helped to develop the idea of community spirit during this difficult economic time.

Like parish governments, the state received funds from a New Deal program for a building to serve the community, the Louisiana State Exhibit Museum, originally the Louisiana State Exhibit Building. This building, resulting from a cooperation between the state and the Federal Emergency Administration of Public Works program, was the largest and most monumental public building constructed in Northwest Louisiana in this era. Today, the building is on the National Register of Historical Places. Harry D. Wilson, then Louisiana's Agriculture and Immigration Commissioner, was responsible for promoting the building and overseeing its construction. Begun in 1937 and completed in 1939, the building had its formal opening on January 15, 1939.[26] Architects E. F. Neild, D. A. Somdal, and E. F. Neild, Jr., received national recognition for their combination of Classical and Modern architecture.

Facing the building's façade, the viewer is conscious of its classical, monumental presentation. The broad steps, flanked by large, copper-lined flower boxes, rise to a podium portico, an architectural form "characteristic of design inspired by the proper Roman temple."[27] For support, the portico has two hand-shaped, elliptical columns made from Texas granite, the largest of this type in the world.[28] The building's symmetrically styled facade and round rotunda are reminiscent of the Pantheon. The two rectangular buildings, flanking the center structure and connected by passageways, resemble wings, a style made popular by Palladio, an early Roman architect.

Most importantly, the design is in keeping with the mood of the times. It has smooth limestone blocks for exterior walls, sharp clean lines with no eaves, and slick plaster walls to confirm its modern appeal. Other modern features include shiny bronze and aluminum grills, handrails with geometric patterns, and machine-fabricated aluminum doors, six at the front and four at each of the other three entrances. Mounted on the walls above the doors of the north portico are four monumental-size frescoes that were, at the time, the only exterior frescoes in the United States.[29] These works, illustrating activities common to the state's economy in the 1930s, serve to blend the classical and modern styles.

The building's original purpose was to showcase Louisiana's agriculture, commerce, and natural resources. Wilson hired Henry Brainard Wright, nationally acclaimed dioramist, to create miniature dioramas in the building's twenty-two cases to illustrate these aspects of Louisiana's economy. Wright completed the dioramas before his retirement in 1963, and they remain today for the 30,000 students and others who visit the building annually to study and review.

Besides being an architectural masterpiece, the building was the center of community activities. The gallery in the west wing gave local art enthusiasts a place to exhibit their works. Scrapbooks housed at the museum document that before the structure was completed, artists used local hotel lobbies, auditoriums, private clubs, and homes for exhibitions.[30] There was no central location for exhibitions, and only a small portion of the community participated. These makeshift facilities were inappropriate for encouraging students to study the arts. However, once the building was in place, art exhibitions became available to residents in all five parishes. The scrapbook contained a collection of articles describing social gatherings held at the museum, including music recitals, flower shows, and dances. The Louisiana State Exhibit Museum, with an annual visitation of over 500,000 in its early years, was the cultural center for the entire region. After serving the community for fifty-seven years, the building is now a historical and cultural museum.

Of the buildings in Northwest Louisiana parishes funded by the New Deal, only one type was for federal use—the post office. There were two post office buildings constructed in the region, one in Many and another in Vivian, a town in northwest Caddo Parish. A letter from the Director of Procurement to Barnes Brothers dated March 3, 1939, confirmed that the federal government funded 100 percent of the cost for the Vivian post office through the Public Buildings Branch of the Procurement Division of the Treasury Department.[31] The document further stated that the Treasury Department accepted the low bid for the building on March 24, 1939, from Barnes Brothers of Logansport, Indiana. The letter documented that the cost of the actual structure was $43,000 and that the government paid an additional $6,000 for the property, the three lots formerly the site of the Methodist parsonage. The fixtures to complete the interior of the structure added extra expenditures of $20,000, making the total price tag for the facility more than $70,000. The grand opening for the building in Vivian was on December 28, 1939.[32]

The building's symmetrically balanced Georgian-styled facade has four windows, two on each side of a central doorway. Typical of the design, a chimney, appearing to be artificial and serving as a vent, decorates each of the two gable ends. The brick building has such modern features as steam-heated radiators and polished marble wainscoting and floors in the foyer. The post office was the most contemporary structure in the town. The community recognized its value, noting that it "is a fine example of the way a building should be built."[33] It was the custom in this period for the postal service to rent property for its rural stations, and the addition of this new attractive facility made the town's people feel as if the government had singled them out for special recognition. The community, making a statement of approval, attended the formal opening, 600 strong.[34] This sentiment for the structure still exists in Vivian, as the citizens recently secured it a place on the National Register of Historic Places.

The buildings constructed in the five parishes of Northwest Louisiana, in conjunction with the New Deal programs and state and local governments, served many functions. They placed workers back into the workplace, the foremost goal of the venture, and housed a wealth of community services provided by various government agencies. The variety of structure types changed the region's cultural landscape, bringing modern conveniences such as increased commerce for locally grown produce, a modern industrial facility for garbage disposal, new layouts for educational buildings, art exhibition galleries, and buildings designed to offer more efficient federal services. The structures' architectural forms represent a diffusion of international styles that influenced designs across the nation. Buildings constructed in Northwest Louisiana with New Deal funds established the standards for modern architectural styles that later graced area skylines and became a valued part of the region's cultural heritage.

ENDNOTES

1. Harry Lloyd Hopkins, *Spending to Save: The Complete Story of Relief,* pp. 13, 41, 166 (Seattle: University of Washington Press, 1936; reprint, Americana Library Edition, Seattle: University of Washington Press, 1972). Page references are to the reprint edition.

2. Arthur W. Macmahon, John D. Millett, and Gladys Ogden, *The Administration of Federal Work Relief,* pp. 1, 18-19 (Chicago: Public Administration Service, 1941).

3. Willard B. Robinson, *The People's Architecture: Texas Courthouses, Jails, and Municipal Buildings,* pp. 163, 246-247, 263, 163, 274 (Austin: Texas State Historical Association, 1983).

4. H.W. Janson, ed., *History of Art*, 3rd ed., pp. 750-751, 761 (New York: Harry N. Abrams, 1983); Robinson, *The People's Architecture*, pp. 262-263, 273-274.

5. Centenary College Executive Committee Minutes, Archives, Sam P. Peters Research Center, Centenary College, Shreveport, December 20, 1933.

6. "Amphitheater Approved for Local Campus," *Shreveport (Louisiana) Times* (January 22, 1936), p. 5.

7. C.W. Short and R. Stanley-Brown, *Public Buildings: A Survey of Architecture* of *Projects Constructed by Federal and Other Governmental Bodies Between the Years 1933 and 1939 with the Assistance of the Public Works Administration,* p. 629 (Washington, DC: U.S. Government Printing Office, 1939).

8. "Municipal Farmers' Market Beehive of Activity," *Shreveport (Louisiana) Journal,* (July 19, 1938), p. 16.

9. Short and Stanley-Brown, *Public Buildings*, p. 471.

10. Karen Kingsley, "Louisiana Building and Their Architects," in Modernism in Louisiana: A Decade of Progress, 1930-1940, n.p. City of Shreveport, *Record of Building Permits, City of Shreveport, La., Beginning January 1, 1931, Ending December 1, 1938*, December 3, 1934.

11. "Work on City Incinerator to be Finished in 90 Days," *Shreveport (Louisiana) Times,* (May 28, 1936), p. 1.

12. Kingsley, "Louisiana Buildings and Their Architects," p. 49.

13. Lewis Mumford, "The Skyline: The Golden Age in the West," *New Yorker,* April 30, 1938, p. 50.

14. Short and Stanley-Brown, *Public Buildings*, p. 471.

15. Kingsley, "Louisiana Buildings and Their Architects," p. 40.

16. "WPA Approves Fire Station and City Hall Building," Sabine *(Louisiana) Index*, January 27, 1939, p. 1; "WPA Projects in City Progressing Nicely," *Sabine (Louisiana) Index*, April 21, 1939, p. 1.

17. "City Hall and Fire Station Building Began Tuesday," *Sabine (Louisiana) Index*, March 10, 1939, p. 1.

18. Samuel G. Wiener, Sr., "Bossier Looks to Future in Building New High School," (Bossier Parish, Louisiana) *School Board Journal* (November 1941), pp. 33-35.

19. Marshall, Lemeul, Telephone Interview, July 26, 1994. Principal, Butler Elementary School, Bossier Parish, Louisiana.

20. Caddo Parish School Board, *Caddo Parish School Board Minute Books, 1925-1955*. Louisiana State University in Shreveport Archives, Shreveport.

21. Bossier Parish School Board, *Bossier Parish School Board Minutes*, Benton, Louisiana.

22. Caddo Parish School Board (*Caddo Parish School Board Minute Books, 1925-1955*).

23. DeSoto Parish School Board, *DeSoto Parish School Board Records*, Mansfield, Louisiana.

24. Plaque, Coushatta High School, Coushatta, Louisiana; Plaque, Hall Summit High School, Hall Summit, Louisiana.

25. "Many High School W.P.A. Project Started Monday," *Sabine (Parish Louisiana) Index*, March 4, 1939, p. 1.

26. City of Shreveport, May 25, 1937.

27. John J. G. Blumenson, *Identifying American Architecture: A Pictorial Guide to Styles and Terms, 1600-1945,* p. 23 (American Association for State and Local History, 1977).

28. Mary Willis Shuey, "Murals in New State Exhibits Building at Shreveport," *Hammond (Louisiana) Progress*, September 9, 1938, p. 10.

29. H. B. Wright, "Dr. Wright's Notebook," Louisiana State Exhibit Museum, Shreveport.

30. *Scrapbook*, Louisiana State Exhibit Museum, Shreveport.

31. Director of Procurement to Barnes Brothers, March 3, 1939, TDL, Vivian Post Office Collection, Record File 001, Vivian Post Office, Vivian, Louisiana.

32. "Vivian Post Office is Dedicated as 600 People View Building," *Vivian (Louisiana) Caddo Citizen*, December 28, 1939, p. 1.

33. "Town Talk," *Vivian (Louisiana) Caddo Citizen*, February 27, 1941, p. 1.

34. "Vivian Post Office."

8

The WPA's Forgotten Muse:
The Civic Symphony Orchestra of Philadelphia

Arthur R. Jarvis, Jr.

In 1927, when the motion picture sound track made live film music obsolete, one unanticipated result was catastrophic unemployment for musicians. More than 20,000 theater musicians had lost their jobs by 1930, and most were dismissed before the stock market crash of 1929.[1] Between 1929 and 1934, the American Federation of Musicians estimated that 70 percent of all musicians were unemployed and many others could not live on their musical income.[2]

The Depression only heightened unemployment problems for musicians because the erosion of skills from lack of use was even more threatening to their future employment. To feed their families, musicians turned to unskilled manual labor that did immeasurable damage to trained musical hands.[3] Swollen, calloused hands lacked the sensitivity needed to create a violin vibrato or to feel string vibrations. Chapped lips from outdoor work made it impossible to blow a delicate reed instrument such as an oboe or clarinet, and lacked the strength for brass trumpets and trombones.

Origins of the Civic Symphony

National relief efforts for musicians started with an experiment by the Civil Works Administration (CWA) in 1934. Under the Local Works Division (LWD) of the Philadelphia CWA, the LWD City Symphony Orchestra of Philadelphia was created. It was conducted by Dr. Thaddeus Rich, who had been a celebrated violinist from the age of nine.[4] The City Symphony was so critically acclaimed that the National Broadcasting Company (NBC) permitted it to use studio facilities and arranged five coast-to-coast concert broadcasts, including one honoring Admiral Richard Byrd's South Pole expedition.[5] The City Symphony held numerous concerts, but the temporary nature of the CWA forced personnel cutbacks, and the ensemble disbanded in spring 1935.

The Works Progress Administration's Federal Project Number One started at the same time the City Symphony disbanded. Under the umbrella oversight of Federal Project Number One, Dr. Rich became the Director for the Federal Music Project (FMP) region that included Pennsylvania.[6] Rich's experience with the LWD City Symphony Orchestra made him one of the few FMP administrators familiar with musical relief efforts.[7] Rich required that musicians demonstrate their skill before audition boards to qualify for FMP relief work.[8] Musicians were accustomed to auditioning for bands and orchestras and the audition requirement caused no controversy.

Auditions ended by November 1935, and 232 musicians began to practice in an old school auditorium at 17th and Plum streets.[9] Three hundred people had registered, but auditions demonstrated that more than sixty did not deserve consideration because they "were not musicians."[10] Eventually, thirteen different performing units were created for Philadelphia, including a smaller chamber orchestra, symphonic bands, dance bands, and a small ensemble.[11]

City Symphony musicians returned to unemployment when that operation ended, but the FMP provided a second opportunity when it created the Civic Symphony Orchestra, Philadelphia's FMP showpiece.[12] J. W. F. Leman, a native Philadelphian, became the resident conductor of the Civic Symphony after a rotating troika of Leman, Dr. Emil Folgmann, and Guglielmo Sabatini shared responsibility during 1936, the first year of operations.[13] Leman was an experienced violinist who had played with the Philadelphia Orchestra under Leopold Stokowski at the same time Rich had been the concertmaster.[14] During much of the Depression, Leman conducted both the Civic Symphony and the Women's Symphony Orchestra of Philadelphia, a private, nonrelief organization that concertized infrequently. In 1939, Leman had a minor stroke, forcing him to curtail many of his musical activities. His Civic replacement, Guglielmo Sabatini, born in Italy and a naturalized American citizen, remained with the orchestra until its last school concerts in January 1943.[15]

The WPA Civic Symphony became the leading orchestra in Philadelphia during the late 1930s and early 1940s, when the Philadelphia Orchestra underwent a difficult leadership transition from Leopold Stokowski to Eugene Ormandy.[16] Stokowski, who had been the conductor since 1912, announced in 1934 that he intended to resign from his Philadelphia duties, prompting the orchestra to create the post of Music Director to temporarily retain his services. Between 1936 and 1941, Stokowski and Eugene Ormandy, a relatively unknown conductor with the Minneapolis Symphony, shared principal conducting duties.[17] Combined with the financial limitations imposed by the Depression, the transition inhibited the experimentation and innovation that made the Philadelphia Orchestra famous. Such an inhibition opened the door for a temporary transition of musical leadership to the Civic Symphony Orchestra.

Except for a brief program of concerts at the Walnut Street Theater in 1939, most Civic concerts were held at either Irvine auditorium of the University of Pennsylvania or the Grand Court of Mitten Hall at Temple University.[18] Neither was ideal for symphonic music. Temple was a lengthy subway ride up Broad Street from center city and one had to be a dedicated aficionado of classical music to search out the Civic in Northern Philadelphia.[19] Irvine Auditorium, although closer to center city entertainment and restaurants, had acoustical problems. It was a barnlike structure that sometimes echoed sound for three seconds. Such reverberations interfered with orchestral precision and affected musical quality. Arthur Cohn, a frequent guest conductor who later became the first curator of the Edwin Fleisher Collection of Music, described the problem as "ghastly, but there was nothing you could do about it because they had to book the orchestra where they could without paying a fee. They had no money for halls."[20]

During seven years of operations, the Civic ranged from sixty to more than eighty musicians. Although most participants came from the defunct City Symphony, others had experience with the Philadelphia, the Cleveland, the Chicago, and several other major American symphony orchestras. Some were naturalized Americans who had earlier careers in European orchestras. Others came from Philadelphia opera houses, theaters, and motion picture pit orchestras. Finally, there was a collection of young musicians who graduated from city conservatories and schools of music during the Depression and found their first job in the Civic.[21] This diversity of experience provided the orchestra with great versatility in meeting the needs of its numerous guest conductors.

Philadelphia was not alone in creating a symphony orchestra to make use of unemployed musicians. By March 1938, thirty-four symphony orchestras had been created by the Federal Music Project. Although the cities included such obvious locations as New York City, which had two full relief orchestras, Chicago, San Francisco, and Los Angeles, symphonic ensembles were also created in San Bernardino, California; Lynn, Massachusetts; Manchester, New Hampshire; and Winston-Salem, North Carolina.[22]

Guest Conductors and Soloists

The conductor is the single most important individual involved with the interpretation of music by an orchestra. Because of directing decisions, the same piece of music may have a vastly different sound under two conductors. In Philadelphia, Stowkowski's showmanship, good looks, and flamboyant public life focused attention on the conductor as the personal embodiment of musical leadership.[23] Aside from the Philadelphia Orchestra, the city had a wealth of classical orchestras that provided numerous opportunities for guest appearances, but the musicianship of the

Civic Symphony and its willingness to introduce contemporary, experimental works made it a heavy favorite for visiting directors during FMP operations.

Leman and Sabatini conducted most Civic concerts, but they encouraged visiting and neophyte leaders. Guest conducting peaked early in the project with twenty-five maestros appearing during the first full season, 1936-1937. Subsequent seasons saw a steady decline in guest leadership. Fifty-nine guest conductors led the orchestra before it dissolved in 1943; forty-six were Americans. This American emphasis was unusual because the vast majority of resident conductors and music directors for established American symphony orchestras of the same period came from Europe. Unusual as it may have been, American leadership of the relief orchestra was important for it demonstrated that home-grown directors were every bit as capable of putting together a talented ensemble as the experienced imported leaders. Stokowski had been born and educated in England and Eugene Ormandy was from Hungary. Contemporaries among the major established orchestras included Arturo Toscanini (NBC Symphony, 1937-1954), who came from Italy; Dimitri Mitropoulos (Minneapolis Symphony, 1937-1949), who came from Greece; and Serge Koussevitsky (Boston Symphony Orchestra, 1924-1949), who came from Russia.[24] The international origins of these conductors underscored the decidedly American leadership of the Civic.

During the Depression, symphony orchestras were male-dominated strongholds.[25] This sexist policy was rooted more in tradition than in necessity for the numerous soloists hosted by the orchestra clearly demonstrated that qualified musicians for many instruments were available in both genders. The only outlet for women who wanted to conduct was a single-gender group. One of the most noted appearances before the Civic, therefore, was the appearance of Ebba Sundstrom, female conductor of the Women's Symphony Orchestra in Chicago. Sundstrom directed the all-male Civic Symphony in January 1938. Even the musicians acknowledged her directing skill by applauding at one of the rehearsals. Despite favorable reviews and preconcert publicity, weather hurt attendance.[26] Although women frequently appeared as soloists, Sundstrom's appearance was the only one by a woman at the podium.[27]

In addition to the conductors, most Civic guest artists were Americans. As a relief agency sponsored by the federal government, Americans had to be given preference by the FMP. At the same time, the worldwide effects of the Depression made it expensive for international performers to travel, and they had no incentive to appear before a relief ensemble. When World War II broke out in Europe in 1939 and trans-Atlantic travel became risky, performances by European musicians virtually disappeared. From the first performance in 1936 until the last in 1943, the Civic hosted exactly 300 different soloists and singers. International soloists made up only 6 percent of the guest appearances. Many local performers appeared before the orchestra on more than one occasion and more than half were from Philadelphia. More instrumental artists appeared than vocal soloists. By far the most popular instruments were the piano and violin. In voice, there were almost three times as many sopranos as other singers. The peak season occurred in 1938-1939, with ninety-nine soloists.[28]

Soloist skills varied widely and there were times when individuals were underprepared. During a guest-conducting appearance by Dr. Arthur Cohn, the piano soloist lost his way in the Brahms' D-minor Piano Concerto, skipping an entire passage in the difficult work. This put him out of tempo with the orchestra and created "a little chaos."[29] To bring the orchestra up to the pianist, Cohn shouted a place letter in the score to the orchestra and the entire ensemble jumped to the proper spot on cue.[30]

Most soloists were young because older, more experienced performers had contracts with established professional orchestras. Some experienced soloists may have tried to revive slumping careers with Civic concerts, but youth and the future were more important than established reputation. Phyllis Moss, Norman and Renee Carol, and John Paul Pintavalle were considered child prodigies when they made their first appearances.[31] For Moss and Renee Carol, such a claim might be a bit of a stretch because both were in their midteens when they first appeared. For Norman Carol, however, such a description would be appropriate. He was nine years old when he debuted with the Civic Symphony, playing Mozart's Violin Concerto Number 3 in G.[32] Pintavalle was only ten years old when he appeared in July 1942.

African American soloists and choral groups appeared with the Civic Symphony on several occasions. City demographics had changed between World War I and the Depression. Black migrants fled the South in large numbers in the early twentieth century due to crop failures, discrimination, Jim Crow rules, and lynchings.[33] Northern cities offered new employment opportunities with large factories and ethnic neighborhoods. By 1930, Philadelphia had become home to 220,000 African Americans, quadruple the prewar population.[34] Furthermore, the Depression drastically altered black party affiliation. When the party of Lincoln failed to help city blacks during the economic crisis, they turned to the reviving Democrats and helped change Philadelphia into a two-party battleground for the first time since the Civil War.[35] At first constrained by their new surroundings, black inhabitants turned to churches for a social life.[36] Part of this social life revolved around church choruses, solo singers, and background music provided by both piano and organ. Where many white musicians gained their training in music schools, conservatories, and private lessons, black soloists got practical experience from an early age by appearing before church congregations.

The black soloist who received the greatest attention was pianist Joseph Lockett. From 1936 to 1942, Lockett appeared with the orchestra seven times with a wide repertoire that included Brahms' Concerto in D-minor.[37]

It was Lockett's only reviewed performance, partly because he shared the stage with guest conductor/composer Arthur Cohn. Critics were divided in their opinion of the presentation, however. One wrote that Lockett "showed a technique amply able to contend with the tremendous difficulties of the work."[38] Another reviewer was less pleased, claiming that "it would be useless to contend that an ideal blend of brilliancy, forcefulness and poetry was achieved."[39]

Whether Lockett was at the highest levels of musical excellence as a soloist was secondary in importance compared to his frequent appearances. He returned because he was a crowd pleaser that drew attention from a new sector in Philadelphia. The Philadelphia *Tribune*, a weekly newspaper for the African American community that usually did not comment on New Deal cultural programs, included articles about Lockett's appearances in advance, drawing a new audience to classical music. This audience carried high expectations into the concert hall because they wanted him to demonstrate that his talent was equal to the task. By fulfilling those expectations, Lockett continually made new friends for the Civic. Part of this increased attention was due to Philadelphian Marion Anderson, the African American contralto who was earning universal acclaim. Anderson, who never appeared with the Civic, may have reached new heights with her Lincoln Memorial Easter Sunday radio concert on April 19, 1939, but Lockett's first Civic concert preceded Anderson's heralded concert by three years.[40] Among other black artists who were Civic guests were the Hoxter Jubilee Choir, mezzo-soprano Constance Stokes, tenor William Ellis, contralto Mary Denby, and pianist Clyde Winkfield.[41]

The numerous guest conductors and soloists with the Civic Symphony showed that FMP concerts offered an opportunity to appear regularly with a professional organization that had high performance standards. Just like the Philadelphia Orchestra, it played music by Beethoven, Tchaikovsky, Brahms, and Bach, as well as a host of new works. It was taken seriously by local critics. For many performers, an appearance with the FMP symphony was their debut. It provided them with the exposure and publicity needed to launch a career. They certainly did not do it for money because guests who appeared with FMP performance units were not paid.[42]

American Emphasis

The Civic Symphony frequently presented entire programs of American music for special occasions. For example, during the FMP-sponsored National Festival of Music week in both 1938 and 1939, programs included works by renowned American composers Henry K. Hadley, W. W. Gilchrist, Edward MacDowell, and Philadelphians James Francis Cooke and Otto Mueller.[43] In June 1939, the Symphony played for the

Highway Safety Patrol commencement exercises; in May 1940, it participated in the "This Work Pays Your Community" week and the Rural May Day Festival at the University of Pennsylvania. On December 5, 1941, only two days before Pearl Harbor, the Civic was featured at the "You Can Defend America" concert presented by the Philadelphia Council for Defense at the Academy of Music.[44] Two months later, the Civic Symphony used Washington's birthday to present a program that included works by Aaron Copland and Deems Taylor, a world premiere by Harry Adjip entitled "To Maalah," and Alexander Laszlo's "Symphonic Improvisations on Poster's 'Oh! Susanna'."[45]

In June 1942, the Civic participated in a War Production Rally hosted by the Industrial Salvage Section of the War Production Board. One month later, it furnished music for a community Air Raid Protection and Bomb Demonstration Rally of more than 6,000 people.[46] These programs not only made use of the FMP's access to American audiences and the emphasis on American music, but they also appealed to the patriotism of the listeners during the difficult early months of World War II. It created motivation and encouragement when unfavorable national war news tested the local character. During the last year of FMP operations, when the use of music by American composers soared, almost any occasion served as a reason to present American classical works.

Philadelphia's WPA Civic Symphony and its programs strongly emphasized American composers, conductors, and musicians. This was mandated by Dr. Nikolai Sokoloff, and was consistent with WPA directives that the cultural projects were to stimulate national awareness.[47] While the FMP existed, 43 percent of Civic concerts included music by American composers. During the last two seasons of operations, the early war years of 1941-1943, 75 percent of the Civic Symphony wartime concerts had at least one piece of music by an American composer aside from the National Anthem.[48] As a point of contrast, from 1935 to 1943, the Philadelphia Orchestra presented American music in less than 27 percent of its programs.[49]

Much of the American music in Civic programs was composed by Philadelphia composers. Fifty-six percent of the American music that can be identified from existing programs was written by Philadelphians.[50] Among these local composers were Samuel L. Lacier, music critic for the Philadelphia *Evening Ledger*; the previously mentioned Arthur Cohn; Dr. Harl McDonald, Professor of Music at the University of Pennsylvania; and Otto Mueller, a member of the Civic Symphony and frequent guest conductor, particularly when his own compositions were scheduled. Other Philadelphia composers included N. Lindsay Norden, James Francis Cooke, and Luigi Carnevale, all of whom also guest conducted. After Guglielmo Sabatini became the Civic conductor, he frequently scheduled his own compositions, including the Prelude to "Il Mare" and "Poemetto Autumnale" for concerts.

Although American music was a feature of the Civic, numerous examples of requests for traditional symphonic standards exist in letters to FMP headquarters in Philadelphia, including one for the "Emperor Waltz" by Strauss and another for Fritz Kreisler's "Liebesfreud and Liesbesleid."[51] Request concerts were nothing new on the Philadelphia scene, Stokowski had made it a practice to end each Philadelphia Orchestra season with a program made up entirely with requests, but by placing the requests throughout the season instead of merely at the end, the Civic Symphony made a shrewd, if calculated, appeal to public relations.[52] Programs were designed for popularity and audiences were invited to address their requests to FMP headquarters. Other examples of requests were shown in programs for April 26, 1940, at which Strauss's "Tales From the Vienna Woods" was scheduled, and February 23, 1941, when Wagner's Overture to "Tannhauser" fulfilled another patron's query.[53]

Public Response

The popularity of the Civic benefited from its use of local soloists. Great public support developed in Philadelphia when people realized that local talent was being both recognized and encouraged. This was reflected by the FMP adding concerts each season as well as constant audience growth.

Another method of judging the success of the Civic Symphony was the turnout. How large were the Civic audiences? People attended concerts only when they believed the performances were worthwhile. Interest was rapidly lost in anything that was boring or repetitive. The FMP not only provided employment for unemployed musicians, but it filled a pressing need in Philadelphia for live music. The Civic Symphony and other units of the FMP benefited from this interest in music. Record numbers turned out to see and hear FMP concerts. More than 6.5 million people attended FMP concerts over the six years of operations, three times the population of Philadelphia during the Depression.[54] The Civic Symphony averaged 1,136 people in the audience per concert.[55] Each of the first three years exceeded this average. Peak average attendance was reached in 1939. This apex was immediately followed by the poorest seasonal attendance when the Civic saw attendance plummet in 1940. This drop was unusual because 1940 was the peak attendance year for the Philadelphia FMP music units.[56]

Poor attendance in 1940 had several causes. Outdoor concerts, which always drove up audience totals with their large audiences, started later than usual, July, because the Civic held concerts in Penn's Irvine Auditorium during June. Another problem was a change of location. Usually, the Civic held concerts on the steps of the Philadelphia Museum of Art during summer months. A well-known location near center city, it was easily accessible by public trolley and subway. Furthermore, Benjamin Franklin Boulevard, the large street between city hall and the museum, had ample parking for people who drove into Philadelphia from nearby communities. Summer concerts frequently attracted audiences of 4,000 to 6,000 people and were the most heavily attended programs of the year. In 1940, however, they were scheduled for Fisher Park in the city's Olney section. Olney is in Northwest Philadelphia, more than six miles from the art museum and far from the theaters, nightclubs, and entertainment facilities of center city. Severely limited parking forced much of the audience to take subways and public transportation through several connections to reach the isolated park. Although the new location fit FMP requirements of taking music to the people, in this case, it also mitigated against large audiences, particularly when the return home had to be made after dark, through strange neighborhoods, on public transportation.

The 1940 decline also may be partially attributed to increased competition from the other FMP music units and municipal music organizations such as the police and fire department bands. Nineteen-forty was the only year when eight units of the FMP provided music in Philadelphia. Why should people endure the difficult trek to the Civic at Fisher Park when another FMP unit was probably within walking distance of their own neighborhood?

Average audience attendance for the Civic Symphony was not an accurate reflection of Civic audience growth. When averages were high from 1937 to 1939, the Civic gave fewer music appreciation concerts than it did in its later years. After 1939, music appreciation concerts in city schools increased dramatically for the Civic. As a result, the number of concerts increased, but so did the audiences. Despite the aberration of 1940, the number of people who turned out for Civic concerts constantly grew, from 65,063 in 1938, to a peak of 179,396 during 1941.[57] That peak year might have been exceeded in 1942, but the music project was terminated at the end of September. In six years, the Civic Symphony drew a total audience of more than half a million people.[58] Civic attendance figures indicated that, as performances improved and program selection included more American music, the audience grew. Even in 1941-1942, the last complete season of FMP operations, when the city's attention was diverted by World War II, the Civic audience did not decline in size.

Local, American, and World Premieres

The Civic Symphony provided a unique opportunity for American composers during the Depression, particularly local people who had worked in obscurity. Not only did the Civic Symphony regularly schedule new music, the FMP actively solicited composers to submit scores for consideration. In early September 1941, a notice appeared in Philadelphia newspapers inviting local composers to submit new works for consideration by any of the Philadelphia WPA units. All music was welcome, including compositions for symphony orchestra, string or wind ensemble, concert band, and dance orchestra.[59] Because of this, the Civic became the city's leading classical orchestra in terms of premieres during the late 1930s, frequently doubling and tripling the number of world premieres presented by the more renowned Philadelphia Orchestra. During its operations, the Civic had seventy-eight world premieres, whereas the Philadelphia Orchestra only offered twenty.[60] Sixty-eight percent of the Civic introductions were local compositions. Many of the titles suggested that composers thought in terms of American sights, sounds, events, and people. They included "Under the Elm Tree," by Otto Mueller; "County Fair," by Evelyn Berchman; "New Sweden on the Delaware," by Dr. Harvey Gaul; "Negro Lament," by Martin Muscaro; and "The Legend of Sleepy Hollow" Suite, by Robert H. Elmore.[61] This meant that social customs, Pennsylvania history, ethnic experiences, and literary themes inspired the composers.

Local premieres were almost as prevalent as world premieres. Seventy-six musical works had Philadelphia debuts between 1935 and 1943. Among the more prominent compositions presented by the Civic Symphony was Aaron Copland's "An Outdoor Adventure," which premiered in the initial 1941-1942 concert.

Despite the prevalence for works by Americans, some European works also premiered. These included Franz Liszt's "Ungarishche Sturm Marsch," Giuseppe Verdi's "Manzoni Requiem," Josef Haydn's Overture to "The Deserted Island," and Giocchino Rossini's "Il Viaggio a Reims."[62]

The premieres of American music played by the Civic Symphony during its operations vastly exceeded the American music introduced by the Philadelphia Orchestra in the same period. From the initial abbreviated season of 1935-1936, through the final complete season of 1941-1942, the Civic Symphony was consistently more receptive to new music. Part of this can be credited to the Civic's nondependence on ticket sales for operating funds, whereas the Philadelphia Orchestra needed paying customers to pay its bills. When experimental or unfamiliar music was programmed, the Philadelphia Orchestra ran the risk of patrons refusing to buy tickets because the concerts did not include interesting music.[63] Funds were not a factor in Civic Symphony programs. As long as the federal government maintained WPA operations, the FMP continued its experiments with new music and provided opportunities for American composers. Their financial support permitted programming flexibility with which no self-supporting orchestra could compete. Therefore, whereas the Philadelphia Orchestra premiered 45 pieces of American music, the Civic Symphony introduced 125 works to Philadelphia, 278 percent more than the world-famous orchestra.

Teaching a New Audience

The Civic Symphony encouraged the creation of new American music, largely by Philadelphians, because FMP leadership realized the nation's musical future rested on the cultivation of a new audience and the encouragement of local composers. Composers drew encouragement from hearing their music before an audience. This new audience was cultivated from the beginning of the first season. Whereas the FMP maintained a minimal charge for admission to its concerts, librarians, social workers, students from public schools, nurses in training, and music students were admitted at no cost.[64] Also, large blocks of tickets for Civic concerts at Irvine Auditorium and Mitten Hall were sold at fifty cents apiece, or less. Summer outdoor concerts were always free. The FMP sent letters to school administrators and music conservatories throughout Philadelphia to encourage attendance.[65] Later, as American defense industries expanded before and during World War II, concert notices were posted at factories and military bases. All servicemen in uniform were admitted free.

FMP bands were frequently booked into junior and senior high schools for music appreciation assemblies during the first four years of FMP operations, but the Civic did not originally operate the same way. At first it offered discounted tickets so selected groups could attend the concerts at Penn and Temple. Under the program of sponsorship that began in late 1939, however, the Civic changed its policy.[66] No longer were students expected to come to the concerts, but music education programs were taken directly to the schools by the orchestra. As a result, the Civic began to appear far more frequently in public school assemblies while maintaining its regular schedule of concerts. Part of this increased youth concert policy was a requirement by the new sponsor of the music program, the Philadelphia Board of Education.[67] The Philadelphia Orchestra had children's concerts at the Academy of Music, but a comparison of the two educational programs demonstrated that the Civic Symphony held far more concerts for students, cultivating a future audience. Each year, the Philadelphia Orchestra played between four and nine youth concerts. Although the Civic held only three music appreciation assemblies in 1935-1936, by 1941-1942 their educational program had expanded to sixty-two school concerts a year.[68] In other words, the FMP brought the music to the students, whereas the Philadelphia Orchestra forced students to seek out the music.

By advertising at military bases and factories, by actively seeking audiences with free student tickets, and by providing low-cost admission to the working class, the Civic Symphony encouraged the cultural democratization of classical music. It greatly expanded the audience for classical music by holding free public concerts on the steps of the Philadelphia Museum of Art. This appeal was helped by having the Civic travel to different city locations for its concerts. Although Penn's Irving

Auditorium and Temple University's Mitten Hall were the principal concert halls for Civic concerts, they were not the only locations to hear the FMP orchestra. Open-air summer concerts in city parks and secondary school assemblies underscored the accessibility of the program. Finally, local radio broadcasts of the Civic demonstrated that the FMP unit had the same public exposure as more renowned orchestras.[69] By having its own weekly program on local radio the Civic Symphony gained additional respect from music patrons.

The Civic and World War II

Not only did the Civic expand its educational program in 1939-1940, it also increased the patriotic emphasis, particularly as the nation edged closer to World War II. The announcement for the August 23, 1939, concert was a harbinger of this patriotism for it indicated the national anthem would be played.[70] This was an unusual announcement because the national anthem was not generally advertised as part of a concert, but simply added to the program. Two years later, however, public announcement of the national anthem was a regular feature.[71]

After the United States entered World War II, adjustments were made in concert policies. Admission charges were lowered even more, particularly for people involved in the war effort, or soon to be involved. Student nurses, for example, were admitted after they paid the Federal Admission Tax of three cents.[72] New slogans appeared on the announcements, including "MUSIC FOR NATIONAL MORALE," "BUY WAR SAVINGS STAMPS AND BONDS NOW!," "FORWARD MARCH WITH MUSIC!," "DO YOUR PART IN THE SALVAGE CAMPAIGN!," and "DO YOUR PART IN CIVILIAN DEFENSE!"[73]

American war participation initiated additional changes. Special programs were held for servicemen at the Philadelphia Navy Base.[74] During scheduled public concerts at Irvine auditorium, the Philadelphia Council for Defense used intermissions for talks on National unity, civilian cooperation with the government, and other aspects of war life by government departments and civil defense organizations.[75] Even the monthly narrative reports displayed the slogan "For Defense Buy United States Savings Bonds."[76]

The war effort began to affect the Civic as the draft and defense industries drew unemployed musicians. The size of the orchestra, which had usually been around eighty musicians, quickly shrank. By September 1942, it was down to fifty-five musicians and most of them were either retired or unfit for the armed services.[77] That same month performances decreased to ten, and five of them were radio broadcasts.[78]

Music projects in some states were not officially terminated until July 1943, but war demands on manpower made it impossible to continue operations that required active, balanced cooperation among a group of musicians.[79] In some states, the need for an orchestra transcended war preparations and when federal funding ended, private support continued operations. Among the musical organizations that owe their existence to a WPA birth are the Oklahoma City Symphony Orchestra, the Symphony Orchestra of Utah, and the Buffalo Philharmonic Orchestra.[80] With the Philadelphia Orchestra already well-established, however, a second professional orchestra was not needed in the city. Newspapers reported that the final public concert of the Civic Symphony took place on Sunday, December 20, 1942.[81] The last announced concert was a Music Appreciation assembly at Furness Junior High School, January 26, 1943.[82]

Conclusions

The social function of the Civic Symphony was just as important as the employment practices of the Philadelphia FMP. By performing in homes for the elderly and schools, by scheduling concerts in hospitals and parks, by appearing at military installations and social centers, the Philadelphia FMP demonstrated that young and old, ill and healthy, servicemen and the general public could enjoy live music. The diversity of locations at which performances were held demonstrated that music was a democratic institution. No longer was it an elitist activity reserved for the well-to-do or for special holidays. Live music became an everyday event that could be enjoyed almost anywhere in the city. Furthermore, making FMP concerts free or low-cost had a decisive effect at encouraging attendance. People who had little or no money for restaurants during the Depression could walk to the nearest park, school auditorium, public square, or social center and be entertained by professional musicians for several hours.

The public concerts of the Civic Symphony had the ability to make people temporarily forget about their daily troubles and relax. With the high social tension caused by the Depression and nagging fears of international chaos at the start of World War II, FMP concerts in Philadelphia served as a diversion for public frustration and anxiety. Music provided an uplifting experience that aided public morale when it was greatly needed. Furthermore, as the city moved from economic recovery to defense preparation, the Civic also changed. Instead of playing only in schools and public parks, they appeared more frequently at defense rallies, bond sales campaigns, and programs for servicemen. The enormous popularity of the program was clearly demonstrated near its end. When work-relief operations were winding down and public projects were no longer necessary to relieve unemployment, requests for concerts, inspirational support, and the emphasis on American compositions increased. During the initial months of World War II, the FMP provided encouragement and focused public attention on the national musical heritage. The emphasis on American music demonstrated that American culture was worth preserving.

Education was a vital function for the Philadelphia FMP. Although much of the Philadelphia public was familiar with the Philadelphia Orchestra through the efforts of Leopold Stokowski, relatively few visited the Academy of Music. That boded ill for the future because few of the city's children were familiar with any orchestra. Only a small number attended the youth concerts provided by the Philadelphia Orchestra. Unless the audience expanded by creating new support among city youth, the orchestra's audience would erode. The Civic worked tirelessly to provide that education, giving musical appreciation concerts throughout the city's public and parochial schools. These were educational assemblies and did far more than merely present music. Conductors and instrument section leaders interspersed performances with explanations about the music and demonstrations of string, brass, woodwind, and percussion sections. They also encouraged musical studies by including student performers in the school concerts. FMP leaders realized that school concerts were, in reality, training sessions for the future, for unless the students enjoyed the experience, the city's musical future was endangered.

Most important of all, however, was the emphasis on American music, presented by American musicians for American audiences. For composers, particularly local people who had been working in obscurity, presentation of their work by the Philadelphia FMP units replaced the "lip service" they received for years. Civic audiences for the FMP were often inexperienced concert goers. Unfamiliar with the classical repertoire, they had not developed discriminating musical tastes. This lack of familiarity benefited American composers because their works received as much attention as the standard repertoire before audiences with open interests. Because the FMP did not have to worry about income and budget, many new works premiered with the Civic Symphony. Even if a musical work was performed only once, before the select Composers' Forum audience, at least it was heard, and the composer could judge its value by comparing it to both the standard repertoire and a host of other new compositions. The Philadelphia musical effort was regional in nature because much of the music was of local origin, but when the local FMP was combined with similar regional efforts taking place in New York, Chicago, Los Angeles, and the smaller Federal Music Projects in the South and Midwest, a national effort resulted that has never been duplicated. Demand for American music increased as the project continued. At first, this was due to lack of familiarity with classical works, therefore, local directors of the project took advantage of the opportunity to bring as much American music to their attention as possible. As war fervor mounted, however, demands for American music served as a patriotic outlet.

Of the four cultural projects in Federal One, which also included theater, writers, and art, the most successful in Philadelphia was the Federal Music Project. Although the principal purpose of the FMP was to provide relief for unemployed musicians, the secondary goal of community service became the guiding principle. In Philadelphia, the significant achievement of the Civic Symphony was not that it provided music for large audiences, but that it placed the music in a local context by creating opportunities for both local composers and soloists. By expanding the repertoire and by revealing the vast talent pool that existed in Philadelphia, the FMP confirmed the local opinion of the city as a regional musical center.

ENDNOTES

1. William F. McDonald, *Federal Relief Administration and the Arts: The Origins and Administrative History of the Arts Projects of the Works Progress Administration*, p. 586 (Columbus: Ohio University Press, 1969).

2. Ibid., p. 587.

3. Nikolai Sokoloff, *A Preliminary Report on the Work of the Federal Music Project*, p. 8 (Washington, DC: Works Progress Administration, 1936).

4. Robert A. Gerson, *Music in Philadelphia*, p. 208 (Philadelphia: Theodore Pressor, Inc., 1940). In 1906, Rich became the concertmaster of the Philadelphia Orchestra, a position he retained for over twenty years. After resigning from the orchestra in 1926, Dr. Rich served on many musical boards and judged musical contests and auditions throughout the city.

5. McDonald, *Federal Relief Administration and the Arts*, p. 594.

6. Ibid., pp. 606-607.

7. Gerson, *Music in Philadelphia*, pp. 222-223.

8. Harry Hopkins to Dr. Thaddeus Rich, October 28, 1935, WPA serial telegrams folder, 1935-1938. Harry L Hopkins papers, Franklin D. Roosevelt Library, Hyde Park, New York.

9. Philadelphia *Evening Bulletin*. n.d. Bulletin microfiche file, Urban Archives, William Paley Library, Temple University, Philadelphia.

10. Ibid., quotation attributed to William C. Mayfarth, city director of the FMP.

11. Generally, a "full" orchestra ranged from 80 to 100 trained musicians, whereas a chamber orchestra was smaller. A chamber orchestra may include all the sections (string, woodwind, brass, and percussion) as a full orchestra, but each one had fewer members. For example, the violins may include only eight instruments instead of twenty. A symphonic band had all the instruments that an orchestra had except the string section. Dance bands were usually small groups of six to fifteen instruments.

12. *Report on the Purposes and Activity of the Civic Symphony Orchestra*, Works Progress Administration, Federal Music Project, Philadelphia. The Report covers from January 1, 1936, to August 31, 1937. WPA Federal Music Project files, Music Department, Free Library of Philadelphia.

13. Although musical seasons usually run from October until April or May of the following year, the fall of 1935 was spent organizing the project, determining the appropriate local units, and rehearsing the musicians.

14. Dr. Nikolai Sokoloff, Leopold Stokowski, Thaddeus Rich, and J. W. F. Leman were all violinists. So was Eugene Ormandy. Violinists frequently became conductors because of internal orchestra organization. The principal violinist, or first chair, is also called the concertmaster. Violins frequently carry the melody, therefore concertmasters evolved in orchestras to become the leaders of the instrumentalists. As indicated by the listed conductors, concertmasters move directly from the violin first chair to the podium, sometimes serving in emergencies as a substitute for scheduled conductors. See Michael Hurd, *The Orchestra*, p. 34 (Secaucus, N.J.: Chartwell Books, 1981).

15. *Report on the Purposes and Activity of the Civic Symphony Orchestra*, p. 4. See also Hope Stoddard, *Symphony Conductors of the U.S.A.*, p. 368 (New York: Thomas Y. Crowell, 1957).

16. Philadelphia Monthly Narrative Reports, "1937 Pennsylvania Narrative Reports" folder, January 1937, January 1939, September 1939, Federal Music Project, RG 69 Records of WPA, Box 3, Entry 352. Pennsylvania Narrative Report January 1940, "1940 Pennsylvania Narrative Records folder," Box 12, Entry 353, RG 69 Records of the Works Projects Administration, Federal Music Project, National Archives, Washington, DC. Shortened hereafter to WPA FMP. The Civic Symphony began under that name, but new work rules, personnel changes, and budget guidelines encouraged name changes. The Civic Symphony Orchestra became the Philadelphia Federal Symphony Orchestra in January 1939; the Philadelphia WPA Civic Symphony in September 1939; and, finally, the Pennsylvania WPA Symphony Orchestra in January 1940. Of the different Philadelphia FMP units, it was the only one to make such drastic changes in identification. For the sake of reader clarity and simplicity, the author has retained the original title of the organization throughout the narrative.

17. David Ewen, *Dictators of the Baton*, pp. 82-83, 200-204 (Chicago: Alliance Book, 1943). Also see Herbert Kupferberg, *Those Fabulous Philadelphians, The Life and Times of a Great Orchestra*, pp. 121-129 (New York: Charles Scribner's Sons, 1969). Ormandy eventually earned a reputation as great as Stokowski's.

18. Use of the Walnut Street Theater by the Civic Symphony coincided with the theater's use by the Federal Theater Project, which presented its plays in the same facility. Conflict was avoided, however, because Philadelphia blue laws did not permit theatrical productions on Sundays, but concerts could be held. This arrangement lasted only for a short period, because a fee had to be paid for the use of the privately owned theater. This led to a curtailment of discounted tickets because income had to cover the cost of the theater rental. The experiment ended when it was found to be economically unsound.

19. Philip Scranton and Walter Licht, *Work Sights: Industrial Philadelphia, 1890-1950*, p. 4 (Philadelphia: Temple University Press, 1986).

20. Arthur Cohn interview with the author, December 12, 1992, in New York City.

21. *Report on the Purposes and Activity of the Civic Symphony Orchestra*, p. 2. Major cities were able to draw from a deep pool of talented and experienced musicians for their FMP units. Small cities and rural organizations with FMP units did not have that luxury. McDonald, *Federal Relief and the Arts*, p. 611.

22. McDonald, *Federal Relief Administration and the Arts*, p. 619.

23. Hope Stoddard, *Symphony Conductors of the U.S.A.*, p. 222-223 (New York: Thomas Y. Crowell, 1957).

24. Norman Lebrecht, *The Maestro Myth: Great Conductors in Pursuit of Power*, pp. 339, 341, 226, 334 (New York: Birch Lane Press, 1991).

25. Sexist attitudes in musical circles have changed very little in the last sixty years. Only Sarah Caldwell, who founded the Boston Opera Group, has led a major musical organization for any extended period in the United States. Ibid, pp. 266, 331.

26. *Philadelphia Evening Public Ledger*, January 14, 1938; Philadelphia *Record*, January 16, 1938.

27. Sundstrom's Civic Symphony appearance did not vault her into prominent guest conducting appearances. In a list of major conductors of the last century she was not included despite her groundbreaking efforts in both Chicago and Philadelphia. Lebrecht, *The Maestro Myth*, pp. 329-342.

28. Numbers include total soloists for all seasons. If an individual appeared in

separate seasons the individual was counted twice.

29. Dr. Arthur Cohn interview with author, December 11, 1992.

30. Ibid.

31. Philadelphia *Inquirer*, January 2, 1938, also WPA Federal Music Project Collection of Posted Notices, n.d. Also Pennsylvania Music Project Narrative Report for July 1942, "Pennsylvania 651.311-June 1942" folder, Box 2440, Central Files by State 1935-1944, RG 69 Records of the WPA and Program announcement for July 7, 1942, WPA Federal Music Project Collection of Posted Notices, ibid.

32. Carol was not the usual fleeting child prodigy who faded after the initial fame. He appeared with the Civic several times and demonstrated his expanding virtuosity by playing the Beethoven Violin Concerto and the Tchaikovsky Violin Concerto in D-Minor. Carol continued his studies at the Curtis Institute and appeared as a soloist when he was a young adult, but he preferred a stable home life to the fame and constant travel of solo performing. He took a position as concertmaster of the New Orleans Symphony, moved to the Minneapolis Orchestra shortly afterwards, and was finally invited back to the Philadelphia Orchestra in 1966 as their concertmaster. Although many concertmasters leave orchestras to take up solo performing or become conductors, Carol retained his chair for twenty-eight years, retiring in July 1994. Philadelphia *Inquirer*, Entertainment section, Sunday, July 31, 1994.

33. Russell F. Weigly, ed., *Philadelphia. A 300 Year History*, p. 531 (New York: W. W. Norton, 1982).

34. Ibid., p. 588.

35. Ibid, p. 589.

36. Ibid.

37. Philadelphia *Inquirer*, December 27, 1936; March 25, April 6, May 16, December 23, 1937; April 2, 1939; and, June 15, 1941.

38. Samuel Laciar, Philadelphia *Ledger*, April 3, 1939.

39. Henry Pleasants, Philadelphia *Evening Bulletin*, April 3, 1939.

40. Ibid., and Marion Anderson, *My Lord, What a Morning, An Autobiography*, p. 188 (New York: Viking Press, 1951).

41. Philadelphia *Inquirer*, August 9,1936; April 5, June 2, 1940; October 1941; and January 18, 1942. The Hoxter Choir was named for its director, Dr. W. Franklin Hoxter. Denby only appeared at school concerts, not the scheduled public concerts.

42. Dr. Arthur Cohn, interview, December 11, 1992. Funds for the Music Project were used only for musicians' salaries. See also Philadelphia *Inquirer*, September 7, 1941. Money for transportation to concerts, arrangement for the use of concert halls, and the actual use of musical scores depended on sponsors who were willing to absorb such costs.Music was a problem for the FMP because music scores were quite expensive. That expense limited the repertoire of the Philadelphia units only briefly. One of the reasons that J. W. F. Leman was appointed conductor of the Civic was because he had an enormous music library. His library was even more important because his scores had multiple arrangements that fit orchestras of different sizes. The problem of scores was further alleviated when Dr. Cohn obtained the permission of Edwin Fleisher to loan the music in his collection to the Philadelphia FMP units. Ibid.

43. Philadelphia *Inquirer*, February 20, 1938; February 19, 1939.

44. Pennsylvania Narrative Report for December 1941, undated letter, Box 2441, RG 69, Records of the WPA FMP.

45. Philadelphia *Inquirer*, February 22, 1942.

46. Pennsylvania Narrative Report for June 1942, July 13, 1942; and Pennsylvania Narrative Report for July 1942, August 13, 1942, Box 2339, RG 69, Records of the WPA FMP.

47. Ashley Pettis, "The WPA and the American Composer," *The Musical Quarterly* XXVI: I (January 1940): p. 102.

48. WPA Federal Music Project Collection of Posted Notices, Music Room, Free Library of Philadelphia. See also the Philadelphia *Inquirer*, 1936-1943.

49. The Philadelphia *Inquirer*. 1935-1943. The percentage was based on the regular season concerts that appeared in the Sunday Arts and Entertainment section each week.

50. Philadelphia and State Narrative Reports, 1936-1942, Boxes 3, 5,10, 12, 2440, and 2441, RG 69 Records of the WPA FMP.

51. M. H. Costell to Civic Symphony, February 16, 1938; Elise D'Antone to J. W. F. Leman, February 16, 1938, Philadelphia Monthly Narrative Report for February 1938, Box 5, Entry 352, RG 69, Records of the WPA FMP.

52. Kupferberg, *Those Fabulous Philadelphians*, pp. 53, 131. The polls used to determine the request programs also revealed the inherent conservatism of the Philadelphia Orchestra audience. Year after year, the same compositions won the vote; Tchaikovsky's "Pathetique" (Symphony Number Six), Beethoven's Fifth, Schubert's "Unfinished," and Cesar Frank's D-minor Symphony.

53. WPA Federal Music Project Collection of Posted Notices, April 26, 1940, and February 23, 1941, Music Room, Free Library of Philadelphia.

54. *Statistical Abstract of the United States 1942*, 64th edition, Bureau of the Census, United States Department of Commerce (Washington, DC U. S. Government Printing Office, 1943). According to the 1940 census Philadelphia had 1,950,961 residents.

55. These averages were skewed high by the large outdoor audiences, which were frequently three to five times the size of the indoor concerts that sometimes had a modest fee. Pennsylvania Narrative Report for June 1940, Box 12 Entry 353, RG 69 Records of the WPA, National Archives.

56. The figures have been calculated by adding the attendance figures from the monthly narrative reports submitted by Philadelphia and Pennsylvania divisions of the Federal Music Project. See Works Progress Administration RG 69, Federal Music Project.

57. The scanty and incomplete records for 1937 make its figures abnormally low. Years for which more complete records existed were therefore compared. See Monthly narrative reports, 1936-1940, Boxes 3, 5, 10, 12, 2439, 2440, 2441, RG 69 WPA FMP.

58. Ibid., This is an underestimation based on figures from the 1937-1942 narrative reports. It did not include audience totals from the 1935-1936 season because they were not classified by unit. It also did not include a large portion of the audience for 1937 because totals were not reported to Washington. Narrative reporting did not become consistent until August 1937; therefore, the only figures for 1937 were those for August, September, and December.

59. Philadelphia *Inquirer*, September 7,1941.

60. Philadelphia *Inquirer*, October 1935-January 1943. A complete record of all concerts listed in the *Inquirer* for both orchestras was made and compared.

61. Titles listed in the Monthly Narrative Reports, RG 69, WPA FMP, 1936-1942.

62. Ibid.

63. Kupferberg, *Those Fabulous Philadelphians*, pp. 88-89.

64. Philadelphia Narrative Report, Federal Music Project, September 1937, Box 3 Entry 352, RG 69, Records of the WPA FMP.

65. Philadelphia Narrative Report, Federal Music Project, October 1937, Box 5 Entry 352, RG 69, Records of the WPA FMP.

66. When the Emergency Relief Act of 1939 continued the funding for the arts projects, a hostile Congress ended total funding for local programs and required local institutions to provide 25 percent of the money to continue the programs. They expected Federal One and its continuing Art, Music, and Writers projects to expire from lack of interest. Philadelphia continued to support these relief programs when various institutions became sponsors.

67. WPA Federal Music Collection of Posted Notices, Free Library of Philadelphia, n.d.

68. Information accumulated from the Philadelphia *Inquirer*, 1935-1943, the WPA Federal Music Project Collection of Posted Notices, and Philadelphia and Pennsylvania Narrative Reports, 1936-1942.

69. Philadelphia *Inquirer*, May 1, 1938. Each Sunday, the *Inquirer* listed the week's upcoming classical radio broadcasts in a column entitled "Symphonic Music on Air This Week." It showed that many major symphony orchestras had radio programs during the Depression. In the last ten years, 1987-1997, broadcasting by major orchestras has declined to the point where very few do so on a weekly basis. The Philadelphia Orchestra did not have a broadcast contract for 1994-1995.

70. WPA Federal Music Project Collection, announcement for August 23, 1939, Civic Symphony concert.

71. Ibid., announcement for October 19, 1941, Civic Symphony concert.

72. Ibid., announcement for February 15, 1942, Civic Symphony concert.

73. Ibid., announcements for March 22, May 3, June 7, and August 25, 1942, Civic Symphony concerts. Slogans were always capitalized on the public notices.

74. Pennsylvania Narrative Report for February 1942, Box 2339, RG 69, Records of the WPA FMP.

75. Pennsylvania Narrative Report for March 1942, *ibid*.

76. Richard Allen to Florence Kerr, July 12, 1942, Pennsylvania Narrative Report for June 1942, ibid.

77. Monthly Services Report for September, October 15, 1942, ibid.

78. Pennsylvania Narrative Report for September 1942, Box 2441, RG 69 Records of the WPA FMP.

79. McDonald, *Federal Relief Administration and the Arts*, p. 617. In Philadelphia the only WPA arts project that continued was the FMP music copying project that operated in the Free Library. By 1943, the copyists were collecting scores from Latin American composers and appealed the pending termination on the basis of Roosevelt's "Good Neighbor" policy. Florence Kerr, Assistant Commissioner of the WPA, granted the extension after a meeting with Arthur Cohn and Franklin Price, Chief Librarian of the Free Library.

80. MacDonald, *Federal Relief Administration and the Arts*, pp. 620-621.

81. Philadelphia *Inquirer*, December 20, 1942.

82. Philadelphia *Inquirer*, January 24, 1943.

III

Popular Culture

9

Don't Let Hitler (or the Depression) Kill Baseball:
Franklin D. Roosevelt and the National Pastime, 1932-1945

Ron Briley

Although a leftist critique of American sports suggests that there is social despair in the idea that athletic contests are "one of the bits of glue that hold our society together,"[1] an examination of American baseball during the 1930s and 1940s reveals that when confronted by the challenges of the Great Depression and World War II, President Franklin D. Roosevelt used the national pastime to ward off despair and retain American pride and morale during a period of crisis. Although his sporting interests were more directed to sailing, hunting, and fishing rather than mass urban spectator contests such as major league baseball, Roosevelt and his speech writers cleverly manipulated baseball metaphors to explain the New Deal and gain political support. Likewise, during World War II, the president provided a "green light" for baseball's survival and use as a morale booster on the home and war fronts.

From his first day in office, the new president confronted a crisis to which the American public expected a governmental response. Thus, in his Second Fireside Chat on May 7, 1933, Roosevelt described his New Deal as a partnership between government and farming and industry and transportation. Making an astute use of baseball metaphors, the president asked the American people to be patient with his programs, explaining, "I do not deny that we may make mistakes of procedure as we carry out the policy. I have no expectation of making a hit every time I come to bat. What I seek is the highest possible batting average, not only for myself but for the team."[2]

The president in 1933 sought to make his goals clear to the American people by appealing to their favorite pastime, the game of baseball. However, in the early years of the Depression, major league baseball was also a depressed industry. In 1929, regular season attendance in the major leagues topped nine million for a record sixth straight year, and in 1930, a tight pennant race in the National League, in which the top four teams finished within six games of each other, was mostly responsible for a major league net income of $1,462,000. Nevertheless, it proved impossible for baseball to escape the impact of the massive economic slump, and in 1931, net income declined to $217,000, and the profit margin of major league teams dwindled to 2.3 percent. Financial prospects for the sport dimmed further in 1932 and 1933 with losses of $1,201,000, a margin of 15 percent in the election year of 1932, with net losses totaling $1,651,000 in 1933, for a "loss" margin of 23.9 percent.[3] Major league baseball was certainly in need of a new deal.

In response to the ravages of the Depression, the *Sporting News*, a self-proclaimed Bible of baseball, warned that "baseball must get in step with the times. Talking about innovations as being 'bad for precedent,' that they hadn't been 'attempted before' and that what 'was good enough yesterday is good enough today,' won't get the game anywhere."[4] Reflecting Heywood Broun's observation in the *Nation* that baseball reigned as the country's number one sport due to "shrewdness, skill, sentimentality, and downright luck,"[5] the baseball establishment maintained a conservative stance, rejecting profit-sharing proposals and refusing to lower ticket prices, while allowing for some limited experimentation with night baseball. While Herbert Hoover was greeted by Philadelphia Athletics fans at the 1931 World Series by booing and chants of "We Want Beer," the magnates of baseball sought to trim expenses by reducing salaries. According to baseball historian Ben Rader, "total payrolls dropped from $4 million in 1930 to $3 million in 1933; by 1933, the average player salary had plummeted to $4,500."[6]

Disgruntled star players, such as the Yankees Babe Ruth and Giants Bill Terry, engaged in celebrated holdouts, but public opinion rarely sided with the players, who had little choice but to accept salary reductions, for the sport's reserve clause bound a player to the team for which he was currently contracted. Under the existing interpretations of baseball's Supreme Court exemption from the nation's antitrust laws, free agency was not an option. Popular resentment against baseball salary squabbles was well reflected in an article for the *Outlook and Independent,* which stated, "Somehow, in these days of breadlines and jobless heads of families, one cannot sympathize too deeply with the wellfed, bankroll-padded baseball holdout."[7]

Although the major leagues were struggling to stay afloat by trimming expenses, minor leagues were imposing salary ceilings, and some organizations such as the Eastern League were forced by Depression conditions to suspend operations. James A. Michener, who during the early 1930s was a high school coach and teacher in Pottstown, Pennsylvania, proclaimed that baseball had passed its period of greatest interest for American youth and was being replaced by other entertainment and sports such as golf. To survive in this crisis mode, many minor league operators resorted to such gimmicks as a pajama parade in Dayton, Ohio, where 700 women marched and bleacher spectators selected the prize-winning "fannette." In Huntington, West Virginia, fifteen chickens, each with a ticket to the next game tied round its neck, were turned loose on the field.[8] Thus, minor and major league baseball were able to survive the Depression, although the nadir was apparently reached during the winter of 1933 when the legendary Connie Mack, principal owner and field manager of the Philadelphia Athletics, broke up his American League champions of 1929, 1930, and 1931 by selling stars Robert Moses "Lefty" Grove, Mickey Cochrane, and George Earnshaw, expecting to realize approximately $300,000 from the transactions.[9]

Having trimmed expenses, baseball, like the nation, seemed poised by 1934 to bounce back from the worst years of the Depression. The baseball establishment appeared willing to embrace Franklin Roosevelt and the New Deal. The recovery program of the president was providing economic growth on which baseball, like other businesses that had stabilized operations, could build. Despite his conservative Republican proclivities and personal dislike for Roosevelt, Baseball Commissioner Kenesaw Mountain Landis, recognizing that baseball's fortunes were tied to the reforms of the Democratic administration, acknowledged, "Steel, factories, railroads, newspapers, agriculture, baseball—we rode down together, and we'll ride back together. The American people love baseball. They will return as paying customers as soon as they have money."[10] Landis could not bring himself to directly endorse the Roosevelt recovery program, but E. G. Brands, editor of the *Sporting News,* which advertised itself on letterhead as the "official publication of organized baseball," wrote to Roosevelt expressing support for the president and asserting that baseball deserved a place in the New Deal coalition. On May 22, 1934, Brands informed the president that "the National Game is keeping step with your recovery program by giving employment to hundreds of young players and thousands of others through the erection of new parks and in creation of many new jobs in connection with the operation of these parks." According to Brands, baseball would continue to play a role in the rehabilitation of the country, and the editor hoped that "news of this co-operation, small as it might be, would help to hearten you in your fight to make the country a better one in which to live."[11]

The baseball public appeared to echo the confidence reported by Brands. The *Literary Digest* reported considerable spring training interest in baseball for the 1934 season and predicted, "nothing will reflect the progress of the Recovery Program and the NRA as much as baseball attendance this year." Opening season, gate receipts seemed to herald better days for baseball, the American economy, and the Roosevelt administration. The New York Giants played to over 73,000 more customers in its first nine games than it had in the same number of games during the 1933 season, whereas the Boston Red Sox surpassed the first six dates of the previous campaign by 145,000 fans. These figures led New York sportswriter Rob Rennie to speculate that the "National Road to Ruin now is a thriving thoroughfare. It has been redecorated. People have come out of the shellholes to which they were blown by the explosion of finance and industry. They are working and playing and seem perfectly content to let a busy tribe of professional worriers do their worrying for them."[12]

Rennie was somewhat optimistic as baseball, like the American economy, was certainly not out of the Depression. However, in 1934, the baseball owners lost only $290,000 in comparison with losses of $1,650,000 in 1933. By 1935, baseball ownership reported the first net profit in four years, but not until the affluent society of post-World War II America did net profits exceed those of 1930.[13] Thus, the New Deal recovery had stopped the decline of baseball revenues without ownership having to alter the basic corporate structure of the game. Cardinal pitcher Dizzy Dean, who led St. Louis to a World Series victory over the Detroit Tigers in 1934, became a symbol of Depression-era baseball. Dean's biographer described the pitcher as "a fourth-grade dropout and one-time cotton picker who laughed at hitters when he struck them out, loved to brag, and said of himself, 'There'll never be another like me." But the folk-hero image of Dean was never to alter the dominant position attained by the lords of baseball. In a May 1935 article for the *Review of Reviews*, Jo Chamberlin praised baseball ownership, observing that for big league club owners, baseball was not all sport. It was a serious big business in which baseball magnates "pit their men and money against each other in competition which makes yacht-raising, horses, or polo seem much like matching pennies." According to this interpretation, Dean was simply a popular commodity who was the property of the St. Louis Cardinals baseball club. By 1936, baseball ownership was comfortable enough for the irrepressible Connie Mack to author a baseball piece for the *Saturday Evening Post* entitled "The Bad Old Days."[14]

Although the *Sporting News* expressly acknowledged Roosevelt and the New Deal as playing a major role in the stabilization of organized baseball, the question remains as to whether the public perceived the president as a champion of the game for boosting American morale during the dark days of the Depression. An examination of correspondence in the Roosevelt Library at Hyde Park indicates that there was considerable public identification of Roosevelt with the game of baseball. And ever the master politician, FDR was not going to ignore what baseball scholar George C. Rable called a public platform in which presidents could "mouth familiar platitudes about sport and patriotism."[15]

The Roosevelt mastery of communication, so well exhibited in the Fireside Chats, produced a sense of intimacy between the president and the American people. It was not uncommon for Roosevelt to receive personal letters from his constituents on any number of subjects, and the topic of baseball proved to be no exception during the president's first term in office. For example, a high school baseball enthusiast from Pennsylvania wrote the president because he had read in the newspaper that Roosevelt was a "Baseball Fan." Accordingly, the young man suggested, "if it would not interfere with governmental circumstances I would be thrilled to receive a short letter from you concerning your choice of the Pennant Winners." In a similar vein, an 18-year-old from Norfolk, Virginia, wanted to know whether the president would sponsor his baseball team by purchasing sixteen uniforms. In exchange for Roosevelt's support, the writer offered to advertise the teams as the NRA Eagles, concluding, "If you can help us President Roosevelt we will be the happiest boys in the world." Realizing that the president received a season pass to National League ballparks but lived in the American League city of Washington, DC, Samuel L. Rubin of Brooklyn asked for the Chief Executive's pass. Rubin wrote, "I am a young man of 29, and have just recovered from a two year's siege of illness. I have been ordered to spend the next few months in the open air, and since I am an ardent baseball fan, you would be doing me a great honor and service, if you should let me have your pass."[16]

In addition to the representative requests from enthusiastic young baseball fans around the country, Roosevelt's baseball correspondence included efforts by Henry Misselwitz of the United Press to develop international baseball between the United States and Japan. Lucile Gibbons, president of the Nassau, New York, Amateur Baseball Alliance, inquired whether the president could not push for the construction of baseball diamonds through the PWA. Gibbons argued, "If the nation has funds with which to build prisons, why not use some of the money as a preventive measure in the checking of crime? Keep our young men and boys interested in clean American sports instead of pool halls."[17] The president could not respond in a personal fashion to this plethora of requests, but he did use baseball imagery and symbolic occasions to identify himself with the national pastime.

But did Roosevelt really enjoy baseball? In a study of Roosevelt's sense of humor and personality, M. S. Venkataramani observes that the president was very fond of stories involving fishing or hunting. A favorite was the account that FDR was almost killed when he was struck a glancing blow by a falling goose or duck that he had shot in flight. Venkataramani, however, includes no baseball anecdotes in his volume. Popular biographer John Gunther also places baseball low on Roosevelt's list of leisure activities, behind such pleasures as sailing, stamp collecting, fishing, and card playing. Gunther describes Roosevelt as a casual fan who liked the game "if it was a lively game full of slugging; a pitcher's duel bored him."[18] Gunther's observation is apparently based on FDR's letter to James P. Dawson of the *New York Times,* which was read at the Fourteenth Annual Dinner of the New York Chapter, Baseball Writers Association of America. The president wrote, "When it comes to baseball I am the kind of fan who wants to get plenty of action for his money. I have some appreciation of a game which is featured by a pitcher's duel and results in a score of one to nothing. But I must confess that I get the biggest kick out of the biggest score—a game in which the batters pole the ball into the far corners of the field, the outfielders scramble and men run the bases. In short, my idea of the best game is one that guarantees the fans a combined score of not less that fifteen runs, divided about eight to seven."[19]

Thus, Roosevelt was a casual fan who did not attempt to discuss the intricacies of the morning box score. Nor is there any indication that Roosevelt enjoyed playing baseball in his youth. Baseball was often perceived in the late nineteenth and early twentieth centuries as a vehicle for the indoctrination of immigrants into the values of American civilization, but Roosevelt, as his biographers suggest, was brought up to be a "Hyde Park gentleman" or at best a "Genteel Reformer."[20] A product of his social class, Roosevelt loved the rigors of sailing. When he contracted polio, however, FDR's range of activities as a sportsman were considerably limited, and perhaps he began to develop an affinity for spectator sports such as baseball. Regardless of whether his health played any role in FDR's growing awareness of the national pastime, as a politician, the president was certainly apprised of the game's symbolic importance to the American people. His most passionate game was politics. For the first eight years of his presidency, Roosevelt attended opening-day ceremonies at Griffith Stadium in Washington, DC, tossing the ceremonial first pitch in an "unorthodox, overhand" fashion. FDR informed Washington Senators owner Clark Griffith that he would attend more games, "If I didn't have to hobble up those steps in front of all those people." The Senators owner responded to the president's plea by erecting a special ramp at Griffith Stadium so the president could have direct access to his box.[21]

Roosevelt also made use of baseball imagery in what was perceived as a tight 1936 reelection campaign against his Republican opponent Alf Landon. Speaking before a capacity crowd at Forbes Field in Pittsburgh on October 1, 1936, Roosevelt announced, "a Baseball park is a good place to talk about box scores. Tonight I am going to talk to you about the box score of the Government of the United States. I am going to tell you the story of our fight to beat down the depression and win recovery. From where I stand it looks as though the game is pretty well 'in the bag.'" Continuing with his baseball metaphor, the president observed that the national scoreboard looked pretty bleak in 1933, but that a change in management gave the country an opportunity to win the game. And with New Deal investment in agriculture, industry, small business, and the American people, the box score was being revised. The president concluded, "Compare the scoreboard which you have in Pittsburgh now with the scoreboard which you had when I stood here at second base in this field four years ago. At that time, as I drove through these great valleys, I could see mile after mile of this greatest mill and factory area in the world, a dead panorama of silent black structures and smokeless stacks. I saw idleness and hunger instead of the whirl of machinery. Today as I came north from West Virginia, I saw mines operating. I found bustle and life, the hiss of steam, the ring of steel on steel—the soaring song of industry."[22]

The landslide reelection of the president in 1936 indicated that the American people supported the new management in Washington and the improving box score of national recovery, even if the Depression game was not yet complete. During his second term, FDR continued his association with baseball, attending games and tossing ceremonial pitches, although not without some embarrassing moments. For example, amidst the bitter political debate surrounding FDR's efforts to alter the composition of the Supreme Court, a plane flew over Griffith Stadium on opening day for the 1937 season, bearing a banner that read, "Play the game, don't pack the court." The irrepressible Roosevelt supposedly laughed heartily and continued to munch peanuts. On opening day of the 1940 season, the president responded to *Washington Post* photographer Irving Schlossenberg's request for just one more photograph opportunity by flinging one additional ball, an errant throw that smashed Schlossenberg's lens.[23] The president was usually able to make more successful application of baseball opportunities and symbols.

Throughout the late 1930s as Americans became increasingly uneasy regarding international affairs in Europe and Asia, baseball was used in popular culture as a comforting reminder of traditional American values. The St. Louis Cardinals "Gas-House Gang" captured the public imagination with their work ethic and desire to win. As Cardinals Manager Frankie Frisch told the *Saturday Evening Post*, "There's no room for sentiment in baseball if you want to win." This doctrine was to prove most applicable to a nation that would soon engage in an era of total war. In addition to the virtues of hard work and success, Americans cherish the mantle of innocence, which in baseball terms is often extolled in the purity of the country boy who makes it to the big leagues. Accordingly, sportswriter J. Roy Stockton championed the virtues of a young Iowa farm boy named Bob Feller who was destined to become one of the greatest pitchers in the history of the game. Feller's message to young boys wishing to climb the ladder of baseball success was "to get plenty of rest and to eat, sleep and think baseball."[24]

Seeking to expound on baseball as a symbol of traditional values in an age of uncertainty, organized baseball prepared for the 1939 opening of the Baseball Hall of Fame and Museum in Cooperstown, New York. Even though ample evidence existed that Abner Doubleday did not develop baseball in Cooperstown and that 1939 was not the centennial of the game, Roosevelt endorsed the project and associated himself with the nostalgic values of baseball. In approaching the Baseball Hall of Fame and Museum, the president echoed sentiments he had expressed in a 1936 letter to C. F. Drake, editor of the *Chicago Cubs News*, calling baseball the national pastime "because it stands for the fair play, clean living and good sportsmanship which are our national heritage." On the eve of the Cooperstown "centennial," FDR sent a similar message, observing that baseball "has become through the years, not only a great national sport, but also the symbol of America as the melting pot. The players embrace all nations and national origins and the fans equally cosmopolitan, make only one demand of them: Can they play the game?"[25] The concept of America as a melting pot would be essential mythology for the American people during World War II (especially in Hollywood productions of the war years), but the reality of American race relations in the late 1930s was better reflected by racial segregation in baseball and the public statement by Yankee outfielder Jake Powell that while serving as a Dayton, Ohio, policeman, his favorite winter sport was "cracking niggers on the head."[26]

As Roosevelt sought an unprecedented third term in the White House and as international affairs replaced the New Deal in the president's attention, there was less time for baseball. Yet, FDR did make opening-day baseball appearances for the 1940 and 1941 seasons, although after the entrance of America into World War II, he would not attend another major league game.[27] As Doris Kearns Goodwin observed in her history of the Roosevelts and the home front in World War II, the Chief Executive had other concerns. Despite labor unrest, racial strife, dislocations in the American family, overcrowding, and profiteering, Roosevelt's leadership was indispensable in keeping the American people focused on military victory.[28]

Nevertheless, it would be impossible for the president to ignore the national pastime. Baseball's presence in the ritual of daily life in America was exhibited in the national fascination with Joe DiMaggio's fifty-six game hitting streak during the summer of 1941 while the country prepared for the war that was engulfing Europe and Asia.[29] And as war clouds gathered, baseball executives were concerned about the game's role in American life and legacy of patriotic service. Thus, National League President Ford Frick, when dispatching his usual season pass to the president, wrote, "At the same time may I not on behalf of my league and myself, volunteer to you such services as we may be able to render in this time of crisis. My own background of experience in the World War plus twenty years of newspaper, advertising and public relations work, together with ten years experience in organizing, regulating, supervising and directing recreational programs is, I think, typical." On the other hand, while Frick was volunteering his services, Clark Griffith was writing Roosevelt adviser General Edwin Watson, suggesting that it was the desire of the government to disturb essential industries, like baseball, as little as possible. Therefore, Griffith proposed that the Army devise a draft plan whereby only one player from each club would be called in a season, except in the event that the government declared a state of national emergency.[30]

After the Japanese attack on Pearl Harbor and declarations of war on the United States by Germany and Italy, baseball's lobbying to be classified as an essential industry for the war effort became more public. During World War I, the 1918 baseball season was cut short as a result of criticism from such organs of public opinion as the *New York Times* and *Stars and Stripes*, which claimed baseball was a drain on resources needed for conducting the war.[31] To deter such complaints during World War II, the *Sporting News* rushed to the sport's defense, maintaining that baseball "has a responsibility to fans and the nation heightened by war. It must go on fighting, buoyed by the fact that it is the fun, the entertainment, the joy, the sports interest of the common people." The publication, however, insisted that baseball was not asking for any special favors as "in all the history of baseball there never was a conscientious objector, or a slacker in the ranks."[32]

Many politicians supported the baseball establishment. Joseph Martin of Massachusetts, Republican leader in the House of Representatives, said it would be foolish to abolish baseball for the duration of the war because the sport was necessary to preserve national morale. On a similar note, Edward A. Kelly, Democratic Representative from Illinois, argued that baseball was needed to provide morale and recreation for the nation during a time of crisis. The colorful Fiorello H. LaGuardia, Mayor of New York City and Director of National Civil Defense, maintained that baseball was the "fun" of the common people and would be his only source of entertainment for the coming summer. Referring to the rumors of Nazi air attacks on New York City, LaGuardia proclaimed, "If we are to be hit, I'd just as soon get hit in Yankee Stadium, the Polo Grounds or Ebbets Field, as I would in my apartment. It seems to me, under the stands in the Stadium is as safe a place as any in the city. I am for baseball now, more than ever."[33]

President Roosevelt, who had consistently identified himself with baseball and used the sport to boost morale during the Depression, had no qualms with applying the same reasoning to the national crisis of World War II. In a letter to Baseball Commissioner Kenesaw Mountain Landis, Roosevelt wrote, "There will be fewer people unemployed and everybody will work longer hours and harder than ever before, and that means that they ought to have a chance for recreation and for taking their minds off their work even more than ever." Although Roosevelt did not believe baseball represented an essential occupation for draft-deferment purposes, he insisted that the professional game should continue even if the league rosters had to be filled with nondraft-age players. The *Sporting News* lauded Roosevelt's decision, calling the president the player of the year for recognizing, "No matter how great its military power in the field, no nation at war is stronger than the morale of the people at home."[34]

Roosevelt's position on the continuation of major league baseball agreed with most Americans, especially those young men in the armed services. The Athletic Round Table of Spokane, Washington, conducted a poll in the spring of 1943 regarding the feasibility of maintaining professional baseball. The results were overwhelmingly in favor of the sport; 95 percent of over 130,00 replies opposed abandoning the national pastime during the war emergency. Of 38,000 sailors polled, 99.5 percent approved conducting baseball business as usual. A Gallup Poll conducted during the same period, utilizing more systematic techniques than the Spokane analysis, did not produce the same spectacular percentages, but did demonstrate a definite sentiment in favor of continuing the sport; 59 percent preferred that baseball be maintained, while 28 percent opposed its operation, and 13 percent remained undecided. The Gallup organization reported that the most typical reply of respondents to the poll was simply, "America wouldn't be the same without baseball." The Spokane and Gallup quantitative conclusions were further substantiated by a letter-writing contest for serviceman conducted by the *Sporting News*. The winning entry, penned by Wayne L. Ashworth of Fort Benning, Georgia, asserted that the game must be continued. Ashworth wrote, "Baseball may suffer setbacks in attendance and gate receipts. Yet do we soldiers discontinue fighting after a few setbacks and defeats? We'll keep fighting until final and complete victory is won—until we can continue to live as free men and to play our sports as free men."[35]

A perusal of correspondence in the Roosevelt Presidential Library also indicates considerable popular support for the president's decision, which was soon followed by a memorandum to Admiral Ernest King requesting that baseball be encouraged for merchant ship crews in Iceland who were encountering morale problems. A school principal in New Jersey wrote, offering congratulation for the president's stand on major league baseball, as the sport was the "greatest civilian morale booster of them all." Some correspondents thought there was little to discuss regarding the central nature of baseball to American life. One postcard in the Roosevelt Papers simply reads, "Don't let Hitler Kill Baseball. Baseball is essential to our country's victory. The soldiers want it, defense workers need it. Need we say more?" Baseball endorsements to the president were also forthcoming from American servicemen such as Marine Staff-Sergeant William Stein, who informed Roosevelt that baseball "keeps our spirits up, gives us something to talk about and promotes sportsmanship." While serving in China and Guam before American involvement in the Pacific War, Stein indicated that he always eagerly read reports of scores and games, for they "brought the states to me very pleasantly."[36]

But not all Americans agreed with the president's perception of baseball's role in the war. After expressing devotion to the national game, Franlau K. Lutz urged FDR to cancel the sport for the duration of the conflict. In simple direct language, Lutz argued, "I can't see a bunch of

Ball Players going around the Country, getting big pay, having a good time, While Millions of other boys are fighting, Dying, Being made Cripples, Being made Sightless for their country. No, Mr. President, I can't get excited over a Ball game as long as we are at war." However, dissenting voices, such as Lutz, were drowned out by numerous letters, exemplified in a note by Richard Berlin to Press Secretary Stephen Early, stating, "The majority of the boys in the army, wherever they are, would say to keep those stars on the diamond where they would do more good."[37]

In addition to a rather voluminous public correspondence regarding baseball's morale role in the war, the White House was besieged by members of the baseball establishment more interested in lobbying for financial gain than in assessing the spiritual and philosophical aspects of the game. Whereas the conservative politics of Landis prohibited much official correspondence between the Commissioner's Office and the White House, unofficial inquiries by individuals such as Clark Griffith and J. G. Taylor Spink, general manager of the *Sporting News*, focused on such issues as the president's support for night baseball, morning games for evening workers, travel restrictions, and, of course, the draft status of major league athletes.[38]

After considerable political maneuvering and lobbying activities, major league baseball did make it through the war years. Although by 1945, it was a rather ragged regiment that included one-armed outfielders and 15-year-old pitchers. Nearly 70 percent of all major league players at the time of Pearl Harbor served in the armed forces during World War II; however, many never saw combat and made their military contributions by playing baseball on service teams. Despite manpower shortages, there is little evidence that the president seriously considered discontinuing the game during the war. In 1944, Lieutenant General Brehan Somervell, Chief of the Service of Supply, informed the New York Chapter of the Baseball Writers' Association that baseball served a crucial purpose in the winning of the war. Somervell stated, "It has been said that the successes of the British army can be traced to the cricket fields of Eton, and I can say that the sandlots and big league ball parks of America have contributed their share to our military success." In March 1945, shortly before his death, Roosevelt indicted that he still had an intuitive grasp for the feeling of the American people regarding the national pastime. In response to a reporter's inquiry as to whether manpower shortages would curtail the current season, the president responded that although the quality of play might deteriorate, he "would go out to see a baseball game played by a sandlot team—and so would most people."[39]

However, the wartime leader was unable to see another baseball game because on April 12, 1945, Roosevelt died from a cerebral hemorrhage. Although he was a casual fan and did not attend any major league games during the war years, FDR demonstrated his ability to understand the values and passions of the American people as he adroitly used the sport of baseball as a metaphor and morale booster to help the American people through the difficult days of Depression and war. Franklin Roosevelt refused to let either Hitler or the Depression kill baseball and endanger American values of teamwork, determination, innocence, success, and democracy embedded within the mythology of the sport. In many ways, the affluent society of post-World War II, which has exposed many of the gaps between American promise and reality, has proven more destructive of baseball than the Depression and World War II. Today, it is difficult to envision baseball, or many other American institutions for that matter, as a symbol around which an articulate and intuitive leader could rally the American people in times of crisis such as was the case for Franklin Roosevelt during the Great Depression and World War II.

ENDNOTES

1. John M. Hoberman, p. 21, *Sport and Political Ideology*, p. 21 (Austin: University of Texas Press, 1984).

2. "The Second Fireside Chat," May 7, 1933, as cited in Samuel I. Rosenman, ed., *The Public Papers and Addresses of Franklin Roosevelt*, vol. 2, p. 164-165 (New York: Russell and Russell, 1950).

3. For the economic conditions of baseball during the Depression era, see U.S. Congress, *Organized Baseball: Report of the Subcommittee on Study of Monopoly Powers of the Committee on the Judiciary*, House Report, No. 2002, 82 Cong., 2 Sess. (1952), pp. 1600-1615; Bill Rabinowitz, "Baseball and the Great Depression," in Peter Levine, ed., *Baseball History*, p. 49-59 (Westport, CT: Meckler Books, 1989) and Ben G. Rader, *Baseball: A History of America's Game*, 126-140 (Urbana: University of Illinois Press, 1994). For additional information on baseball in the 1930s, see Richard C. Crepeau, *Baseball: America's Diamond Mind, 1919-1941* (Orlando: University Presses of Florida, 1980); David Voigt, *American Baseball: From the Commissioners to Continental Expansion* (University Park: Pennsylvania State University Press, 1970).

4. *Sporting News*, October 3, 1932.

5. "It Seems to Heywood Broun," *Nation*, 129, October 23, 1929, p. 457.

6. Rader, *Baseball*, p. 138.

7. "The Spotlight on Sports," *Outlook and Independent*, 160, January 27, 1932, pp. 116-117. For additional contemporary articles that supported the baseball establishment's timid approach to the Depression, see John Kiernan, "Big League Business," *Saturday Evening Post*, 202, May 31, 1930, pp. 10, 17, 149-154; and Billy Evans, "Big League Over-Head," *Saturday Evening Post*, 206, August 5, 1933, pp. 16-17, 60.

8. "Hard Times Hit the Minors," *Literary Digest,* 114 July 30, 1932, p. 37; "Is the American Boy Quitting Baseball," *Literary Digest*, 106 July 12, 1930, pp. 34-35; and "Minor Leagues Take Heart," *Literary Digest*, 114 August 20, 1932, p. 33.

9. "The Break-up of the Athletics," *Literary Digest*, 116 December 23, 1933, p. 26.

10. G. H. Fleming, ed., *The Dizziest Season*, p. 19 (New York: William Morrow, 1984). For background information on Landis, see J. G. Taylor Spink, *Judge Landis and Twenty-Five Years of Baseball* (New York: Thomas Y. Crowell., 1947).

11. E. G. Brands to Franklin Roosevelt, May 22, 1934, President's Office File, Box 170, "Baseball," Franklin D. Roosevelt Library, Hyde Park, New York.

12. "America Cries 'Play Ball' in a Recovery Season," *Literary Digest*, 117, April 14, 1934, pp. 30-31; and Rob Rennie, "A Year Ago Baseball Games Were a Gage of National Melancholy, but Today Fans Flock to Make All Sports Events a Measuring Rod of Recovery," *Literary Digest*, 117 June 16, 1934, p. 25.

13. U.S. Congress, *Organized Baseball*, p. 1600.

14. Robert Gregory, *The Story of Dizzy Dean and Baseball During the Great Depression*, p. 2 (New York: Penguin Books, 1932); Jo Chamberlin, "Safe At Home!," *Review of Reviews*, 91, May, 1935, pp. 47-49; and Connie Mack, "The Bad Old Days," *Saturday Evening Post*, 208, April 4, 1936, pp. 16-17, 96-99.

15. George C. Rable, "Patriotism, Platitudes and Politics: Baseball and the American Presidency," *Presidential Studies Quarterly*, 19, Spring, 1989, pp. 363-372.

16. Allen V. Russell to Franklin Roosevelt, June 1, 1935; Vincent Pezzella to Franklin Roosevelt, n.d.; and Samuel L. Rubin to Franklin Roosevelt, April 15, 1935, President's Office File, Box 170, "Baseball," Franklin D. Roosevelt Library, Hyde Park, New York.

17. Henry F. Misselwitz to Stephen Early, September 21, 1934; and Lucile Gibbons to Stephen Early, February 25, 1935, President's Office File, Box 170, "Baseball," Franklin D. Roosevelt Library, Hyde Park, New York.

18. M. S. Venkataramani, *The Sunny Side of FDR*, p. 259-260 (Athens: Ohio University Press, 1973); and John Gunther, *Roosevelt in Retrospect*, p. 96-100 (London: Hamish Hamilton, 1950).

19. Franklin Roosevelt to James P. Dawson, January 23, 1937, in Rosenman, ed., *Public Papers and Addresses of Franklin Roosevelt*, vol. 6, p. 10.

20. Steven A. Riess, *Touching Base: Professional Baseball in the Progressive Era* (Westport, CT: Greenwood Press, 1980); James MacGregor Burns, *Roosevelt: The Lion and the Fox, 1882-1940*, p. 6; (New York: Harcourt, Brace & World, 1956), p. 6; and Frank Friedel, *Franklin D. Roosevelt: A Rendezvous with Destiny*, p. 3-15 (Boston: Little, Brown, 1990).

21. William B. Mead and Paul Dickson, *Baseball: The Presidents' Game*, p. 71-80 (Washington, DC: Farragut, 1993).

22. Campaign Address at Forbes Field, Pittsburgh, "The Only Way to Keep the Government Out of the Red Is to Keep the People Out of the Red," October 1, 1936, in Rosenman, ed., *The Public Papers and Addresses of Franklin Roosevelt*, vol. 5, pp. 401-408.

23. Rable, "Patriotism, Platitudes and Politics," p. 368; and Mead and Dickson, *The Presidents' Game*, p. 76.

24. Frank Frisch, "The Gas-House Gang," *Saturday Evening Post*, 209, July 4, 1936, pp. 12-13, 55-57; and J. Roy Stockton, "Bob Feller--Storybook Ball Player," *Saturday Evening Post*, 209, February 20, 1937, pp. 12-13, 66-70.

25. "Are We Celebrating a Fake 'Centennial?,'" *Current History*, 50, June, 1939, 53-54; Franklin Roosevelt to C. F. Drake, August 5, 1936; and Franklin Roosevelt to National Baseball Museum, Cooperstown, New York, April 19, 1939, President's Personal File, Box 227, "Baseball," Franklin D. Roosevelt Library, Hyde Park, New York.

26. "Why the Yankees Win," *Nation*, 147, September 17, 1938, p. 258.

27. Mead and Dickson, *The Presidents' Game*, p. 73. In 1942 and 1944, Vice-President Henry Wallace did the opening-day honors for Roosevelt, although his performances were eccentric. In 1942, Wallace stunned the crowd by tossing the ceremonial ball over the players' heads and all the way out to second base, some two

hundred feet from his seat. In his last opening-day performance, Wallace threw the ball to Senators pitcher Alex Carrasquel. Wallace explained that he singled out Carrasquel, a Venezuelan, to emphasize the administration's "Good Neighbor Policy" toward Latin America. In a more subdued fashion, wartime manpower chief Paul V. McNutt performed the ceremony in 1943, and following FDR's death on April 12, 1945, House Speaker Sam Rayburn, wearing a black armband, substituted for the new president, Harry Truman.

28. Doris Kearns Goodwin, *No Ordinary Time: Franklin and Eleanor Roosevelt, The Home Front in World War II*, p. 10 (New York: Simon & Schuster, 1994).

29. Michael Seidel, *Streak: Joe Di Maggio and the Summer of '41* (New York: Penguin Books, 1988).

30. Ford Frick to Franklin Roosevelt, April 5, 1941, President's Office File, Box 170, "Baseball"; and Clark Griffith to General Watson, April 12, 1941, President's Personal File, Box 7299, "Clark Griffith," Franklin D. Roosevelt Library, Hyde Park, New York.

31. For the impact of World War I on major league baseball see Fred Lieb, "The Great Exhumation," *Collier's*, 109, May 16, 1942, pp. 22, 60-61; and Harold Seymour, *Baseball: The Golden Age*, pp. 244-255 (New York: Oxford University Press, 1971).

32. *Sporting News*, December 11, 1941, January 18, 1942. For the role of the *Sporting News* in baseball and World War II see "Bible of Baseball: *Sporting News*," *Saturday Evening Post*, 214, June 20, 1942, pp. 9-10. For more specialized accounts of baseball during the World War II see William B. Mead, *Even the Browns: The Zany, True Story of Baseball in the Early Forties* (Chicago: Contemporary Books, 1978); Richard Goldstein, *Spartan Seasons: How Baseball Survived the Second World War* (New York: Macmillan, 1980); and Bill Gilbert, *They Also Served: Baseball and the Home Front, 1941-1945* (New York: Crown, 1992). For general accounts of the American domestic scene during World War II, see John Morton Blum, *V Was for Victory: Politics and American Culture During World War II* (New York: Harcourt Brace Jovanovich, 1976); and Richard Polenberg, *War and Society: The United States, 1941-1945* (Philadelphia: Lippincott, 1972).

33. *New York Times*, January 9, 1942; *Sporting News*, February 12, 1942.

34. Franklin Roosevelt to Kenesaw Mountain Landis, January 16, 1942, in Rosenman, ed., *Public Papers and Addresses of Franklin Roosevelt*, vol. 7, p. 62; and *Sporting News*, January 22, 1942.

35. *New York Times*, March 25, 1943; "Batter (If Still There) Up," *Newsweek*, 21, May 3, 1943, p. 82; and *Sporting News*, April 16, 1942.

36. Franklin Roosevelt to Admiral Ernest King, July 11, 1942; Ronald Decker Glass to Franklin Roosevelt, April 14, 1942; Ted Eckhardt to Franklin Roosevelt, February 23, 1943; Staff-Sergeant William Stein to Franklin Roosevelt, February 9, 1943, President's Office File, Box 170, "Baseball," Franklin Roosevelt Library, Hyde Park, New York.

37. Franlau K. Lutz to Franklin Roosevelt, October 13, 1942; and Richard Berlin to Stephen Early, February 6, 1943, President's Office File, Box 170, "Baseball," Franklin Roosevelt Library, Hyde Park, New York.

38. For examples of baseball establishment correspondence to the White House, see Clark Griffith to Stephen Early, March 2, 1943, President's Personal File, Box 7299, "Clark Griffith"; Thomas Kirby to M. H. McIntyre, January 19, 1942, President's Office File, Box 170, "Baseball"; and J. G. Taylor Spink to Franklin Roosevelt, January 28, 1944, President's Personal File, Box 227, "Baseball," Franklin Roosevelt Library, Hyde Park, New York.

39. "Baseball Gets Mandate from Army to Carry On," *Recreation*, 38, August, 1944, p. 274; and "995th Press Conference," March 13, 1945, in Rosenman, ed., *Public Papers and Addresses of Franklin Roosevelt*, vol. 8, p. 592.

CULTURAL CHRONOLOGY

Oct	1929	Stock Market crash triggers America's largest economic crisis
Mar	1933	FDR inaugurated
Mar	1933	Civilian Conservation Corps (CCC)—first of the New Deal programs—created
May	1935	Works Progress Administration (WPA) created—the most enduring New Deal Symbol
Aug	1935	Federal Arts Project established
		Federal Music Project established
		Federal Theater Project established
		Federal Writers' Project established
		Indian Arts and Crafts Board
		Historical Records Survey established
Mar	1936	Federal Dance Project established
Jan	1937	Rep. Martin Dies, Jr. and the House Committee on Un-American Activities criticize New Deal
May	1936	Pare Lorentz's film, *The Plow that Broke the Plains* released
May	1937	Pare Lorentz's film, *The River* released
Aug	1938	U.S. Film Service established
Apr	1939	Opera singer Marian Anderson in concert at the Lincoln Memorial
July	1939	Federal Works Agency established replacing the WPA

July	1939	John Steinbeck's *Grapes of Wrath* published
Nov	1940	FDR wins unprecedented third term against Wendell Wilkie
Nov	1941	James Agee *Let Us Now Praise Famous Men* published
Dec	1941	Pearl Harbor attacked
Nov	1944	FDR reelected to fourth term by defeating Thomas Dewey
Apr	1945	FDR dies

BIOGRAPHICAL DIGEST

Agee, James R. (1909-1955). Author of the Great Depression-era classic *Let Us Now Praise Famous Men* (1941), dealing with Alabama sharecropper families and illustrated with photographs by Walker Evans.

Alsberg, Henry G. (1881-1970). Director of the Federal Writer's Project (1935-1939), and administrator of the American Guide Series published about each state as well as other geographical units.

Anderson, Marian (1897-1993). African American opera singer who performed at the Lincoln Memorial after her concert in Constitution Hall was canceled by the Daughters of the American Revolution in 1939 because of her race. The alternate site was arranged with the help of Eleanor Roosevelt who resigned her DAR membership over the incident. The open-air concert attracted a crowd of some 75,000.

Benton, Thomas Hart (1898-1975). A major figure in twentieth-century American art who painted many murals with elongated, twisted figures and historical themes which became models for the New Deal art projects. Abstract painter Jackson Pollock was one of his students, and Harry Truman a close friend.

Burns, James MacGregor (1918—). A major political biographer whose authoritative *Roosevelt: The Lion and the Fox* (1956), the first of a two-volume biography, established his national reputation.

Cahill, Holger (1893-1960). Director of the Federal Art Project (1935-1943), whose appreciation of the relationship between democratic life and popular culture was fundamental to his successful administration of the federal arts program.

Caldwell, Erskine (1903-1987). Novelist best known for *Tobacco Road* (1932) and *God's Little Acre* (1933) portraying impoverished Georgians. His works provided justification for the New Deal's Resettlement Administration and Farm Security Administration.

Capra, Frank (1897-1991). Legendary Hollywood movie director who won three Academy Awards for best director in the 1930s. His Hollywood films celebrated the common man as a hero during the Great Depression. He also produced award-winning war-time documentaries while serving in the U.S. Army during World War II.

Civil Works Administration (CWA). Experimental plan created in 1933 from the Public Works Administration and directed by Harry L. Hopkins. It generated public employment, priming the economy through minimum wages paid to otherwise employed opera singers, teachers, and others. Despite its success, the program was terminated in 1934.

Civilian Conservation Corps (CCC). The only New Deal program which originated with Franklin Roosevelt himself. Designed for young adults between the ages of 17-24, some 2.5 million men served from 1933-1945. One of the most expensive agencies on a per capita basis, the CCC was successful in restoring national historical sites, building national parks, fighting forest fires, reforestation, undertaking other conservation efforts, as well as providing basic literacy skills for many of its enrollees.

Collier, John (1884-1968). Commissioner of Indian Affairs (1933-1945) who offered the Native Americans the New Deal, including creation of the Indian Arts and Crafts Board in 1935.

Dies, Martin, Jr. (1900-1972). Democrat from Texas who served in Congress 1931-1945 and 1953-1959. Initially a New Deal supporter, he became a national critic as chairman of the House Committee on Un-American Activities after the 1936 presidential election. He opposed the WPA, unions, immigrants and the Communist Party.

Evans, Luther H. (1902-1981). Director of the WPA Historical Records Survey (1935-1939).

Evans, Walker (1903-1975). Photographer for James Agee's *Let Us Now Praise Famous Men* (1941), containing his famous pictures of sharecroppers' and tenant farmers' cabins in Alabama. Earlier he had worked for the photographic unit of the Farm Security Administration.

Federal Art Project (FAP). Begun in 1935 with active support from Franklin and Eleanor Roosevelt, it provided work relief for up to 6,000 artists annually. Best known for its murals on public buildings, the Index of American Design led to some 20,000 photographic reproductions that helped to popularize American folk art and hundreds of community art centers. Artists included William de Kooning, Jackson Pollock, and Thomas Hart Benton, who painted many of the nation's post office murals.

Federal Dance Project (FDP). This program was beset with multiple problems from its start, in 1936. Problems among the dancers, directors, private studios, and eventually with conservative members of Congress led to its termination by 1940.

Federal Music Project (FMP). Created in 1935 as part of the WPA, it provided jobs annually for some 10,000-15,000 musicians and is considered today as having been a vastly successful project.

Federal One. A common term applied to the artistic work of relief projects, formally known as Federal Project No. 1 of the WPA, including the Federal Art Project, Federal Music Project, Federal Writers' Project, Federal Theater Project, and the Historical Records Survey.

Federal Theater Project (FTP). Started under the direction of Hallie Flanagan in 1935, it soon became embroiled in political controversy after FDR's enemies questioned the political values of both the actors and the productions. Representative Martin Dies (D-Texas), chairman of the House Un-American Activities Committee, saw to it that funding was terminated in 1939, as he did with the Federal Dance Project. Nonetheless, the FTP provided leading roles for actors such as Burt Lancaster and Burgess Meredith.

Flanagan, Hallie (1880-1969). Director of the Federal Theater Project from 1935-1939, employing nearly 12,500 people in 28 states during its peak. The program was terminated in 1939 after criticism from the House Un-American Activities Committee.

Goodwin, Doris Kearns (1942—). Political scientist who wrote *No Ordinary Time. Franklin and Eleanor Roosevelt: The Home Front in World War II* (1994), which provides wonderful insight into the Roosevelt White House.

Great Depression. The stock market crash of October 24, 1929 triggered the largest economic crisis in U.S. history. More than 5,000 banks closed and more than a quarter of the labor force was unemployed in 1933. Millions of citizens lost their savings, farms, and homes. The New Deal restored hope, but it took World War II to return prosperity.

"Happy Days Are Here Again" (1929). Written by Jack Yellen and Milton Alger for a movie, "Forever Rainbows," the song became FDR's theme song at the 1932 Democratic National Convention in Chicago and symbolized hope during the Great Depression.

Hickock, Lorena (1893-1968). A journalist and friend of Eleanor Roosevelt who left journalism to travel the nation and write private reports for Harry Hopkins. Her findings contributed to the creation of the Civil Works Administration.

Historical Records Survey (1935-1941). Originally a part of the Federal Writers' Project, it later became an agency of the WPA's Federal One, directed by Luther Evans. A variety of records and archives at the state and local level, as well as congressional and executive materials, were catalogued and inventoried.

Hopkins, Harry L. (1890-1946). While governor of New York, Franklin Roosevelt in 1931 appointed Harry Hopkins deputy director of the state's Temporary Emergency Relief Administration. As president in 1933, FDR appointed him to head the Federal Emergency Relief Administration (FERA), the Civil Works Administration (CWA) from 1933-1934, and the Works Progress Administration (WPA) from 1935-1938. Secretary of Commerce from 1938-1940, he was one of FDR's closest advisors. Hopkins advocated work relief for actors, artists, historians, and others. He remained a White House adviser throughout FDR's administration.

Ickes, Harold L. (1874-1952). In 1933, FDR selected Ickes as Secretary of the Interior and as the head of the Public Works Administration (PWA). He was a close associate of Eleanor Roosevelt in promoting civil rights, including Marian Anderson's concert at the Lincoln Memorial.

Indian Arts and Crafts Board. A five-member body created from the 1935 Indian Arts and Crafts Board Act which Secretary of the Interior of the Interior Harold Ickes had supported. The board encouraged the distribution of Indian arts and crafts by giving them government trademarks, created reservation craft guilds, organized art classes, and promoted Indian-made products.

Kerr, Florence S. (1890-1975). A college friend of Harry L. Hopkins appointed by him in 1935 as a regional (Chicago) director of the Division of Women's and Professional Projects within WPA. She oversaw sewing and library projects, the Federal Art Project, Federal Writers' Project, and the Federal Theater Project. In late 1938, she became assistant administrator of the WPA and director of the Women's and Professional Projects. Early the following year, the WPA became the Works Project Administration within the new Federal Works Agency (FWA). She directed the Division of Professional and Service projects until the WPA ended in 1943. The next year she became the director of the new public services of the FWA.

La Guardia, Fiorello H. (1882-1947). Known as "the Little Flower," La Guardia was the popular and dynamic three-term mayor of New York City (1933-1945), who became famous for reading comic strips over the radio and guest conducting the New York Philharmonic Orchestra. He formed a partnership with the New Deal in return for urban assistance from the CWA, FERA, PWA, and WPA.

Lange, Dorothea (1895-1965). Famous photographer who documented the Great Depression in photographs. The photos formed the book, *An American Exodus: A Record of Human Erosion* (1939). Her work for the New Deal's Resettlement Administration led to its enlargement and transformation into the Farm Security Administration (FSA) in 1937. She also documented the Japanese American relocation and the Charter of the United Nations.

Leuchtenburg, William (1922—). American political historian who wrote the classic one-volume work on the New Deal, *Franklin D. Roosevelt and the New Deal* (1963), and the only study on how subsequent presidents evaluated and used FDR's legacy, *In the Shadow of FDR: From Harry* Truman to Ronald Reagan (1983).

Lorentz, Pare (1905-1992). A film critic and author hired by the Resettlement Administration in 1935 to produce the following year a documentary film on the Dust Bowl, "The Plow that Broke the Plains," with a musical score by Virgil Thompson. A decade after the largest natural disaster in American history, the Mississippi River Flood of 1927, Lorentz made "The River," also scored by Virgil Thompson in 1937. The award-winning film dealt with the Mississippi River and its tributaries and covered the unexpected Ohio River flood with an epilogue showing the beginning of the Tennessee Valley Authority (TVA). After FDR saw the film he made immediate plans to establish the United States Film Service (USFS).

Macleish, Archibald (1892-1982). The "Poet Laureate of the New Deal," appointed Librarian of Congress from 1939-1943, where he served as FDR's speechwriter; the director of the Office of Facts and Figures and assistant director of the Office of War Information; and from 1944-1945 Assistant Secretary in charge of forming the United Nations Educational, Scientific, and Cultural Organization (UNESCO). He also wrote *The*

Irresponsibles (1940), and other books during World War II, urging artists and intellectuals to fight Fascism.

New Deal (1932-1945). The term that FDR began using in 1932 to describe the administration's political and economic policies. Scholars use it to describe his presidential philosophy in dealing with the Great Depression.

Oakies. The slang term applied to those who migrated mostly by automobile on Route 66 from southwestern states to California during the 1920s and 1930s. The migration was prompted by agricultural conditions (economic decline, overproduction, mechanization, soil depletion, and severe drought). The migrants received some aid from the Federal Transient Service (FTS), the Resettlement Administration (RA), and the Farm Security Administration (FSA). A chain of camps was eventually constructed and defense industries during World War II served to integrate them into California.

Public Works Administration (PWA). Created out of Title II of the National Industrial Recovery Act (NIRA) in 1933, the PWA became a primary source of public construction during the Great Depression, financing projects from 30 percent federal funds and 70 percent local funds. Harold L. Ickes, its director, saw to it that more than 34,000 quality projects were well planned during the New Deal, pioneering direct federal allotments to municipal governments.

Public Works Art Project (PWAP). The first national art program funded by the federal government in late 1933 from a Civil Works Administration (CWA) grant to the Treasury Department. Art connoisseur and Treasury lawyer Edward Bruce directed the project that provided work relief for more than 3,600 unemployed artists who produced murals and sculptures for public buildings. After the PWAP ended in 1934, similar projects were initiated by the WPA.

Roosevelt, Anna Eleanor (1884-1962). Eleanor Roosevelt married her distant Franklin D. Roosevelt in 1905. After rearing five children, she became a social reformer and champion of women in governmental positions, wrote a syndicated newspaper column "My Day," and held press conferences only for women. Increasingly she promoted civil rights for the poor and powerless (blacks, young people, women, and workers). In many ways, she was her husband's political partner and social conscience.

Roosevelt, Franklin D. (1882-1945). America's greatest president of the twentieth century and the only president who served more than two terms (1932-1945). An active and flexible personality, he successfully adapted the presidency to meet the political challenges of the Great Depression with the ad hoc programs of the New Deal and the military threat of the Axis powers during the World War II.

Schlesinger, Arthur, Jr. (1917—). Award-winning American historian who authored the three-volume classic biography of Franklin Roosevelt *The Age of Roosevelt* (1957, 1959, 1960).

Shahn, Benjamin (1898-1969). A muralist who rejected modern art in favor of social liberalism, Shahn painted for the Federal Art Project (FAP) of the Works Progress Administration (WPA) during the late 1930s. He was influenced by Mexican muralist Diego Rivera and later worked with him. Shahn's murals captured scenes of poverty, immigration, and workers. He painted the mural of the Social Security building in Washington, D.C., and later designed posters for the Office of War Information.

Sinclair, Upton B. (1878-1968). Best known for his exposé of the Chicago meat-packing industry, *The Jungle* (1906), Sinclair was one of the leaders in American social criticism. In 1934 he ran unsuccessfully for the governorship of California on the slogan "End Poverty in California." He wrote about plutocracy and the suppression of organized labor in *The Flivver King: A Story of Ford America* (1937); *Little Steel* (1938), about state-owned industrial co-ops in *Co-op* (1936), and anti-fascism in *Dragon's Teeth* (1943).

Sokoloff, Nikolai (1886-1965). Russian child prodigy who became the director of the Cleveland Orchestra (1920-1935) until accepting an appointment as director of the successful Federal Music Project of the WPA. He promoted orchestral performances during his reign from 1935-1939.

Steinbeck, John (1902-1968). Novelist from Salinas, California, who won a 1962 Nobel Prize. He wrote perhaps the best strike novel, *In Dubious Battle* (1936), and the classic *Grapes of Wrath* (1939), dealing with the plight of "Oakies" who were lured to California by promises of agricultural jobs. He worked in various government agencies after Pearl Harbor until the end of World War II.

Survey of Federal Archives. The legislation which created the National Archives required a description of federal records outside Washington, D.C. With a grant from the WPA, Federal Project No. 4 divided the nation into 34 regions and began work in 1936. The next year the inventory of archives continued under the Historical Records Survey and the National Archives. Finally completed in 1942, the surveys amounted to more than 500 published volumes.

Treasury Relief Art Project (TRAP). Begun in 1935, TRAP provided murals and sculptures for federal buildings without art funds. It involved several hundred artists. In 1938, TRAP was transferred to the Federal Art project.

United States Film Service (USFS). Created by FDR in 1938 after the president saw Pare Lorentz's "The Plow That Broke the Plains" and "The River," which had been sponsored by the Resettlement Administration and the Farm Security Administration. The USFS was placed under the National Emergency Council with funding from the WPA, PWA, and Farm Security Administration, and directed by Lorentz, who produced "The Flight for Life," and "Power of the Land" in 1940. After opposition from the private film industry, Congress terminated the USFS in 1939. FDR took money from relief agencies to continue the work in the Office of Education and then he new Federal Security Agency in 1939. The next year, Congressional critics terminated the USFS.

Warren, Robert Penn (1905-1989). Author of *All the King's Men* (1946), the greatest American political novel of the twentieth century which captured the essence of a charismatic autocrat. The fictional account parallels the life of Huey Long to a large extent.

Woodward, Ellen S. (1887-1974). After Eleanor Roosevelt and Frances Perkins, Ellen Woodward was often considered the third most important woman in the New Deal. She was appointed by Harry Hopkins to direct the Women's Division of the Federal Emergency Relief Administration (FERA), and director of women's relief work under the Civil Works Administration (CWA) and the Works Progress Administration (WPA). Every state and the District of Columbia had a jobs program for women. In 1936 she directed the WPA white-collar professional projects for writers, musicians, actors, and artists. From late 1930-1946, she served on the Social Security Board.

Works Progress Administration (WPA). The WPA was created in May 1935 from the Federal Emergency Relief Administration (FERA). It was directed by Harry Hopkins who replaced relief (welfare) for work. Though conservative critics criticized its more than 11 million dollar budget, it employed more than 3 million people at its peak. In 1939 the WPA was moved into the new Federal Works Agency. The National Endowment for the Humanities (NEH) and the National Endowment for the Arts (NEA), begun in the 1960s, is a legacy of the WPA cultural projects, as well as numerous buildings, parks, and other public works from the 1930s.

LIST OF CONTRIBUTORS

Graham Barnfield is a Regular Visiting Lecturer in Communication Studies at Sheffield Hallam University, England. Between 1992 and 1996, he held a postgraduate research studentship at Hallam's Communications, Media and Communities Research Centre. His recently completed doctoral thesis was entitled 'Co-opting Culture': State Intervention in and Party Patronage of Literary and Popular Culture, 1929-1941." His articles have appeared in numerous journals and periodicals.

Ron Briley received his B.A. and M.A. degrees from West Texas State University. He is pursuing his doctoral studies at the University of New Mexico. Currently, he is a history teacher and Assistant Headmaster at Sandia Preparatory School in Albuquerque, New Mexico, and an adjunct history professor at the University of New Mexico-Valencia Campus. Briley has published over twenty articles on baseball history and on film in American culture.

Francine Carraro is the Executive Director of the National Museum of Wildlife Art in Jackson, Wyoming. Formerly professor of art history at Southwest Texas State University, San Marcos, Texas, she received her Ph.D. from The University of Texas at Austin in 1989. A specialist in American art, her essays have appeared in a variety of journals and she has curated a number of exhibitions. She is the author of *Jerry Bywaters: A Life in Art* (The University of Texas Press, 1994), and a contributor to *Prints and Printmakers of Texas* (Texas State Historical Association, 1997), and *Suspended License: Censorship and the Visual Arts* (University of Washington Press, 1997).

Byron W. Daynes is a professor of political science at Brigham Young University. He is the author of numerous articles and books, including *The New Deal and Public Policy*.

Arthur R. Jarvis, Jr. is an adjunct assistant professor at the Abington campus of the Pennsylvania State University. He holds a Ph.D. from Penn State. He has published two articles in *Pennsylvania History*. His chapter in this book is part of a larger study about all four New Deal cultural projects and their operations in Philadelphia.

Philip Parisi is a journalist and editor with the Texas Historical Commission, the state agency for historic preservation. He researches and writes articles on history and historic preservation. Currently, he is writing a book on the Texas post office murals.

William D. Pederson is professor of political science and Director of American Studies at Louisiana State University in Shreveport. He has authored numerous articles and edited several books, including *The New Deal and Public Policy* and *FDR and the Modern Presidency*.

Ronald D. Tallman is Dean of the College of Arts & Sciences at Roosevelt University in Chicago. He is a specialist in Canadian history.

Lynn Y. Weiner is associate professor of history and associate dean of the College of Arts & Sciences at Roosevelt University in Chicago. She also directs the Center for New Deal Studies.

Nancy Beck Young is assistant professor of history at McKendree College in Lebanon, Illinois. She co-authored *Texas, Her Texas: The Life and Times of Frances Goff*. She is also completing a biography of Wright Patman.

Mary Robinson Zimmerman is the Director of Education and Public Programs at the Louisiana State Exhibit Museum in Shreveport, Louisiana. She received her B.A. in 1990 and her M.A. in 1995 from Louisiana State University in Shreveport.

INDEX

Abe Lincoln in Illinois, 29
Academy of Motion Picture Arts and
    Sciences, 20, 26
Academy of Music, 103, 108, 110
Aceves, Jose, 74
Adjip, Harry, 104
The Adventures of Ozzie and Harriet,
    34
Agee, James, 30-31
Age of Roosevelt, 23, 42
Air Raid Protection and Bomb
    Demonstration Rally, 104
Albrisio, Conrad Alfred, 4, 84, 85
Alger, Horatio, 22
Allen, James, 22, 23, 24
Alpert, Hollis, 33
Altvater, Elmar, 45, 46
Amateur Baseball Alliance, 123
American Federation of Musicians, 98
American League, 120, 123
American Regionalism, 85
American Scene Movement, 4, 64, 74
Anderson, Marian, 145
Ankeney, John, 64, 65
Annie, 2, 19, 21, 34, 35
Anson, Texas Post Office, 69
Apollo-13, 21
Architectural League, 2, 4, 91
architecture, 5, 48, 51, 82, 84, 85, 86,
    89, 94
Arnautoff, Victor, 68
Arnold, Edward, 28
art, 1, 42, 43, 44, 45, 47, 48, 50, 51
Arthur, Jean, 26
Ashworth, Wayne L., 128
Athletic Round Table, 127
Atlantic Charter, 31

Bach, Johann Sebastian, 103
Barnes Brothers, 45
Barnfield, Graham, 2, 3
Barrow, Clyde, 34
baseball, 1, 5, 119-130
Baseball Hall of Fame, 127
Baseball Writers' Association of
    America, 122

Bass, Sam, 77-78
Bataan, 30
Beethoven, 103
Before the Fencing of Delta County,
    69
Bellamy, Ralph, 30
Benet, Stephen Vincent, 26
Bennett, Babe, 26
Benton, Thomas Hart, 4, 66, 67, 74,
    85
Benton High School, 93
Berchman, Evelyn, 107
Berlin, Richard, 128
Berryman, C.K., 13
Biddle, George, 49-50, 55
Bossier High School, 92-93
Bossier Parish, 92, 93
Boston Red Sox, 121
Boston Symphony Orchestra, 101
Boy Rangers, 27
Brahms, Johannes, 102, 103
Brands, E.G., 2, 5, 6, 121
Briley, Ron, 1
Broadway, 32, 33, 34, 35
Brookings Institution, 46
Broun, Heywood, 120
Bruce, Edward, 49, 50, 52, 53, 54, 55,
    56
Buffalo Philharmonic Orchestra, 109
Burns, James MacGregor, 15
Byrd, Richard, 98
Bywaters, Jerry, 3, 65, 66, 67, 69, 70,
    146

Caddo Parish, 86, 88, 93, 95
Cagney, James, 22, 25
Cahill, Holger, 43
Campobello Island, 14
Capra, Frank, 26, 27, 34
Carnevale, Luigi, 104
Carol, Norman, 101
Carol, Renee, 101
Carraro, Francine, 3, 4, 63
Centenary College, 90
Center for New Deal Studies, 10, 11,

Center for New Deal Studies, 10, 11,
    147
Center of Progress Exposition, 89
Chamberlin, Jo, 122
Chicago Cubs News, 125
Chicago Symphony Orchestra, 100
Chicago World's Fair, 89
Churchill, Winston, 15, 23
City Symphony Orchestra of
    Philadelphia, 98, 99, 100, 103,
    104
civil rights movement, 21, 34
Civil Works Administration, 50, 66,
    73, 90, 98
Civilian Conservation Corps, 47
Cleveland, Grover, 52
Clinton, Bill, 19, 20
Cochrane, Mickey, 121
Cohn, Arthur, 100, 101
Cold War, 4, 30, 31, 32
College Art Association's Emergency
    Work Bureau, 47
Collier, Alberta, 84
Collins, Richard G., 32
Columbia University Medal of
    Excellence, 55
Commission of Fine arts, 42, 43, 47,
    48, 49, 52, 57
Commonweal, 30, 31, 33
Communist Party, 32
Composers' Forum, 111
Confessions of a Nazi Spy, 21, 30
Cooke, James Francis, 103, 104
Cooper, Gary, 26
Cooper, John Milton, 31
Cooper, Texas Post Office, 69
Copland, Aaron, 104, 107
Cosmopolitan Studios, 23
Cotton Pickers, 68
Council of Fine Arts, 48
counterculture, 34
Coushatta High School, 93
Cowboys Receiving the Mail, 68
Cowley, Malcolm, 58
Crisis of the Old Order, 42
Crist, Judith, 35
A Current Affair, 35
Curry, Stuart, 74

Daddy Warbucks, 34
Dallas Morning News, 63
Dallas Museum of Fine Arts, 64
Dallas Post Office Terminal Annex,
    64
Dallas Times Herald, 63
Darro, Frankie, 24
Davies, Joseph E., 30
da Vinci, Leonardo, 70
Davis, Ronald L., 29
Dawson, James P., 123
Dean, Dizzy, 122
Deeds, Longfellow, 26
Delano, Frederic, 52
Deluxe Stamp Works, 16
DeMille, Cecil B., 23, 24
Democratic National Committee, 33
Democratic National Convention, 33
Denby, Mary, 103
Department of Fine Arts, LSU, 83
DeRidder, Louisiana Post Office, 84
DeSoto Parish, 88, 93
De Stijl School, 89
Detroit Tigers, 122
de Zapp, Count Rudolphe, 50
DiMaggio, Joe, 126
Dmytryk, Edward, 32
Doe, John, 27, 28
Dole, Bob, 19, 21, 35
Donehue, Vincent, 32
Doubleday, Abner, 125
Douglas, Helen Gahagen, 20
Douglas, Melvyn, 20
Dozier, Otis, 68
Drake, C. F., 127
Dyson, Michael Eric, 19

Early, Stephen, 156
Earnshaw, George, 121
Eastern League, 120
Ebbets Field, 127
Eccles, Marriner, 46
Edinger's Bakery, 11
Edwin Fleisher Collection of Music,
    100
Eisenstein, Sergei, 25
Electra, Texas Post Office, 69
Ellis, William, 103

Elmore, Robert H., 107
El Paso, Texas Federal Building, 75
Emergency Relief Appropriations Act, 47
End Poverty in California, 20
Fala, 12
Farber, Manny, 31
Father Knows Best, 34
FDR After 50 Years, 1, 63
Federal Art Project, 43, 48, 73, 82
Federal Bureau of Investigation, 25
Federal Emergency Administration of Public Works, 82, 86, 88, 94
Federal Music Project, 5. 11, 98, 98, 100
Federal Theater Project, 47, 58
Federal Works Agency, 52, 77
Feller, Bob, 125
Ferguson, Otis, 28
Ferrer, José, 32
Finney, Albert, 34
First Municipal Art Exhibition, 55
First One Hundred Days, 24, 46
Fisher Parks, 106
Folgmann, Emil, 99
Fonda, Henry, 29
Forbes Field, 124
Ford, John, 28
Fort Worth, Texas Federal Courthouse, 77
Fourteen Points, 31
Franklin and Eleanor Roosevelt Institute, 10
Franklin D. Roosevelt Presidential Library, 12, 16
Freman, Frank, 32
Frick, Ford, 126
Frisch, Frankie, 125
Furness Junior High School, 109

Gabriel Over the White House, 12, 19, 21, 23, 29
Garson, Greer, 32
Gaul, Harvey, 107
Geer, Will, 32
General Service Administration, 70
German Bauhaus, 89
Gibbons, Lucile, 123
Giddings, Texas Post Office, 68

Gilchrist, W. W., 103
Gill, Brendan, 33
Gingrich, Newt, 25, 34
G-Men, 25
Goff, Lloyd, 69, 147
Golden Gate International Exposition, 84
Goodwin, Doris Kearns, 126
Grand Court of Mitten Hall, 99
The Grapes of Wrath, 21, 29
Great Depression, 2, 22, 64, 88, 119, 130
Griffith Stadium, 124, 125
Grove, Robert Moses "Lefty", 121
Gunther, John, 14, 123

Hadley, Henry K., 103
Hall Summit High School, 93
Hammond, Judd, 23, 24
Hard Copy, 35
Harding, Warren G., 48
Hardy, George, 90
Hartung, Philip, 30, 33
Haskell, Molly, 34
Hayden, Sterling, 31
Haydn, Josef, 107
Hays, Will, 25, 29
Hearst, William Randolph, 23, 24
Henderson, Roy Buchanan, 85
Hermann, Edward, 34
Hitler, Adolf, 128, 129
Hoellering, Franz, 27
Hogue, Alexandre, 65, 67, 69
Hollywood, 2, 1-36, 125
Hollywood Ten, 32
Hollywood vs. America, 19
Holmes, Oliver Wendell, 21
Hoover, Herbert, 23, 26, 46, 88, 120
Hopkins, Harry L, 47
House Committee on Un-American Activities, 21, 32, 134
Houston Ship Channel, 4
Howe, Louis, 30
Howells, John Mead, 51
Hoxter Jubilee Choir, 103
Hurd, Peter, 69, 76-77
Huston, John, 34, 35
Huston, Walter, 23, 30
Hyde Park, 10, 122, 124

I Am a Fugitive From a Chain Gang, 20
Ickes, Harold, 58
International Style, 91-92, 96
Irvine Auditorium, 99-100, 102
It Happened One Night, 25
Italian Renaissance, 64

Jackson, Andrew, 23
Jacobs, Joseph M., 13, 15
Jagger, Dean, 32
Jarvis, Arthur R., 5, 98
Jefferson, Thomas, 20, 51
Joad Family, 26
Johnson, Lyndon, 19
Jones, Alfred Haworth, 28
Jones, Roessle Olschner, 91
Jouffroy, Alain, 49

Kael, Pauline, 35
Kalfatovic, Martin, 70
Kaufmann, Stanley, 35
Keene, Tom, 25
Kelly, Edward A., 218
Kennedy, Edward, 127
Kennedy, John F., 21, 32, 33, 34
Keynes, John Maynard, 46
Kids, 21
King, Ernest, 128
Korean War, 32
Koussevitsky, Serge, 101
Kreisler, Fritz, 104

Lacier, Samuel L., 104
LaGuardia, Fiorello H., 127
Landis, Kenesaw Mountain, 127, 129
Landon, Alf, 124
Laszlo, Alexander, 104
Laurie, Lee, 51
The Law–Texas Rangers, 77
Lea, Tom, 75, 76
League of Nations, 34
Leave it to Beaver, 34
Leman, J.W.F., 99, 100
Leuchtenburg, William, 22, 33
Lewis, Ross, 12
L'Exposition International des Artes,
    Decoratifs Modernes, 89

Life, 30
Lincoln, Abraham, 11-12, 15, 29, 27,
    28
Lincoln Memorial, 27, 103, 145
Linden, Texas Post Office, 68
Lippman, Walter, 24
Liszt, Franz, 107
Literary Digest, 121
Local Works Division, 98
Lockett, Joseph, 102, 103
Longfellow, Henry Wadsworth, 15
Longstreet High School, 93
Longview, Texas Post Office, 69
Lorentz, Pare, 25-26, 34
Louisiana Department of Agriculture,
    and Immigration, 83, 86-87
Louisiana Leader, 84
Louisiana State Capitol, 84
Louisiana State Exhibit Museum in
    Shreveport, 94, 95
Louisiana State University, 84
Louisiana State University-
    Shreveport, 1, 146, 147
Lowery Collection, 15
Luce, Henry, 31
Lutz, Franlau K., 128
Lynes, Russell, 81

MacDowell, Edward, 103
Mack, Connie, 121, 122
MacLeish, Archibald, 52
Macmahon, Arthur, 88
Madison, James, 52
Magafan, Jeanne, 69
Many High School, 93
Markowitz, Gerald E., 82
Marling, Karal Ann, 70
Marshall, Lemuel, 93
Mart, Texas Post Office, 79
Martin, Joseph, 127
Massey, Raymond, 29
Mayer, Louis B., 2, 20
McDonald, Harl, 103
McKenzie, Ralph, 84
McKinzie, Richard, 49
McLennan Looking for a Home, 74
McMahon, Audrey, 47
Mechau, Frank, 77
Medved, Michael, 19
Meet John Doe, 21, 26, 27, 28

Mexican muralists, 54
MGM, 23
Michelangelo, 70
Michener, James A., 120
Milwaukee Journal, 12
Minneapolis Symphony, 99, 101
Misselwitz, Henry, 99
Mission to Moscow, 21, 30-31
Mitchell, Anne, 28
Mitchell, Rossell Edward, 50
Mitropoulos, Dimitri, 101
Modern Museum of Art Film Library,
   26
Monroe, James, 52
Moore, Charles, 47, 49, 52
Mooringsport High School, 95
Morison, Samuel Eliot, 16
Moscow Film Festival, 24
Moss, Phyllis, 102
Motion Picture Producers and
   Distributors of America, 26
Mozart, Wolfgang Amadeus, 102
Mr. Deeds Goes to Town, 26
Mr. Smith Goes to Washington, 26
Mueller, Otto, 103, 104, 107
Mumford, Lewis, 91
Muni, Paul, 22
Mural Painters of America, 55
murals and frescoes, 4, 42, 74, 81, 84
Murphy Brown, 19
Muscaro, Martin, 107
Museum of American Political Life, 9
Museum of Modern Art, 56, 84
My Son John, 32

Nakoni, Peta, 77
The Naming of Quanah, 77
The Nation, 20, 24, 27, 28, 120, 130
National Endowment for the Arts, 71
National League, 28, 119
National Origins Act, 44
National Press Club, 28
National Recovery Administration,
   25, 121
National Register of Historic Places,
   95
Nazi Germany, 30
NBC, 98, 101
NBC Symphony, 101
Neild, E.F., 94

New Deal, 1, 2-3, 4, 10, 11, 12, 13,
   14, 15, 19, 20, 21, 22-24, 30, 35,
   43, 45, 48, 50, 54, 55, 58, 63, 64,
   65, 67, 68, 70, 71, 73, 81, 82, 86,
   95, 96, 103, 119, 121, 122, 145,
   146
New Frontier, 21, 32
New Iberia Parish Courthouse, 84
The New Republic, 24, 28, 30-31, 33
New Yorker, 33, 35
New York Giants, 121
New York Times, 30, 122, 126
New York Yankees, 120
Nixon, Richard, 20, 30
Norden, Martin, 33
Norden, N. Lindsay, 102
Northeast Technical School, 85
Norton, D.B., 28
Nye, Gerald, 29

O. Pioneers, 76
O Pass of the North, 76
Obregon, Alvaro, 50
Odysseus, 75
Offe, Clause, 45
Office of Facts and Figures, 52
Office of War Information, 26, 30
Oil, Cattle, and Wheat, 70
Oklahoma City Symphony Orchestra,
   109
Old City Hall (Dallas, Texas), 65
Orchard, Louise, 51
Ormandy, Eugene, 99, 100
Our Daily Bread, 25, 30
Outlook and Independent, 20

Paine, Joseph, 26
Paddadio, 100
Pantheon, 93
The Paper Curtain, 33
Paramount Pictures, 33
Parisi, Philip, 3, 73
Park, Marlene, 82
Parker, Bonnie, 34
Parker, Quanah, 78
Parks, Larry, 32
Pearl Harbor, 103
Pelican High School, 93
Pells, Richard, 42

Philadelphia Athletics, 120, 121
Philadelphia Board of Education, 108
Philadelphia Civic Symphony, 3, 98,
    99, 101, 102, 103, 104, 106, 107,
    108, 109, 110, 111
Philadelphia Council for Defense,
    103, 109
Philadelphia Evening Ledger, 104
Philadelphia Museum of Art, 105, 108
Philadelphia Navy Base, 109
Philadelphia Orchestra, 109, 110
Philadelphia Symphony Orchestra, 2
Philadelphia Tribune, 103
The Plow That Broke the Plains, 25,
    134
Polo Grounds, 127
post office murals, 4, 73, 74, 77
Powell, Jake, 126
Powers, Tom, 22, 23
The President Vanishes, 21
Preston, James, 12
Public Buildings Administration, 52
Public Enemy, 22, 24
Public Works Administration, 3, 50,
    92
Public Works of Art Project, 35, 48,
    63, 73
Purdy, Jim, 24

Quayle, Dan, 19

Rable, George C., 122
Rader, Ben, 120
Rains, Claude, 27
Reagan, Ronald, 34, 35
Rennie, Rob, 121
Resettlement Administration, 25
Review of Reviews, 122
Rich, Thaddeus, 98, 99
Rife, A. J., 98
Rivera, Diego, 53, 68, 74, 85
Robert, Lawrence, 49
Robinson, Edward G., 32
Robinson, J.M., 13
Robinson, Willard B., 89
Rocky Mountain High School, 93
Roffman, Peter, 24
Roosevelt, Eleanor, 33, 51, 54, 63,
    101

Roosevelt, Franklin D., 35, 43, 47, 48,
    53, 119
Roosevelt, Theodore, 23, 48, 79
Roosevelt University, 10, 147
Rosenman, Samuel, 14
Rosenwald Fellowship, 84
Rossini, Giocchino, 107
Rowan, Edward, 70, 73, 75, 77
Rubin, Samuel L., 123
Ruth, Babe, 120

Saarinen, Eero, 51
Sabatini, Guglielmo, 99, 100, 104
Sabine Parish, 92
San Francisco Coit Tower, 53, 68
San Francisco World's Fair, 84
Sandburg, Carl, 23
Saturday Evening Post, 32, 122, 125
Schary, Dore, 21, 33, 34, 35
Schick, Nat, 77
Schlesinger, Arthur, Jr., 23, 42
Schlossenberg, Irving, 126
Schulberg, Budd, 32
science fiction, 32
Section of Fine Arts, 48, 53, 73, 82,
    85
Sherwood, Robert, 20
Short, C.W., 91
Shreveport Farmers' Market, 91
Shreveport Municipal Incinerator, 91
Shreveport Public Works Department,
    89
Shreveport Symphony Orchestra, 90
Sims, John, 26
Sinclair, Upton, 2, 20
Smith, Al, 33, 44
Smith, Jefferson, 27
Smithsonian Institution, 10, 51
Sobchack, Vivan C., 29
Sokoloff, Nikolai, 104
Somdal, D. A., 94
Somervell, Brehan, 126
Southwest Review, 68
Soviet Union, 30
*Spending to Save: The Complete
    Story of Relief*, 88
Spink, J. G. Taylor, 128
Sporting News, 120, 121, 122, 128
St. Louis Cardinals, 122, 125, 126
Stalin, Josef, 30

Stanley High School, 93
Stanley-Brown, R., 91
Stanwyck, Barbara, 27
Stark, Ray, 34, 35
Stars and Stripes, 127
Stein, William, 128
Steinbeck, John, 29, 43
Stell, Tom, 69
Stewart, James, 37
Stockton, J. Roy, 125
Stokes, Constance, 103
Stokowski, Leopold, 104, 110
Strauss, Johann, 104
Sundstrom, Ebba, 101
Sunrise at Campobello, 21, 32, 33, 34
Supreme Court, 84, 120, 125
Symphony Orchestra of Utah, 109

Taft, William Howard, 48
The Taking of Sam Bass, 48
Tallman, Ronald, 1
The Taming of the Shrew, 7
Taylor, Deems, 103
Tchaikovsky, Peter Ilyich, 103
Teichmueller, Minette, 77
Temple University, 100, 108
Temporary Emergency Relief
    Administration, 47
Tennant, Allie, 69
Terry, Bill, 120
Texas Rangers, 2, 73, 77
This Day and Age, 23
Thalberg, Irving, 2, 30
Time, 28, 33, 35
Toscanini, Arturo, 100
Treasury Department Section of
    Painting and Sculpture, 3, 45, 82
Treasury Relief Art Project, 48, 51
Treaty of Versailles, 31
Trotsky, Leon, 30
Troy, William

Union Station (New Orleans,
    Louisiana), 84
United Nations, 31
U.S. Department of the Interior, 52
U.S. Department of Justice, 49
U.S. Department of the Treasury, 50,
    51, 63, 65, 73, 95, 100, 103, 104

University of Pennsylvania, 103, 104

Venkataraman, M.S., 123
Verdi, Giuseppe, 107
Vidor, King, 25
Vietnam War, 30, 34
Vivian, Louisiana Post Office, 95
Vogue, 34

Wagner, Richard, 105
Walker, Robert, 32
Walnut Street Theater, 100
War Production Board, 104
Warner Brothers, 22, 24, 30, 32
Washington, George, 11, 15, 17
Washington Masquerader, 23
Washington Merry-Go-Round, 23
Washington Post, 126
Washington Senators, 124
Washington Star, 13
Watson, Edwin, 126
Weiner, 1
Wellman, William, 11
Wheeler, Burton K., 15
Whitney Museum of Modern Art, 84
Why We Fight, 26
Wiener, Samuel, 91
Wild Boys of the Road, 24, 30
Willoughby, Long John, 27-28
Wilson, 30, 31-32
Wilson, Harry D., 94
Wilson, Woodrow, 7, 11, 16, 48, 52
Winkfield, Clyde, 103
Women's Symphony Orchestra of
    Chicago, 101
Women's Symphony of Philadelphia,
    99
Wood, Grant, 2, 74
Works Progress Administration, 82,
    99
World Series, 120, 122
World War I, 13, 20, 30, 22, 126, 127
World War II, 1, 26, 31, 35, 101, 102,
    104, 106, 107, 108, 119, 122, 126,
    127, 129, 130
Wright, Henry Brainard, 94

Yankee Stadium, 127
Young Mr. Lincoln, 29, 30

Zanuck, Darryl, 29, 31
Zimmerman, Mary R., 4